Quo Vadis Univer-Cities?

"Congratulations on this Univer-Cities Conference 2016 hosted by Vice-Chancellor Caroline McMillen to carry on this important conversation on univer-cities and the symbiotic link between universities and cities. I speak with my experience in teaching and research at Caltech and living in Pasadena. This relationship between Caltech and Pasadena provides yet another especial example of the ideas you have generated on the symbiosis celebrated by your univer-cities, well documented in this volume."

— **Professor Rudolph A. Marcus,**
Nobel Laureate for Chemistry,
John G. Kirkwood and Arthur A. Noyes
Professor of Chemistry,
California Institute of Technology.

"We used to speak of town and gown, but today it's 'univer-cities' that grab the headlines: the virtuous cycle of research and innovation that universities and their regions create and sustain. There are many challenges, but the abundant future of every metropolis depends on it."

— **Professor Richard Bender,**
Professor of Architecture and Dean Emeritus,
College of Environmental Design,
University of California, Berkeley.

"Universities can and must continue to play a pivotal role in societal transformation — through pursuing innovations, shaping thought leadership, cultivating synergies, and enriching networks — to advance the frontiers of knowledge and benefit the world we live in.

Univer-Cities offers a strategic and apt illumination of the complexity of inter-related issues confronting contemporary cities, and on themes which are both universal and urgent."

— **Professor Tan Eng Chye**,
President,
National University of Singapore.

"A well rounded higher education system should embed the engagement of the community in the nurturing of leaders. Only then will they understand the needs of the society. With the right eco-system, graduates are empowered to be a catalyst for change, and will be able to contribute to the global yet local univer-city of Singapore with an anchored sense of purpose."

— **Chua Thian Poh** DUBC, JP;
Alternate Member to Council
of Presidential Advisers;
President, Singapore Federation of Chinese Clan
Associations; Chairman & CEO, Ho Bee Land
Limited; Co-Founder, NUS Chua Thian Poh
Community Leadership Centre.

"Newcastle, New South Wales, Australia epitomises all that is vital about the univer-city: a high-powered research university, linked to hospitals, business, and industry. Cambridge similarly has, in its innovative bio-medical campus, grown an environment where different interests can communicate and interact. Each has a distinctive role but they have the greatest impact by being brought together. The university searches for new knowledge without preconceptions, philanthropic bodies and businesses provide support for research and its applications, and the hospitals deliver the resulting health care and well-being through new drugs and treatments. The chapters in this volume demonstrate the vitality of such clusters and the challenge of creating them."

— **Professor Jane Clarke**,
President of Wolfson College,
Cambridge Wellcome Trust Senior Research Fellow,
and Professor of Molecular Biophysics, Cambridge.

"Univer-Cities Narrative — Your drive, vision and enduring commitment to build institutions of the learned and for the learners are admirable. I have had the privilege and pleasure to witness firsthand how you took time, effort and personally invested with heart and mind to choreograph the conference programme, and the line-up of speakers with a narrative which only you know and could envision. The notes which you carefully crafted and were hand-written to acknowledge a mix of contributors and humble souls earned respect from many present in the conference dinner. There was no lack of intellectual thought-provoking moments as the conference unfolded throughout the day. Seriousness of the topic aside, you threw in the humour, showed us the solidarity of the Advisory Board Members, and the camaraderie and wisdom in curating a global conference, well captured in this volume. Thank you Anthony and I look forward to Univer-Cities 2019."

— **Winnie Eley**,
Deputy Vice-Chancellor, International and
Advancement, University of Newcastle.

UNIVER-CITIES

STRATEGIC DILEMMAS OF MEDICAL ORIGINS AND SELECTED MODALITIES
WATER, QUANTUM LEAP & NEW MODELS

VOLUME III

UNIVER-CITIES
STRATEGIC DILEMMAS OF MEDICAL ORIGINS AND SELECTED MODALITIES
WATER, QUANTUM LEAP & NEW MODELS

VOLUME III

EDITOR

ANTHONY SC TEO

World Scientific

NEW JERSEY · LONDON · SINGAPORE · BEIJING · SHANGHAI · HONG KONG · TAIPEI · CHENNAI · TOKYO

Published by

World Scientific Publishing Co. Pte. Ltd.

5 Toh Tuck Link, Singapore 596224

USA office: 27 Warren Street, Suite 401-402, Hackensack, NJ 07601

UK office: 57 Shelton Street, Covent Garden, London WC2H 9HE

National Library Board, Singapore Cataloguing in Publication Data

Name(s): Univer-Cities (Conference) (2016 : Australia) | Teo, Anthony S. C., 1944–   editor.

Title: Univer-cities. Volume III, Strategic dilemmas of medical origins and selected modalities : water, quantum leap & new models / editor, Anthony SC Teo.

Description: Singapore : World Scientific Publishing Co. Pte Ltd., [2018] | Includes bibliographical references and index.

Identifier(s): OCN 1021867598 | ISBN 978-981-3238-72-5 (paperback)

Subject(s): LCSH: Community and college--Congresses. | University towns--Congresses. | Medicine--Study and teaching (Graduate)--Congresses.

Classification: DDC 378.103--dc23

British Library Cataloguing-in-Publication Data

A catalogue record for this book is available from the British Library.

For any available supplementary material, please visit
http://www.worldscientific.com/worldscibooks/10.1142/10952#t=suppl

Typeset by Stallion Press
Email: enquiries@stallionpress.com

Printed in Singapore

To the idea of the New Silk Roads redefined by univer-cities

CONTENTS

Foreword
Koh Boon Hwee, Chairman
Board of Trustees
Nanyang Technological University, Singapore   xv

Acknowledgements   xvii

About the Contributors   xxi

Welcome Address
Caroline McMillen, Vice-Chancellor and
President, University of Newcastle, Australia   xxxix

Keynote Address
Leszek Borysiewicz, Vice-Chancellor,
University of Cambridge, UK   xli

Chapter 1   Univer-Cities: Strategic Dilemmas of
Strategy & Leadership — Medical Origins & Select
Modalities   1
Anthony SC Teo

Part I
The Trans-Disciplinary Impact on Academic Evolution:
From Medicine to Global Univer-Cities   **25**

Chapter 2   Dilemma & Strategy: Shaping the University
of Newcastle, Australia   27
R. John Aitken and H. Le Gresley

Chapter 3   Medicine in Cambridge   45
Gordon Johnson

Chapter 4   Meeting Societal Challenges Through Medical
Education and Research: LKCMedicine,
NTU-ICL Singapore   59
Bertil Andersson

Chapter 5   Univer-City of Zurich: An Evolutionary-Medical
Perspective   77
Frank Rühli and Maciej Henneberg

Part II
Univer-Cities 2013 Updates:
Berkeley, Ottawa, Hong Kong   **85**

Chapter 6   University of California, Berkeley in the Bay
Region: The Present and Future of a Public
Research University   87
Emily B. Marthinsen and John J. Parman

Chapter 7   An Architecture of Light: Ottawa, the City of Light   101
Roseann O'Reilly Runte

Chapter 8   Re-Inventing the University of Hong Kong in Both
Mortar and Spirit: Building the Centennial Campus   111
John Malpas

Part III
Ecosystems of Globalising Univer-Cities:
Strategic and Evolving Implications   **127**

Chapter 9   Safe Water for the Developing World: Rhetoric
and Reality   129
Asit K. Biswas and Cecilia Tortajada

Chapter 10   On Strategy for Developing an Innovative
University: S-Factor, S-Gap and Vector Delta (δ)   151
Nam P. Suh

Chapter 11   Multi-Campus Internationalisation of Higher
             Education Institutions   177
             Gabriel Hawawini

Chapter 12   A Singapore University Catering to the Needs
             of a Population Amidst a Volatile and Changing
             Economy   205
             Cheong Hee Kiat

Appendices   **231**

Appendix 1: Advisory Council of the Univer-Cities
             Conference 2016   233
Appendix 2: Programme of the Univer-Cities Conference 2016 237
Appendix 3: About the Unique Univer-Cities Design   241

Index   **243**

FOREWORD

"This univer-cities narrative has made pleasing progress since Volume I on *Univer-Cities: Strategic Implications for Asia: Readings from Cambridge and Berkeley to Singapore.* That first volume envisaged the UC2013 Conference on *Univer-Cities of the Future: Strategic View of the Future from Berkeley and Cambridge to Rising Asia and Singapore* followed by UC 2016 on *Strategic Dilemmas of Medical Origins and Select Modalities — Water, Quantum Leap and New Models.*

I am delighted to pen this Foreword to encourage this niche avenue of fomenting new ideas with top academic leaders meeting collegially and mulling modalities that hold potential for theoretical underpinnings for higher education's future, fidelity to its societal mission and aiding to resolve humanity's challenges. It is a perennial challenge to prepare for succession; who is to educate the educators of multi-billion univer-city institutions devoted to the transient present, to focus them on the future, socio-economic and human progress and eventually, survival.

Universities risk alienation from their host cities and wider society. Such has so poignantly emerged in America with the envisaged tax on perceived elitist universities and their largesse of endowments and reducing donors' tax incentives.

Univer-cities as an evolution from earlier times like Cambridge 800 years ago and needing active nurturing will help academic leadership avoid being blind-sided by nascent trends that seem to unexpectedly spring upon these timeless institutions.

I hope that this univer-cities discourse will address the disruptive side of globalisation, innovation, technology on the nature of work, employment and enterprise; and the unsustainable rise of inequality in human socio-economic life.

For water and other resources to open new vistas in medicine and public health and addressing self-sufficiency in water may seem easier than constantly adjusting higher education to continual socio-economic restructuring and ameliorating inequality **or creating** the quantum leap for research-intensive universities as posed by MIT Professor Suh in this volume.

Koh Boon Hwee
Chairman, Board of Trustees
Nanyang Technological University and
Chairman
Credence Partners Pte Ltd.

ACKNOWLEDGEMENTS

Praise be to the Univer-Cities Conference Advisory Councillors and academia's leading light Sir Borysiewicz who set the stage for the impact of medical origins and the global context of univer-cities redefining the New Silk Road. Councillor Gordon Johnson our historians' historian puts it in the language of history, "The univer-city is a complex being and not simply evolved. It is, in the end, a fragile human creation, requiring constant attention to flourish."

May I acknowledge the many accomplished academic leaders who contributed to the univer-cities conversation in "perfect serenity" of open, uninhibited and collegial discourse. Classicist Professor Morpeth said of the proceedings: "Clarity with ease amongst equals, drawing on the past, present and future yet not encumbered nor overly indebted to the past."

To Vice-Chancellor Runte and the Berkeley Three: Emeritus Dean Bender, Assistant Vice-Chancellor Marthinsen and John Parman, my thanks. This fragile human creation of univer-cites is morphing to the continuum of Duo-Univer-cities as in Carleton-Ottawa to the emerging Tri-Univer-cities of Berkeley, UC San Francisco and Stanford — equivalent to the economy of Holland, nudged together through citizen Zuckerberg's mission-purpose US$3 billion investment in public health. Such an initiative optimises the complementarity of medico-health research collaboration and applied results as directly as possible to the citizenry and not simply more mortar. The future has arrived at UT Southwestern Dallas — Parkland Memorial Hospital where there is medical and community collaboration.

To the academic leaders who are not blindsided but instead steadfastly maintain their commitment to the "re-societalisation" through their univer-cities; who grapple with the dilemmas of medical origins and contending disciplines, strategy and leadership; and who evoke the grace of unrelenting charm tempered with understanding and prescience: VC Caroline McMillen, Bertil Andersson, Gordon Johnson, Graeme Jameson, John Malpas, Nam P. Suh, John Aitken, Tan Sri Sharifah amongst the many thought leaders who contributed to this 12-chapter Volume III; and the venerable Lee Foundation led by Chairman Dr Lee Seng Tee FBA whose generous S$150 million underpinned the setting-up of the NTU-Imperial Lee Kong Chian School of Medicine — pray I thank you all.

For if a strategic view of the future is to pre-empt and prevail, we look to examples like Cambridge whose emerging bio-medical research campus approaches that phase (like the gamete sperm and the recent research implying an active host); globally innovative universities like KAIST and NUS; NTU that rose to 11th position globally, boosted by the new medical school; and others.

To Berkeley's indomitable Emeritus Dean Richard Bender who joined me to advise NTU on place-making to 2025 as he did with the Mori Foundation and Waseda, Elon Musk, Roosevelt Island's rebirth and heightened univer-city engagement — ever my respect.

To Winnie Eley and the UoN's UC2016 Team at the jubilee Hunter Medical Centre who made everything so seamless and woven for success by acclamation, celebrated at Merewether's Surfhouse under the rare blue moon.

To Yeo Chee Kiong our resident artist and sculptor for the continuity in design and legend of the cover of the Univer-Cities Series.

To my wife Margaret on our 50th anniversary, three sons and six grandchildren, my everlasting love. 'Tis a labour of love with friends and imagineers — the future for our grandchildren is upon us as we are passing through with our precious ones Xuan, Jun, Wen, Yin, Kai and En.

Sequel — To President HK Cheong of UniSim, now Singapore University of Social Sciences (SUSS), for bearing the torch to host Univer-Cities Conference 2019 (from 17 to 18 November 2019) focusing on the theme of aligning univer-cities to mid-career up-skilling and tertiary life-long learning. The discussion will be set against a back drop of the continual economic restructuring and disruption through globalization; and unsustainable rising inequality needing re-modelled third millennium social contract? Papers and interest of academic leaders can be directed to hkcheong@suss.edu.sg or UC2019 Convenor at ascteo@univer-cities.com

Through World Scientific Publishing's Chua Hong Koon and Triena Ong, the three univer-cities volumes are dedicated to the endeavour that case studies can provide a rich vein for developing theory per theorist Kathryn Eisenhardt of Stanford.

Anthony SC Teo
Adjunct Professor
Lee Kuan Yew School of Public Policy
National University of Singapore

ABOUT THE CONTRIBUTORS

 **R. John Aitken**

Pro Vice-Chancellor, Health and Medicine,

University of Newcastle, Australia

PANELIST

Laureate Professor Aitken's research career began with a PhD in reproductive biology from the University of Cambridge. Following post-doctoral positions at the Institute of Animal Genetics, University of Edinburgh and the University of Bordeaux, he managed two task forces within the Human Reproduction Unit of the World Health Organisation. In 1977, he joined the Medical Research Council's Reproductive Biology Unit, University of Edinburgh, to establish a research group in gamete biology with clinical outreach into infertility. In 1992, John was awarded an Honorary Professorship within the Faculty of Medicine of Edinburgh University and in 1998 he received an ScD degree from the University of Cambridge in recognition of his research contributions to gamete biology. In the same year he moved to the University of Newcastle, NSW, as Chair of Biological Sciences and, later, Director of the ARC Centre of Excellence in Biotechnology and Development.

John Aitken has published over 600 research articles, given more than 350 invited lectures and filed 13 patents. His work has been cited more than 37,000 times (h-index of 102). Since arriving in Newcastle he has generated more than $40 million in research income and has been continuously funded by both the ARC and the NHMRC. In 2005 he received the ST Huang-Chan Memorial Medal from the University of Hong Kong, was appointed a Laureate Professor by the University of Newcastle and received the 2005 Scientist-of-the-Year award from the Hunter Medical Research Institute. In 2012 he received the Simmet Prize, the highest honour bestowed by the International Congress on Animal Reproduction, and was named as the New South Wales Scientist-of-the-Year. In 2016 he was awarded the Carl G. Hartman prize, the most prestigious international award in reproductive science and only the second time in its long 47-year history that this award has been bestowed on someone outside of North America.

Bertil Andersson

President,

Nanyang Technological University, Singapore, 2011–2017

PANELIST

A world-renowned Swedish plant biochemist, Professor Bertil Andersson is a pioneer of photosynthesis research who has authored more than 300 papers with over 14,000 citations.

He was NTU Provost, Chief Executive of the European Science Foundation in France, Rector of Linkoping University in Sweden, as well as Chairman of the Nobel Committee for Chemistry and a Trustee of the Nobel Foundation. Since becoming President of NTU in 2011, he has led it to distinction as the world's best young university that is also ranked 11th globally and leads the top Asian universities in normalised research citation impact.

A Fellow of Imperial College London, he was instrumental in Imperial College London establishing a medical school with NTU in Singapore. He has received the Austrian Wilhelm Exner Medal and the Singapore President's Science and Technology Medal, both top honours for lifetime achievement. He serves on the boards of international foundations, societies and public agencies.

Asit K. Biswas

Distinguished Visiting Professor,

Lee Kuan Yew School of Public Policy, National University of Singapore

PANELIST

Professor Asit K. Biswas is one of the world's leading authorities on water and environment. He is Co-founder of the Third World Centre for Water Management, Mexico. He was a member of the World Commission on Water, and a founder of International Water Resources Association and World Water Council. He has been senior advisor to 19 governments at Prime Ministerial and Ministerial levels; six Heads of United Nations Agencies; two Secretary-Generals of OECD; Past President of International Water Resources Association; and advisor to CEOs of four major MNCs on strategic issues.

Among his numerous awards are Stockholm Water Prize, considered to be the Nobel Prize in water-related activities, and five honorary doctorates from major universities. Reuters selected him as being one of the top 10 water trailblazers of the world. In 2015 he was named the world's second most influential water industry leader and recevied the "Hind Rattan" (Jewel of India) award. He is author of 83 books and over 650 scientific and technical papers. His work has been translated into 39 languages. He is a regular commentator to the global media on politics, international relations, business, water, energy, flood and environmental issues.

Leszek Borysiewicz

Vice-Chancellor,

University of Cambridge, 2010–2017

SPEAKER (video in absentia)

Sir Leszek Borysiewicz is Chairman of the Board of Trustees of Cancer Research UK. He was Chief Executive of the UK's Medical Research Council from 2007, and from 2001 to 2007 was at Imperial College London, where he served as Principal of the Faculty of Medicine and later as Deputy Rector.

Born in Wales to Polish parents, he went on to the Welsh National School of Medicine, later taking up clinical and research posts in London. In 1988 he moved to the University of Cambridge as lecturer in Medicine. He went on to be Professor of Medicine at the University of Wales for ten years until 2001. As Deputy Rector of Imperial College, Sir Leszek was responsible for the overall academic and scientific direction of the institution, particularly the development of inter-disciplinary research between engineering, physical sciences and bio-medicine.

Concurrently with his position at Imperial College, Sir Leszek was also Governor of the Wellcome Trust, a founding Fellow of the Academy of Medical Sciences, Chairman of the National Health Service (NHS) (Wales) R&D Grants Committee and acting Director of NHS (Wales) Research and Development, a member of the Council of Cancer Research UK, a non-executive Director of North Thames Regional Health Authority and a member of the MRC Council. He was elected a Fellow of the Royal Society in 2008.

Professor Borysiewicz was knighted in the 2001 New Year's Honours List for his contribution to medical education and research into developing vaccines, including work towards a vaccine to combat cervical cancer.

Cheong Hee Kiat

President,

Singapore University of Social Sciences

Professor Cheong Hee Kiat is the founding President of the Singapore University of Social Sciences (SUSS), formerly known as SIM University (UniSIM). He was Deputy President and Dean of the School of Civil and Environmental Engineering in Nanyang Technological University (NTU) Singapore before taking up his current appointment in 2005.

Prof Cheong has served on various local and international university accreditation and academic committees and boards, and is currently also Chairman of the Singapore Bible College. He obtained his PhD from the Imperial College, London.

He is a registered Professional Engineer, a Fellow of the Institution of Engineers Singapore and the Academy of Engineering, Singapore.

Gabriel Hawawini

Emeritus Professor of Finance,

and former Dean, INSEAD

PANELIST

Professor Hawawini is Emeritus Professor of Finance at INSEAD, held the Henry Grunfeld Chair in Investment Banking from 1996 to 2013 and served as dean from 2000 to 2006, spearheading the school's global expansion. He is also a Visiting Professor at the Wharton School of the University of Pennsylvania where he received the Helen Kardon Moss Anvil Award for Excellence in Teaching (1988).

Prior to joining INSEAD in 1982, he taught at New York University, Columbia University, and the City University of New York where he received the Presidential Award for Distinguished Faculty Scholarship (1982). He has authored 16 books, two online courses and over 70 research papers. His most recent books include *Finance for Executives: Managing for Value Creation* (2015) and *The Internationalization of Higher Education and Business Schools: A Critical Review* (2016).

Gabriel is the recipient of the Fulbright Award for Global Business Education (2004), the French Legion of Honor (2005) and The Chief Executive Leadership Award (2006) of the Council for Advancement and Support of Education.

He chaired the Equis accreditation board of the European Foundation for Management Education (2004–2011) and served on the board of directors of Vivendi, S&B Minerals, and Rémy Cointreau. He is currently a trustee of the University of the People, an advisor to Momentum Invest, and a member of the advisory board of several higher education institutions around the world, including MIT Sloan and Carnegie Mellon University in Qatar.

Gabriel received his bachelor's and master's degrees in chemical engineering from the University of Toulouse (1971 and 1972) and his doctorate in economics and finance from New York University (1977). He was awarded Honorary Doctorates from the University of Liège in Belgium (2005), the Art Center College of Design in Pasadena, California (2005) and the American University in Cairo (2010).

Sharifah Hapsah Syed Hasan Shahabudin

President,

National Council of Women's Organisations of Malaysia

CHAIR

Tan Sri Dato' Seri Emerita Professor Sharifah Hapsah Shahabudin, a medical doctor, is a former Vice-Chancellor of Universiti Kabangsaan Malaysia (UKM), and current President of the National Council of Women's Organisations of Malaysia. She is also Senior Consultant in the Prime Minister's Department overseeing the Permata programme. She combines her academic and social activist work in gender equality and child development to strengthen community engagement projects in UKM. Notable projects include the Centre for Education of the Gifted and Talented, Centre for Empowering Youths-at-risk, the Children's Hospital and the Yunus Centre for Social Business. She promotes knowledge and technology transfer for wealth creation and social well-being by nurturing a culture of innovation and entrepreneurship in research, teaching and service in UKM living laboratories across Malaysia. Her latest contribution is a chapter on "Institutional Governance for a Shared Glocal Engagement Mission" in the GUNI *Higher Education in the World 6* publication entitled "Towards a Socially Responsible University: Balancing the Global with the Local".

Graeme Jameson AO

Director, Centre for Multiphase Process,

University of Newcastle, Australia

CHAIR

Laureate Professor Graeme Jameson has a background in the hydrodynamics of bubbles and particles, especially relating to the minerals industry. He has made significant advances in separating valuable minerals from rock using the flotation process. He applied this knowledge to the development of a radical new flotation cell, known as the Jameson Cell. It is in use in 26 countries worldwide, for the recovery of valuable minerals and fine coal. The Cell is also used for environmental purposes, to remove contaminants from industrial wastewaters and biological effluent streams.

Laureate Professor Jameson has received many awards and medals, the most recent being the inaugural Australian Prime Minister's Science Prize for Innovation in 2015, elected a Foreign Member of the United States National Academy of Engineering (NAE) in 2015, named NSW Scientist of the Year in 2013, and was the recipient of the prestigious Lifetime Achievement Award of the International Mineral Processing Congress in 2016.

Gordon Johnson

Deputy Vice-Chancellor,

University of Cambridge, 2002–2010

CHAIR AND PANELIST

Gordon Johnson is a Cambridge-educated histo-rian. He went to Trinity College, Cambridge in 1961 and following his first degree wrote a PhD thesis on early Indian Nationalism. He was a Fellow suc-cessively at Trinity and Selwyn Colleges and then President of Wolfson College, Cambridge (1993–2010). Dr Johnson chaired Cambridge University Press from 1993 until 2009. He edited *Modern Asian Studies* from 1971–2008 and was General Editor of the *New Cambridge History of India*. He was Director of the Centre of South Asian Studies in Cambridge from 1983–2001. He served two terms as President of the Royal Asiatic Society until 2018. *Provincial Politics and Indian Nationalism* (CUP, 1973) is the book resulting from his thesis. He has also published a *Cultural Atlas of India* (1995) and *University Politics: FM Cornford's Cambridge and his Advice to the Young Academic Politician* (CUP, 1994; centenary edition 2008). He is currently writing a book about Cambridge University Press.

John Malpas

Former Vice-President,

University of Hong Kong

PANELIST

John Malpas is Emeritus Professor of Earth Sciences and was Vice-President and Pro Vice-Chancellor of the University of Hong Kong from 2000 until 2013. He was responsible for strategic planning and university infrastructure and resources, including human resources. Between 2006 and 2012 he was responsible for large-scale campus development in response to the change from a three-year to a four-year undergraduate curriculum in the Hong Kong education system. He was educated as an earth scientist at Oxford University (MA and DSc) and Memorial University of Newfoundland (MSc and PhD), and has undertaken award-winning research into the origins of the world's oceans.

Before coming to Hong Kong in 1994 he was Dean of Graduate Studies at Memorial University, and held various senior positions in scientific organisations including Joint Oceanographic Institutions, the Geological Association of Canada, Canadian Geoscience Council, National Research Council of Canada, and Canadian Centre for Advanced Research. He was a member of the University Grants Committee of Hong Kong (2006–2013). In 2012 he was awarded an Honorary Doctorate from the Hong Kong Academy of Performing Arts. In 2013 he became President of Centennial College in the University of Hong Kong.

Emily Marthinsen

Campus Architect,

University of California, Berkeley, USA

PANELIST

As Campus Architect at the University of California, Berkeley, Emily Marthinsen is responsible for campus physical and environmental planning. Her portfolio includes project planning and design, sustainability, city and private development partnerships and campus long range development planning. Until December 2017, she was an Assistant Vice-Chancellor at UC Berkeley.

She has a Bachelor of Arts in Geography from the University of Chicago and Master of Architecture from UC Berkeley. She is a licensed Architect in California and has over thirty-five years of relevant work experience at UC Berkeley and with design and planning firms in Berkeley, San Francisco, Washington DC, Alexandria, and Virginia.

Emily Marthinsen is a Fellow of the American Institute of Architects (AIA), and a member of the Society for Campus and University Planning (SCUP) and the Association of University Architects (AUA). She is incoming Chair of the National AIA's Public Architects Advisory Group and is a frequent presenter and writer on campus planning issues.

Caroline McMillen

Vice-Chancellor and President,

University of Newcastle, Australia

SPEAKER AND HOST

Professor Caroline McMillen joined the University of Newcastle as Vice-Chancellor and President in October 2011. She has previously served in academic leadership positions at Monash University, the University of Adelaide and the University of South Australia. Professor McMillen is an inaugural Fellow of the Australian Academy of Health and Medical Sciences, and a Bragg Member of the Royal Institution, Australia. She holds a Bachelor of Arts (Honours) and Doctor of Philosophy from the University of Oxford, and completed her medical training graduating with an MB, B Chir at the University of Cambridge. She has held international and national roles in medical and health research, industry engagement and innovation strategy and policy development.

Professor McMillen is a Director of the Board of Universities Australia; the Australian Business Higher Education Round Table (BHERT); and the Universities Admissions Centre (UAC). Professor McMillen is also a BusinessEvents Sydney Ambassador.

She has served on a range of international disciplinary bodies and industry groups as well as government leadership groups focused on innovation, defence, and manufacturing.

As a medical researcher, Professor McMillen is internationally recognised for her work on the impact of the nutritional environment before birth on the risk of developing cardiovascular disease and obesity in adult life and is an inaugural Fellow of the Australian Academy of Health and Medical Sciences, and a Bragg Member of the Royal Institution, Australia.

John J. Parman

Senior Associate,

Gensler

PANELIST

John J. Parman is a Senior Associate at Gensler, a global design consultancy. In this role, he serves as an advisor to the firm's Headquarters Group in San Francisco and to the Managing Principals of its international regions. Until May 2017, he was the editorial director of its Communications Studio. The long-time writing partner of UC Berkeley Professor Richard Bender, Parman is an editorial adviser to ORO Editions' architecture and planning research imprint, *Architect's Newspaper* (California edition), and *Room One Thousand*, the annual publication of UC Berkeley's College of Environmental Design. He writes regularly for the Seattle-based design quarterly, *Arcade*, and is a founding contributor to a new journal, *Architecture, Design + Research*, sponsored by the Association of Collegiate Schools of Architecture. He co-founded the award-winning quarterly, *Design Book Review*, which he published from 1983 to 1999.

Frank Rühli

Director, Institute of Evolutionary Medicine,

University of Zurich, Switzerland

PANELIST

Professor Dr Med. Frank Rühli, PhD, USMLE, Exec. MBA is a Professor of anatomy and Founder and Director of the globally unique Institute of Evolutionary Medicine, Medical Faculty, University of Zurich. He is Director of the future Medical Museum and Head of the Medico-historical collection, University of Zurich. Dr Rühli is also a steering committee member of two University Research Priority Initiatives. He has held visiting researcher status and professional appointments, respectively, at Harvard University, University Hospital Zurich and University of Adelaide. His main expertise is the study of ancient human remains; he has acquired ca. US$17m of third-party funding and has ca. 200 scientific publications. Dr Rühli serves in multiple professional bodies, science and museum advisory boards and political organisations (e.g. President, Health Care Commission Free Democratic Liberal Party FDP Switzerland). He serves in the rank of a lieutenant-colonel responsible for Medical Scenarios, Staff Operational Training, Swiss Armed Forces.

Roseann O'Reilly Runte

President and CEO,

Canada Foundation for Innovation

PANELIST (video in absentia)

Roseann Runte is President and CEO of the Canada Foundation for Innovation. She has previously served as President of Carleton University, Old Dominion University, Universite Sainte-Anne and Principal of Glendon College. Her publications include works on literature, cultural and economic development and university research as well as creative writing which was recognised by the poetry prize from the Academie Francaise.

Dr Runte holds degrees from the State University of New York and the University of Kansas and honorary degrees from many institutions. She has been President of the Canadian Commission for UNESCO, a member of the executive of the Club of Rome, and has served on numerous boards ranging from financial to medical, carrier and shipbuilding to cellular research, from the arts to social services and environmental stewardship.

Her work has been recognized with awards including the Order of Canada, the Royal Society of Canada, the Palmes Academiques, the Order of Merit, the Order of King Leopold of Belgium and the Order of Malta.

KEYNOTE ADDRESS

I have followed the proceedings of the first two Univer-Cities Conferences with interest, and I am delighted to have been asked to send a message to this the third meeting.

Healthcare provides the key theme at this year's conference, so it is particularly appropriate that Newcastle University, with its strengths in medical research and healthcare education, should be hosting the meeting.

We, too, in Cambridge have a proud tradition of medical research. The teaching of medicine at Cambridge in fact dates back to 1540 when Henry VIII endowed the University's first Professorship of Physic, Dr John Blyth. Much has changed in what is nearly half a millennium since then. But one thing has remained constant — in Cambridge it is our mission. We are told "to contribute to society through the pursuit of education, learning, and research at the highest international levels of excellence".

This sounds a simple request. But it is also complex and challenging. For universities today are both rooted in their society and expected to resolve increasingly complex global problems.

These apparently contradictory demands are at the heart of the Univer-Cities Conference. How can we be rooted in our local, regional and national context while building international networks to address the kinds of problems facing humanity today. At the same time, we are expected to educate for a world where technology has transformed the pace of change.

Nowhere is this complex mix of interests more difficult to bring into a creative balance than in the field of medicine and healthcare. Research has transformed patient outcomes. Yet global inequality means this research does not lift the poorest as high as those in developed countries.

Modern technology can help. We are seeing the development of a new "Silk Road" carrying ideas and practices across Asia and the Pacific.

But we need more than technology. We need a commitment — a commitment to pursue research across disciplinary boundaries, from "pure" research to the direct application of new knowledge to new products, approaches and policies.

And that is where our local, regional and national roots come in. These give us the grounding, the connection to the people we are here to serve — in other words, the society of Cambridge's mission statement. Nowhere is this more important than in the field of medicine and healthcare.

The concept of "univer-cities", bringing together these diverse threads and building a new "Silk Road" of connected institutions, is a way of bringing these ideas to life.

I look forward, therefore, to hearing about your meeting in Newcastle and to reading the papers from the panels. I am sorry to miss the discussions. I send my best wishes for your conference and for the continuation of such an incredibly important project.

Thank you

Sir Leszek Borysiewicz
Chairman
Board of Trustees of Cancer Research UK,
and
Vice-Chancellor
University of Cambridge, (2010–2017)

CHAPTER ONE

UNIVER-CITIES: STRATEGIC DILEMMAS OF STRATEGY & LEADERSHIP — MEDICAL ORIGINS & SELECT MODALITIES

ANTHONY SC TEO

"How wonderful that we have met with a paradox. Now we have some hope of making progress"
Nobel Prize-winning physicist Niels Bohr

"To me, you are America"
President Xi Jinping, when asked in 2012 why he chose Muscatine, Iowa instead of visiting Washington, DC

Introduction

The Univer-Cities Conference 2016 at the University of Newcastle picked up the torch from Conference 2013 at Nanyang Technological University. The Univer-Cities discourse started with a focus on Implications for Asia Vol. I, Strategic View of the Future Vol. II to the present focus on Dynamics of Univer-Cities with Medical Origins that is Volume III in the series. Different, Complex and Integrative?

University of Newcastle Vice-Chancellor Professor Caroline McMillen through her academic leadership and unrelenting charm was our Host and Co-Chair of this conference. Deeply committed to this narrative which is well documented in her Volume II chapter "Recasting the City of Newcastle as a Univer-City: The Journey from 'Olde' Newcastle-upon-Tyne to the New Silk Road", Professor McMillen and her Project Team created an outstanding conference and milieu for robust deliberations in 2016.

The Univer-Cities Conference 2016 (UC2016) continued its tradition of the trinity of unique engagement amongst collegiate academic leaders *primus inter pares*: evolving conversation, multi- & trans-disciplinary; continuity update; and published proceedings.

We are most grateful for the diversity and trans-disciplinary input of thought leaders amongst whom are Vice-Chancellors, Presidents, PVCs, DVCs, AVCs, architects & policymakers from disciplines like anthropology, architecture, bio-engineering, business, campus development, chemistry, disruptive economics, environment, history, hydrology, law, medicine, plant biology, psychology as well as writers, classicists, musicologists, pharmacologists, *et al.* Our Univer-Cities Conference Advisory Councillors include Nobel Laureate for Chemistry CalTech Professor Rudolph Marcus; Plant Biologist Professor Bertil Andersson, NTU President & Nobel Trustee; Emeritus MIT's Ralph & Eloise Cross Professor Nam-Pyo Suh; and Emeritus Berkeley's Environmental Design Dean & Chair Professor of Architecture Professor Richard Bender.

Interesting Times 2016: Unexpected, Dilemmas & Paradoxes
Before we delve into the proceedings of UC2016, let's note the big elephant in the conference room. Our conference took place at the time of the US Presidential Election in November 2016. Two aspects of evolving ecology of the past seemed to converge. Firstly, the rural and suburban voted for radical change from "America is great when it's good" to "Make America great again". The first epigram is innocuous yet prescient as it highlights the 33-year relationship of China's President Xi Jinping and the now US Ambassador Terry Granstad to Beijing (then Iowa Governor, meeting a young and promising Hebei agriculture official in the cornfields of Muscatine in the great granary state of Iowa) — a potential re-supplier of grain to narrow the US trade deficit with the PRC!

Secondly, with US univer-cities in mind, we are reminded of the Morrill Land-Grant Acts of 1862 that led to the setting-up of modern research universities to develop the mechanisation of agriculture. Examples are institutions such as MIT, where the mission is so reflected in its founding constitution, and Texas A&M (Agricultural and Mechanical) University, the fourth largest US research-intensive land, sea and space grant institution in collaboration with NASA, NIH, NSF and Office of Naval Research. In academic disciplines, it melded from STEM (science, technology, engineering & mathematics) to

A&M's STEAM (with "A" returning as "Agriculture") and more. Convergence and trans-disciplinarity are to trump academic silos.

Continuity: Past, Present & Future

The past is not another country as described by VC McMillen who gave a tour de force from Homeric times of *The Mighty Dead* to the 21st century. Ambitious inter-continental visions of the University of Newcastle (UoN) from its medical origins with a strong engineering focus confronted the alignment of "dilemmic strategy and dilemmic leadership".

What made UC2016 different— was it the conversation? A classicist, Professor Morpeth of UoN, may have a point: that the discourse has a *professorial style* — which he takes to mean: "That quality where knowledge and mastery of the art and craft of the profession of letters, develops its own distinctive style of presentation which takes the intellectual argument, exploration or observation to another plane or level effortlessly." This can be said of many, and Cambridge Don Johnson and UoN VC McMillen would probably win a straw poll (and pleasingly, Stockholm Water Prize Awardee Professor Biswas was invited to a colloquium, in February 2017 by HH Pope Francis through the Pontifical Academy of Sciences, on water as a human right leading to an expected Rome Declaration; and potentially an encyclical).

We are carving a niche of *"thinking paths"* which inspired Darwin, a narrative in which univer-cities would redefine the New Silk Road. The cornerstone of our conversation is the commitment to peek into or "live the future". We view the challenges through our collaborative vision inspired by imagination, insight and intuition that grapples with the creative balance. This conversation is weaved out of the dilemmas of strategy and leadership in one of humanity's beloved institutions, the university *(with a long view strategy)* and the city *(a relatively shorter one)*. The univer-city evolves seemingly, symbiotically from its origins, a millennium ago, in Bologna, Cambridge, Oxford and Paris.

The prequel and the ensuing five pillars make the University of Cambridge so successful. The five pillars comprise two abilities — to deliver excellence in education and research; and three commitments — to collegiality, being a truly global university *and* service to society.

In his Keynote Address Sir Borysiewicz stated: "These apparently contradictory demands are at the heart of the Univer-Cities Conference. How can we be rooted in our local, regional and national context while building international networks to address the kinds of problems facing humanity today. At the same time, we are expected to educate for a world where technology has transformed the pace of change. Nowhere is this complex mix of interests more difficult to bring into a creative balance than in the field of medicine and healthcare."

Creative Balance, Dilemmas & Paradoxes: To be sure, "paradoxes invite consideration of alternatives that are interdependent as well as contradictory" (Smith, Lewis & Tushman, 2016). This affects strategy as well as core leadership and the widening society of stakeholders. Nobelist Niels Bohr shares this view enabling progress whereas Kissinger thinks of strategic co-existence.

I envisage dilemmas and paradoxes are on a continuum betwixt human and nature's condition. So I am partial to address the human dilemmas of leadership and paradoxes of nature. Iconic is whether Time Travel could bring us to the Past when we're in the Present. Stephen Hawking, the Cambridge Lucasian Professor of Mathematics, is grappling with this Space-Time paradox framing it for best experimental parameters in a limited "finite region" of the universe (Hawking, 2013).

Sir Borysiewicz's video Keynote Address serves both as a *prequel* of the medical origins at Cambridge in 1540 with the appointment of Sir John Blyth and the *sequel* that UC2016 is held at the University of Newcastle befitting its reputation in research in medicine and healthcare with the lead-off address by Newcastle's Laureate Professor John Aitken, Pro Vice-Chancellor (Faculty of Health and Medicine).

1. **UoN & Strategy Dilemma:** Professor Aitken presented the core theme by framing it as the *strategy dilemma*. The future strategic role of the Faculty of Health and Medicine (FHM) with the other faculties is as a *regional* university with responsibility to society and always collegiate and in open collaborative ways:

> a clear vision for 2025 which will see the institution standing as a global leader distinguished by a commitment to equity and excellence and to creating a better future for its regions through a focus on innovation and impact.

At its origin, the Medical School pioneered problem-based learning spearheaded by founding Dean Maddison (and then Professor Saxon White who was an active delegate at UC2016 asserting for more humanities). Aitken embraces the indispensability of *collegiality* (and technology as an enabler) in total agreement with Sir Borysiewicz.

Aitken postulates a way to address the strategy dilemma of medicine and other disciplines in that "health and medicine constitute an ideal nucleation point in the development of such an open collaborative approach". Such an approach nurtures convergence and a creative destruction of silos (benign and evolving) of faculties and disciplines. This aids the transversing of the states from multidisciplinary and cross-disciplinary to highly sought trans-disciplinarity of research.

Trans-disciplinary research at the University of Newcastle coalesces its multi-disciplinary research in the Hunter Medical Research Institute (HMRI) with some 1,500 home grown and foreign talent research scientists. Professor Jennifer Martin best profiles its trans-disciplinary approach, bravely taken as a

> 'reductionist step' back to basic science in order to understand why people respond to medications so differently. All of the leadership of our team is from outside of Newcastle! But we have all moved here because of the freedom and support from the University and the encouragement to think broadly and internationally. Newcastle is a very exciting place to be at the moment.

The strategy dilemma of university and society reveals the tension and the attendant commitment: "Society in general will only ever accept what researchers do, if the outcomes of their labours are measured in terms of social and economic impact." The corollary that is proposed is therefore to "develop an integrated language, administrative framework and physical infrastructure that facilitate rather than discourage such interactions". Doubtless, this is a Herculean task. However, this is just what was embarked upon as described by Professor Malpas in his chapter "Re-inventing the University of Hong Kong". Malpas opined: "The whole process to me boils down to the right people, right place, right time. It was a God-given opportunity and a real team effort."

Aitken reflects on the emerging reality of creating innovative value for the university and the broader set of stakeholders of the university:

the univer-city, government, health service and industry extending to society at large. Recalling Sir Borysiewicz's comment on "creative balance" and a silver lining: "paradoxes invite consideration of alternatives that are interdependent as well as contradictory with a view of 'dynamic equilibrium'" (Smith, Lewis & Tushman, 2016) rather than solely anchored on consistency (of being wrong or right).

To be sure, a new thoughtful matrix and process of review would be needed as distinct from the publication orientation pursued by research-intensive universities. Newcastle, Australia's seventh largest city — together with its University's innovation initiatives, new urban redevelopment city-centre campus with it business and law schools — is an emerging smart city. Novocastrians who possess an engaged and radical streak (Bennett, Cushing & Eklund, 2015) would trust and verify Aitken's words of the value of a "fair go for all". In situ action is needed to counter global trends of inequality in healthcare accessible by the rich vis-à-vis the less well off towards assuaging Sir Borysiewicz's concerns. The apparent inequality in Cleveland (and quite a number of other cities) of private medical excellence co-existing with segments of poverty of care is glaring, yet there is hope in the expressed policy vision of the incoming WHO chief: to reduce that inequality globally, potentially aided by fast and "brilliant technologies" (Brynjolfsson & McAfee, 2016). However, the consensus is not clearcut, as recent research emerges: there is Yale's Starman Dilemma Proposition — fair inequality versus unfair equality?

Cambridge Sequel in Scale & Scope: The disruptive innovations of the Cambridge Bio-medical Campus (CBC) and the phenomenon of the Cambridge Silicon Fen share a common feature that erupted only in the past half century. However, one is mindful of the nascent power of evolution of the univer-city of the Cambridge market town, and an over 800-year collegiate continuity through its 345 Regents or Vice-Chancellors drawing leadership from amongst its community of scholars (Johnson, 2015).

There was the innocuous strategic move of the Addenbrooke Hospital in the midst of Cambridge (now morphed into the Judge Business School) to the outer southern border and the founding of CBC, one of the largest world-class medical and health science research and teaching clusters and the biggest in Europe with some 12,000 scientists and heath science professionals. This is no less than the univer-city's strategic view of the future with decided preemption to lead and prevail (Teo, 2015).

Centres of research now include the Li Kashing Cancer Centre, the Hitchison-MRC Research Centre, $0.5 billion AstraZeneca-MRC Centre for Lead(ing) Discovery for "regulating biological processes", Wellcome Trust-MRC Cambridge Stem Cell Institute, laboratories and the teaching hospital and healthcare services. To be sure, although managed by the University of Cambridge, the broader societal stake-holders, amongst others, are the Cambridge University Hospitals-NHS Foundation Trust, MRC, Cancer Research UK, Addenbrooke's Hospital and University of Cambridge Medical School and the status accorded by the NIH-Biomedical Research Centre.

Two underlying strains intertwine in this narrative. As a pre-eminent magnet for global talent, if Nobel Prize awardees colour the rainbow of thought leadership, the pool connected with Cambridge breakthrough research now nears the magical 100. Crick and Watson of double-helix and Nobel fame half a century ago interweave this and brilliant technologies. The ARM start-up in the Cambridge Silicon Fen (of Trinity and Jesus College beginnings) was valued in a UK-Japan transaction at over $30 billion. It leads in digital conver-gence, mobility and increasingly as an indispensable utility in human communications and enabling unbeknownst healthcare outreach.

Nuevo NTU-ICL Lee Kong Chian School of Medicine: The new kid on the block is Nanyang Technological University (NTU) in Singapore, and its joint-enterprise of the Lee Kong Chian School of Medicine and Imperial College, London. With a strategic vision of pio-neer medical innovations for a future healthcare system (amongst NTU's Five Peaks of Excellence), the new community of physicians would be able to operate and manage multi-professional teams in the emerging healthcare systems and combine strengths of recent bio-engineering-medical with the University's capabilities. The strategy also addresses the needs of the silvering population and enhancing the con-text of tropical health through its collaboration with the centennial Tan Tock Seng Hospital and its famed complementary specialty as a teaching hospital-partner. Freer from legacy issues, NTU has implemented a new pedagogy of "Team-Based Learning"; now assayed at LKCSM it is immigrating to Imperial for adoption despite its earlier rejection. These are early days — in comparison UoN's "Problem Based Learning" morphed through fifty years of refinements, and it may not be a totally "either or" issue.

According to NTU President Bertil Andersson who has led NTU to rank 11th globally in 2017 from 13th, the challenge is to meld the original mission of engineering to collaborate in more trans-disciplinary ways. Records will show some 300 research projects related to medicine across the faculties were anchored on strong bio-medical engineering and experimental bio-medicine capabilities. Although their close collaboration with Imperial College helps, the presidency has imbued a set of strategic vector deltas (see Nam's Chapter 10 in this book) into the trajectory of the university. A closer reading of Bertil Andersson's chapter will show similarities with the Nam approach in re-launching KAIST in the early 2000s with radical faculty renewal, new research initiatives (and innovations to fast proto-typing accomplishments) and richer fund-raising endowments to propel it in 2014 to second place amongst Asia's universities.

Professor Andersson has, however, ensconced himself in the international eco-system twinned with Singapore's steady and rare high public commitment (3% of GDP) to national research funding of about S$15 billion. For his decade of contributions and headlined quantum leap of NTU, he received the highest innovation award from Singapore's Agency for Advanced Science & Research. My summary of his achievements of the formative past decade at NTU may be aptly noted in retrospect to my farewell retirement address when I profiled Bertil as Moses with two tablets — Ten Commandments on research integrity and Five Commandments on the Five Peaks of Excellence. Promised lands are inadvertently a distance away (and so his successor has his work cut out — to lead with the existing Bertil structure and contending sub-structures; fuse them into his own in continuity; or change anew? This proposition deserves testing — leaders can create that transformation; managers, however, can handle the normal productivity gains which are ever more difficult to achieve!

2. **UoN's Inter-continental Univer-City Quilt & UC Future:** The unique development of UC 2016 was the confluence of the academic and thought leadership of University of Newcastle VC Caroline McMillen. She weaved the perspective from the Greco-Roman odyssey and scholarship to the unending pursuit of the truth in higher education and the unfolding fourth industrial revolution *envisaging an inter-institutional and inter-continental quilt of engagement* (Royal Society, 2011) — and the ensuing human dilemmas.

   The totality of the approach and experience itself was a heroic enterprise that can be considered "good" as a body of accomplishment and thought. There are two takeaways: the creative balance of the McMillen debt to *The Mighty Dead* does not seem to be onerous or usurious; and through informal conversations, comes the insight that good leaders understand their mission, people and the unknowns (people and events). Good leaders choose to cut into the "right dilemmas of strategy" drawing upon the wisdom of sequence, timing and angle of approach or repose. Indelicate as it may seem, at crucial times inner core colleagues recognise and understand why, without verbalising them. It calls to mind an answer and a comment in a graduate seminar at the Judge Business School by the then Cambridge Vice-Chancellor Dame Alison Richard on the human dilemma of a woman in a man's world of Cambridge academia. Professor Richard, a noted anthropologist bar none on the lemurs of Madagascar, replied: "Understand primates, men are no different." And on the dilemma of leadership and speed, Stirling Moss observed that if you feel you are in control, you are not going fast enough!

   These apparently contradictory demands are at the heart of every IHE leader's lonely struggles and are brought to focus at the univer-cities conferences (UC). These conferences reveal the ever evolving eco-system of the univer-cities conversation to explore the dynamic creative balance. There is interim time in between, to think and research. And we are not only referring to UC3, but also 4, 5, 6 & 7 with a different focus for each:

   UC1 Strategic Implications For Asia.
   UC2 Strategic View of the Future, from Berkeley and Cambridge to Singapore and Rising Asia.

UC3 Strategic Dilemmas of Medical Origins.

UC3.5 in 2018: Discussions with Advisory Councillor NTU President Bertil Andersson are exploring the suggestion of having a niche conversation in between the acclaimed UC2016 hosted by UoN's VC Caroline McMillen and the anticipated UC2019. It is envisioned as being smaller (35 to 50), by invitation only to *coloris d'automne*, from 16 to 17 September 2018 somewhere between London, Stockholm and Vienna. It will focus on a poignant contemporary issue that poses both tectonic danger and opportunity for leadership in academia to mull the future(s) in their strategic narrative with engaged and not unexpectedly more restive stakeholders; vis-à-vis responsibility to society (Sir Borysiewicz's address at UoN). The meeting will be centred around a "Thought Leader of Focus" who is a respected collegiate leader, rich in research, experience and wisdom, with erudite dispensation willing to engage, no-holds-barred, and best aligned to the chosen issue.

UC4 in 2019 Strategic aligning to continual economic restructuring, resolving inequality & revisiting the social compact in the face of Brexit, US 2016 and more. The epigram of President Xi presages the rise of rural and suburbanites who feel left behind and vote for radical change and leaders of indeterminate risk and reward — the happenstance of President Donald J. Trump. In human affairs, globalisation and more insidiously technology may become society's dilemma of threat and nemesis.

3. **UC2016 Offerings:** The community of academic leaders at UC2016 delivered thought-provoking topics: Carleton VC Roseann O'Reilly Runte's "An Architechture of Light: Ottawa, the City of Light" ideas (versus Paris' city of light); HKU Professor John Malpas' "Reinventing the University of Hong Kong in Both Mortar and Spirit", Berkeley AVC Emily Marthinsen's "Univer-city of California, Berkeley in the Bay Region"; INSEAD Dean Hawawini's "Multi-Campus Internationalisation of Higher Education Institutions"; Stockholm Water Prize Professor Biswas' "Safe Water for the Developing World"; and MIT Emeritus Cross Professor Suh's "On Strategy for Developing an Innovative University: S-Factor, S-Gap and Vector Delta."

There was a pleasing development with regard to the paper by Professor Biswas. He exceeded himself with a distinctly unique chapter for our Volume III. He reports:

> There has been an unexpected development. It seems that His Holiness Pope Francis read some of my work in this area. He has decided to bring in some of the leading theologians, water and development experts, politicians, public officials, some important CEOs and NGOs. The Pope will participate in this meeting which is being organized by the Pontifical Academy of Sciences in the Vatican, 23–24 February 2017. He wants it to be focused on **water and sanitation as human rights** and how these rights can be expeditiously achieved. The Pope would like this meeting to come out with a Rome declaration (decided) and possibly and encyclical (yet to be decided).
>
> I have been specifically requested to help the Pontifical Academy for this meeting so that it will come out with some meaningful outputs and impacts.
>
> Thus, I plan to complete my paper on what I said in Newcastle and supplement it with additional material. Accordingly, the paper I am writing for you will serve dual purpose: the second one will be the main background document for the Vatican meeting.

4. **Modality of Water & the Univer-City:** Professor Asit Biswas asserts the efficacy of a univer-city dealing with the universal issue — shortage of water to sustain cities. He decries the urgent need of resources and attention to confront this unavoidable challenge to life and calls upon univer-cities to devote more thought leadership and resources to enhance human quality of life. Professor Biswas and his co-author Dr Tortajada report that universities all over the world have failed miserably to critically examine the reality. In South Asia alone, 1.7 billion people do not have access to water that is safe enough to drink. Globally some 3.5 to 4.0 billion people now do not have access to clean water, which is nearly five times the currently believed number.

It is my view that over the past decade Professor Biswas at the National University of Singapore and Professor Ng Wun Jern, Executive Director of Nanyang Water and Environmental Research Institute (NEWRI), have seen dividends through:

local and international academia and industry partners, consciously seeks to realise societal and economic value from the outcomes of the collective R&D efforts … with well over 400 post-doctoral and post-graduate researchers work the eco-system of research organisation, university, city, state (*which is now close to being water independent*), region, and global partners. (Teo, 2013)

5. **HKU remakes HKU:** This was a case of *"the right people, right place, right time. It was a God-given opportunity and a real team effort".*

Re-inventing the University of Hong Kong was in both mortar and spirit: physically, pedagogically, curriculum revisited, learning commons, interlinked research-faculty-student facilities, the easy and erstwhile unheard of accessibility with the city, major land swap of a water reservoir (to an Earth Science based mountain cavern-reservoir) with the government to connect the 100-year original campus with the eastern campus by the South China Sea! This was possible thanks to the accidental co-leadership of the dynamic duo team of the *"right people, right place, right time"*: the then VC Lap Chee Tsui and Earth Science Professor (hailing from Memorial University via Rhode Island School of Oceanography) together with New Centennial College President Professor John Malpas. For completeness, the medical campus is a follow-up phase with the HK$1 billion endowment raised by VC Tsui and Chancellor Victor Fung and donated by benefactor Dr Li Kashing.

I would like to note my remarks on visiting the remade HKU and viewing the ten-minute video that Professor Malpas screened at the Newcastle conference on management and human affairs — when skill equates to meet the challenge, flow ensues (Csikszentmihalyi, 1990). I had toured the new campus twice and spoke with a variety of individuals along the way. The reborn Centennial HKU and the city of Hong Kong are testament to the consultants in the Hideo Sasaki tradition of strategic place-making and the paradox of *continuity and change.*

The confluence of HKSAR Higher Education's shift to a 4-year undergraduate study, or in short "334", was not achieved without its challenge. These were numerous: overdue reconstruction, the duet of academic leadership, comprehensive consultations with all stakeholders, available funding, review of curricula as reiterated by Cambridge Don Cartledge "unexamined curriculum is not worth teaching" (Too,

2001), pedagogical redesign, nuevo experiential learning, sustainability, creative application of earth science upon the centred reservoir bowl transformed into an auditorium and a multi-level conference centre (a replacement water reservoir was created in the adjacent mountains), strategic flow of learning commons with enclosed secure communication domes, agoras engendering cross and trans-disciplinarity of interaction, and researching new knowledge and innovation. To have completed all this below budget and within timelines despite risks of typhoons, disputatious Hong Kongers and more, is remarkable. It is testimony to the quiet and revolutionary boldness of the academe's dynamic duo — Tsui et Malpas.

The connectivity released by the elevated 300-metre Roman Road and theavatars of floating multi-purpose buildings with visible wind turbines and solar energy deserving the Leeds award tell of the holism and boldness of this unique enterprise. Other place making or campus planning are more episodic, segmented, incremental and oftentimes fragmented over space and time. This can happen even though lovely plans and timelines are published for successors or remain undone as academic inertia sometimes translate to the proposition of the uncertainty that comes with change, self-serving proof that no-change is best! (Johnson, 2008). There are many takeaways and process lessons to be learnt for it is not product we are seeking, it is competence, vision and commitment to a philosophy of liberal education that is profoundly telling. Weaving the mosaic of place making with the underlying community of scholars' concepts of a liberal education is a process:

> A process which teaches one how to learn, how to think, and how to take a broader perspective of life. It also teaches one how to be flexible and at the same time reliable, how to live a happier life; but above all, it encourages one to become a better human being. At the same time, a liberal education is designed to develop intellectual ability (and create new knowledge) and can therefore prepare individuals for a variety of employment opportunities. (Malpas, 2015)

The same was also said of the contributions by the first graduates of the University of Paris to their city, a thousand years ago.

Contextually it is still an evolving work in progress, evident at the recent colloquium on liberal education at NTU's Institute of Advanced Studies at the panel comprising the recently established Yale-NUS College's inaugural President Pericles Lewis and Shantou's Provost Professor Gu Pei Hua.

Reflective of the video's stirring music is the city's endorsement of Professor Malpas by the HK Academy of Performing Arts in conferring him an honorary doctorate. Just as Darwin thrived upon thinking paths, and Da Vinci on art, music was a key to Einstein's sensibilities. Such trans-disciplinary engagement involving music has a rich tradition at the University of Newcastle. Recently performing at a UN sustainability conference, UoN's Dr Philip Matthias linked *musicology and the univer-city* from cross-cultural European-aboriginal music to music and rehabilitative healthcare.

There are always edges and space for armature to occur (Bender, Marthinsen & Parman, Volume, 2013) for we do not know how human use of space, habitation and integrative purposes will be developed in future times.

6. **Armature & Tri-Univer-City:** And so we come to the armature of the potential tri-univer-city of Berkeley, University of California San Francisco (UCSF) and Stanford where economic output is equivalent to the GDP of the Nederlands.

Our Univer-Cities Conference Advisory Councillor and Berkeley doyen, Professor Emeritus Richard Bender, put paid to the mortar creation of a new global campus at Richmond Bay. Together with John Parman they refocused on the emerging tri-univer-city dynamism of Berkeley, UCSF and Stanford in the context of the greater San Francisco area (with the California economy surpassing that of France and Brazil). Berkeley and UCSF in their long tradition of research were committed to "public benefit" and Stanford to "economic benefit".

The New Lunar Year of the Rooster in 2017 heralded good fortune with the enormity of the Zuckerberg-Chan US$3 billion gift for health research connecting three of the region's powerhouse universities complementary yet competitive: Berkeley's pure science and biotech, UCSF's biotech and medical research and Stanford's applied science, technology and medical research. The power of this

Conclusion

The defining narrative of the Univer-Cities Conference held at the University of Newcastle were the ensuing issues of the **dilemma of strategy** from medical origins growing into a more comprehensive research university, and the associated **dilemma of leadership**. If white seahorses follow the normal seahorse of Darwinian evolution, is there the exceptional **black seahorse** like the proverbial "black swan effect" (Taleb, 2010) that makes the quantum jump? This little niche *black seahorse univer-city of UoN:Newcastle* improbably punches above its weight and in all likelihood could create the "Vector Delta" envisaged by Professor Suh.

In sum, Zalesnik postulates that leaders brave the unknown and managers stay in the zone of the reality, challenging as it is. It is noteworthy that his detailed early case histories of human dilemmas of leadership at that time focused on Henry Ford and General Douglas MacArthur who blazed into the early 20th century frontiers of cars and wars. The former succeeded in revolutionising the auto industry in particular and mobility in general. The latter distinguished himself, after acing at West Point, in wars and battlefields in the Philippine-Pacific theatre and was Pro Consul or "Gaijin Shogun" (Valley, 2000) of Japan in post-WWII reconstruction and Japan's subsequent rise to economic primacy. However, he was dismissed by President Truman after his brilliantly massive and successful landing behind the enemy lines at Inchon — but then seeking total victory, triggered China's entry into the Korean War. These were psycho-sociological studies. To be sure, for completeness this opens another deeper narrative of the microcosm of human and individual sense of self and dynamics for the mantle of leadership.

It would be interesting to run an analysis of the correlation between leadership and manager-ship vis-à-vis discontinuous 'Vector Delta' and normal (productivity progress) curves. To be sure leaders need also to manage.

In the interim, my conjecture is from the deliberations and interactions with academia and top-level appointments that the Vector Delta mission needs leadership of a high order like Sir Borysiewicz; Michael Crow who pioneered the new gold standard of research-intensive universities and set to transform Arizona State University, famed not for traditional disciplines but project and problem resolution oriented Mars

Rover research and proto-typing and the Walter Cronkite journalism centre (I interviewed him during his study visit to NTU with State Congressional leaders); Nam Pyo at KAIST; Bertil Andersson at NTU; Caroline McMillen at UoN; and possibly many others. Like all, they sub-scribe to the Churchillian dictum delivered at Harvard during World War II: the price of greatness is responsibility (Sir Borysiewicz, 2014).

In our undoubtedly complex world where homo sapiens may risk the fate of Neanderthals, dilemmas and paradoxes possess both interdepend-ency and contradictory elements. Hence possessing a strategic sense of dynamic equilibrium (Smith, Lewis & Tushman, 2016) is a desired tempera-ment to cope with uncertainties instead of seeking consistency for neat-ness of consistency.

Nucleation around medical discipline (or any other like engineering or liberal arts as some niche colleges have achieved success and acclaim) is an option with dynamism that our cases in this narrative have shown promising takeaways. A twin radical idea of social and economic impact specification and measurement of research to the univer-city and society is to create a new and enduring foundation for mutual understanding, purpose and sustainability.

Dilemma resolution needs collegiality, hard work, skill, will and the common good. Obamacare survived 8 years of repealing onslaught includ-ing the penultimate early 2017 attempt despite the Republicans' control of the Executive, Congress and Senate (but the attempts are still a work in progress). Many reasons are cited but one which will likely stand the test of time is that dilemma resolution needs hard, hard work, skill and the will to read with wisdom the societal compact. The proponents of Obamacare undertook 14 months of extensive and intensive consulta-tions, detailed trade-offs of dilemmas of affordability, coverage, taxation, co-pay, fines, individual mandates, exchanges and substitutes, and so forth. Such issues were collegially resolved even without eventual Republican votes to pass Congress and the Senate. The deadly comparison is the Republican "repeal and replace" Obamacare with the American Health Care Act, done in a couple of weeks bereft of such mutual engagement, with questionable transparency and rushed to legislate. It was withdrawn by themselves in Congress before any formal voting, later passed with a one vote margin and stalled in the Senate. Sir Borysiewicz, Aitken and others are devoted to the quintessential collegiality in IHEs, ungainly at times but a truism might be said: if you find collegiality an expensive investment, try bi-partisanship and gridlock — a corollary to Harvard's Bok who is reputed to have said, if you think education is expensive, try ignorance.

In summary, the narrative band-width of case discussions in this volume includes:

- *Global pre-emption at Cambridge bio-medical research centre; the advantage of being the nuevo joint-venture medical school,*
- *Evolutionary medicine work for univer-cities,*
- *Carleton-Ottawa City of Bright (Ideas),*
- *Hay of serendipity at* HKU; *armature yields dividends at Berkeley with UC San Francisco and Stanford,*
- *"One University in two Global Cities",*
- *Water as a human right,*
- *The disruptive "Nam Vector Delta",*
- *Translating the academe leaders' self-discovery: "Who is to mentor and educate the educators to succeed in the new paradigms and times, be it the age of anger, unreason and paradox."* (Handy, 1994),
- *The emerging dilemma of inequality: fair inequality versus unfair equality as propositioned in recent Yale studies.*

In some niche way, we are on the way with the Eisenhardt proposition of phased stages building theories from case studies.

Univer-Cities Conference 2019: UC4 will *Revisit the social compact* in the face of growing inequality. It will on ongoing *strategic alignment of univer-cities* to the *continually restructuring economies* reacting to disruptive technology, globalisation and redefining the nature of work, processes and new competencies. President HK Cheong leads the university, UniSim, now refocused as Singapore University of Social Sciences (SUSS). It is dedicated to mid-career and societal dynamics enabling individuals and organisations to reposition in the emerging new economies. UniSim will be the veritable host of UC2019 on 17–18 November 2019 in Singapore.

The new gold standard: Professor Sharifah's précis of praise for UC3 echoes our sentiments completely: Sir Borysiewicz's masterly Keynote

Address and Professor Caroline McMillen's superb leadership in hosting and co-chairing such a stunning conference; Caroline's erudite UoN Vision, creating a new gold standard for the univer-cities conferencess, echoing all the sentiments expressed so eloquently by Anthony, Bertil, Biswas, Gordon and Nam; and for her attention to diversity despite myriad duties comes my gratitude to the thoughtfulness in arranging the halal meals right up to providing a space for prayers. It speaks volumes of Caroline and the University and Newcastle.

References

Bender, R., E. Marthinsen & J. Parman (2013). "Berkeley: Campus and Community". In Anthony S.C. Teo, ed., *Univer-Cities: Strategic Implications for Asia — Readings from Cambridge and Berkeley to Singapore*. Singapore: World Scientific Publishing Company-Imperial College Press.

Bennett, J., N. Cushing & E. Eklund, eds. (2015). *Radical Newcastle*. Sydney, NSW: University of New South Wales Press.

Borysiewicz, L. (2014). "Responsibility: The annual address of the Vice-Chancellor, Professor Sir Leszek Borysiewicz". Retrieved from <http://www.v-c.admin.cam.ac.uk/professor-sir-leszek-borysiewicz/speeches/responsibility>

Brynjolfsson, E. and A. McAfee (2016). *The second machine age: Work, progress, and prosperity in a time of brilliant technologies*. New York, NY: W.W. Norton & Company.

Carroll, L. (1998 Centenary Edition). *Alice's Adventures in Wonderland and Through the Looking Glass*. London, UK: Penguin Books.

CNN (2016). "China's Xi Jinping keeps Iowa close to his heart". Retrieved from <http://edition.cnn.com/2016/12/07/asia/china-iowa-xi-jinping-branstad-trump/>

Christensen, C.M. (1997). *The Innovator's Dilemma: When New Technologies Cause Great Firms to Fail*. Boston, MA: Harvard Business School Press.

Christensen, C. M. & M. Overdorf (2000). "Meeting the challenge of disruptive change". *Harvard Business Review* 78, no. 2, pp. 66–76.

Cohen, G. A. (2008). *Rescuing Justice and Equality*. Cambridge, MA: Harvard University Press.

Crow, M. M. & W. B. Dabars (2015). "A New Model for the American Research University". *Issues in Science and Technology* 10, no. 2, pp. 55–62.

Csikszentmihalyi, M. (1990). *Flow: The Psychology of Optimal Experience*. New York, NY: Harper & Row.

Davis, S. M. (1989). "From 'future perfect': Mass Customizing". *Planning Review* 17,no. 2, pp. 16–21.

Eisenhardt, K. M. (1989). "Building theories from case study research". *Academy of Management Review* 14, no. 4, pp. 532–50.

Handy, Charles (1994).*The Age of Paradox*. Cambridge, MA: Harvard Business School.

Hawking, S. (2013). *My Brief History*. New York, NY: Bantam Books.

Johnson, G. (2015). "Cambridge: From Medieval Market Town to Univer-city". In Anthony S. C. Teo, ed., *Univer-cities: Strategic View of the Future: From Berkeley and Cambridge to Singapore and Rising Asia*. Singapore: World Scientific Publishing Company.

Johnson, G. (2008). *University Politics: F.M. Cornford's Cambridge and His Advice to the Young Academic Politician* (2nd ed.). Cambridge, UK: Cambridge University Press.

Kanter, Rosabeth M. (1995).*Thriving Locally in the Global Economy*. New York: Simon & Schuster.

Krishnamurti, J. (1929). "Truth is a pathless land". Retrieved from <http://www.jkrishnamurti.org/about-krishnamurti/dissolution-speech.php>

Malpas, J. (2015). "Message from the President". *Centennial College Prospectus 2015/16*.Retrieved from <https://www.centennialcollege.hku.hk/f/upload/1343/CentennialCollegeProspectus2015-16.pdf>

Mitroff, I. I. (1995). Review of the book *The Age of Paradox* by C. Handy. *The Academy of Management Review* 20, no. 3, 748–50.

Moore, R. (1966). *Niels Bohr: The Man, His Science, & the World They Changed*. New York, NY: Alfred A. Knopf.

Royal Society (2011). "Knowledge, networks and nations: Global scientific collaboration in the 21st century". London. Retrieved from http://royalsociety.org/uploadedFiles/Royal_Society_Content/policy/publications/2011/4294976134.pdf.

Smith, W. K., M. W. Lewis, & M.L. Tushman (2016). "'Both/And' leadership. *Harvard Business Review* 94, no. 5, pp. 62–70.

Taleb, N. N. (2010). *The Black Swan: The Impact of the Highly Improbable* (2nd ed.) New York, NY: Random House.

Teo, Anthony S. C., ed. (2015). *Univer-cities: Strategic View of the Future: From Berkeley and Cambridge to Singapore and Rising Asia*. Singapore: World Scientific Publishing Company.

Teo, Anthony S. C., ed. (2013). *Univer-Cities: Strategic Implications for Asia — Readings from Cambridge and Berkeley to Singapore*. Singapore: World Scientific Publishing Company-Imperial College Press.

The Star (2016). "Canadian society today is a more just society than it once was". Retrieved from <https://www.thestar.com/news/canada/2016/06/03/canadian-society-today-is-a-more-just-society-than-it-once-was-top-judge-says.html>

Too, Y. L., ed. (2001). *Education in Greek and Roman Antiquity*. Boston, MA: Brill.

Valley, D. J. (2000). *Gaijin Shogun: General Douglas A. MacArthur Stepfather of Postwar Japan 1945–1951*. San Diego, CA: Sektor Company.

Xi Jinpeng (2012). "To me, you are America". *Muscatine Journal*. Retrieved from <http://muscatinejournal.com/news/local/to-me-you-are-america/article_f72a4782-584c-11e1-98b4-0019bb2963f4.html>

Yglesias, M. (2017). "Why Republican efforts to 'repair' Obamacare are doomed to fail". Retrieved from <https://www.vox.com/policy-and-politics/2017/2/3/14493946/repair-obamacare>

Zaleznik, A. (1966). *Human Dilemmas of Leadership*. New York, NY: Harper & Row.

Zaleznik, A. (1992). "Managers and Leaders: Are They Different?" *Harvard Business Review* 70, no. 2, pp. 126–35.

About the Author

Anthony SC Teo is Adjunct Professor, Lee Kuan Yew School of Public Policy, National University of Singapore.

PART I

THE TRANS-DISCIPLINARY IMPACT ON ACADEMIC EVOLUTION: FROM MEDICINE TO GLOBAL UNIVER-CITIES

CHAPTER TWO

DILEMMA & STRATEGY: SHAPING THE UNIVERSITY OF NEWCASTLE, AUSTRALIA

R. JOHN AITKEN AND H. LE GRESLEY

"Come gather around people
Wherever you roam
And admit that the waters
Around you have grown
And accept it that soon
You'll be drenched to the bone
And if your breath to you is worth saving
Then you better start swimming or you'll sink like a stone
For the times they are a-changing"

Bob Dylan: Nobel Prize for Literature 2016

Introduction

The University of Newcastle is a young upstart of an institution established in 1968 in response to a public campaign that went on for more than 20 years and culminated in the burning of placards on the steps of City Hall. Originally, Newcastle University College had been an offshoot of the University of New South Wales (UNSW), accepting its first students in 1952. However, the people of Newcastle were not satisfied with this arrangement and, in 1962, the Vice-Chancellor of UNSW, Sir Philip Baxter, relented and work began transforming the fledgling college into an autonomous university. Given its history, it is not surprising that running deep in the veins of the University of Newcastle is an appreciation that this institution was created to serve the needs of the entire community, regardless of colour, culture, circumstance or creed; equity and equal opportunity are part of its DNA. It is a reflection of the proud, independent, resilient spirit that characterises the people of the Hunter region and their desire to see "a fair go for all". The University is a direct reflection of the powerful sense of community that characterises the region and has seen Novocastrians triumph over earthquakes, floods and sudden unexpected changes in fortune. The latter includes the precipitous loss of heavy industry when BHP, which had been making steel in Newcastle since 1915, suddenly closed its gates in 1999. This single event saw the retrenchment of 2,000 workers as well as 1,000 contractors and the disappearance of an industry that had defined the entire city for 84 years. However, rather than catapult the city into a state of post-industrial decline, this event triggered a renaissance in the region that has seen it transform from a bastion of heavy industry to a beacon of innovation.

Critically, this transformation has been led by the University, which along with the Local Health District, has now become the largest employer in the region. The city has rapidly discarded its Steel City tag and is now a thriving modern univer-city featuring a dynamic and diverse industrial sector as well as a highly innovative, exciting cultural scene. It is no accident that Newcastle was the birthplace of one of most success-ful award–winning rock bands Australia has ever produced (Silverchair) and was voted one of the top 10 cities in the world by the Lonely Plant Guide in 2011. In the space of 18 years, Newcastle has gone from a heavy industry City of Steel to a Global Innovation Hub with the University at its core. The University of Newcastle has become a catalyst for interna-tional research and innovation and nowhere is this contribution better evidenced than in the field of health and medicine.[1] Indeed, in keeping with the theme of this Univer-Cities volume, the Faculty of Health and Medicine has become a major focal point for the future growth and development of the University of Newcastle and its strong sense of con-nection with, and sense of responsibility to, the community. This chapter explores how this particular Faculty has become an agent for change within the institution and a major focus for Newcastle's contribution to the univer-cities narrative.

Faculty of Health and Medicine

The Faculty of Health and Medicine was founded in 1975 under the leadership of David Maddison and rapidly gained an international reputation for excellence and innovation in teaching and learning. Its problem-based curricula coupled with early clinical experience starting in the first year of the degree programme, offered students a different approach to the study of medicine compared to other universities that typically delayed the clinical experience. From its earliest days the Faculty has challenged the nuanced inequities that prevail in the experience of health and well-being. As a result, the Faculty has trained more than twice as many Aboriginal doctors as any other university in Australia. Furthermore, an emphasis on ensuring access to rural medicine has led to the development of a formal partnership between the University of Newcastle and the University of New England to deliver a Joint Medical Program (JMP) in association with their Local Health Districts (Hunter New England and Central Coast). The all-new MD degree offered out of this inter-sector alliance focuses on graduates capable of delivering evidence-based clinical practice as necessitated by contemporary medical practice, and who will be fully equipped to play a key role in shaping the future of healthcare in our community (Fig. 2.1).

Because the Faculty has become the focal point of clinical research and training for an entire region, it has expanded its programme-base beyond medicine to include biomedical science, pharmacy, nursing, midwifery and a wide range of allied health sciences. As a result, the Faculty of Health and Medicine at the University of Newcastle is one of the most comprehensive Faculties of its kind in Australia and, probably, the world. Overall, the Faculty brings together a wide variety of undergraduate, postgraduate and professional training programmes including 15 undergraduate and 19 postgraduate coursework degrees. These programmes are delivered to a diverse student cohort of 7,500 students and support more than 450 Higher Degree by Research (HDR) candidates. To deliver this platform of health education and research the Faculty engages 327 academic, 288 professional and over 1,000 conjoint staff who not only orchestrate a wide variety of accredited educational programmes but also account for approximately half

Fig. 2.1 The Tamworth Education Centre is an important feature of the Faculty of Health and Medicine's commitment to training health professionals to work in a rural setting.

of the University's research income, including a consistently powerful performance in national competitive grant rounds.

The dominant role that the Faculty is playing in meeting the health workforce needs within the region is clearly emphasised by the employability of its graduates. The Graduate Destination Survey (2012–2014) indicated that almost 90% of students surveyed from health-related study areas are in full time employment, four months after graduating. This included 92.3% of Nursing and Midwifery graduates (5th out of 32 universities in Australia); 100% of medical graduates (equal 1st in Australia out of 19 universities) and 90% of Rehabilitation students (6th out of 20 universities). The global reputation earned by the Faculty is also evidenced by its top 150 world listing in the 2016 QS World University ranking system, while its School of Nursing and Midwifery has received a global top 50 classification.

The Dilemma — Our Raison D'être

The dilemma highlighted in the title of this chapter refers to the role that the Faculty of Health and Medicine might play in the future development of our University and the institution's place in the world. As a regional University, it could be argued that we are already catering for the workforce needs of our local community very effectively and that there is no need to effect significant change in the educational and research programmes that we are currently offering. However, the University of Newcastle no longer sees itself as an institution focusing solely on the tertiary education needs of the local community, any more than the Universities of Oxford or Cambridge, isolated in small rural towns distant from London, would see themselves as regional universities. The University of Newcastle, like the Universities of Oxford and Cambridge, sees itself as a global university, engaging in world-class research and education with partners from across the globe but concentrating on issues that have currency within the local and national community. In other words, a University that is globally engaged but regionally focused. In 2016, the University of Newcastle released a New Futures Strategic Plan incorporating a clear vision for 2025 which will see the institution standing as a "global leader distinguished by a commitment to equity and excellence and to creating a better future for its regions through a focus on innovation and impact".[2] This is a vision that cannot be carried on the shoulders of any single faculty working in isolation. Indeed, to achieve the kind of global relevance and scale indicated in the New Futures Strategic Plan will necessitate an integrated response from the entire institution and a clear commitment to an interdisciplinary mode of working.

In the 21st century, faculties, no matter what their pedigree, can no longer catalyse institutional growth if they are siloed, protecting their academic turf with a selfish eye on retention of their student load and the corralling of their research productivity. Protectionist policies do not work in the world of international trade and they are no way to run a university. If any academic institution is to remain competitive in the future, it has to learn how to abandon the discipline-specific structures and behaviours that have driven productivity and income in the recent past. Indeed, if we are to meet the challenges of the 21st century with a university system that is flexible, nimble, adaptive, relevant, impactful and has the potential for growth, we have to transform the culture that has underpinned the intellectual architecture of universities since their inception more than 900 years ago. In the future we have to be capable of harnessing the full range of intellectual firepower locked up within academic institutions and traverse academic, service and industry boundaries in order to address problems of such complexity and scale that their resolution will have a significant impact on society. This movement will involve a change of emphasis from the current discipline-led strategies and a reorientation of capacity to areas of greatest opportunity through inter- and multi-disciplinary structures that enable a truly holistic trans-disciplinary synthesis. The journey to trans-disciplinarity will be a difficult one because it will entail the reversal of decades of siloed activity on the part of faculties which, to maintain their integrity and viability, have learned to protect their intellectual territory, typically aided by convoluted jargon that isolates rather than informs and reinforced by KPIs that encourage isolationist behaviours. If we do not issue the trumpet call of change, the very walls that were designed to protect faculties, will simply secure their isolation and demise.

Importance of Globalization

A second important element of the University of Newcastle's New Futures Strategic Plan to promote growth is to internationalise both the curriculum and the research portfolio. The digital age has resulted in unparalleled advances in our capacity to communicate with each other. With enhanced communication comes the realisation that the major issues facing our regions are typically faced by communities all over the world. They are not unique to our local community or restricted to our specific geographical location. They are largely a reflection of the human condition and our struggle to live peacefully and sustainably with the environment in all of its cultural, physical, economic and political dimensions. It seems logical therefore that the resolution of this struggle will be facilitated by collaborations that not only cross discipline and sector boundaries but also the borders that arbitrarily divide our world into constituent nations. Research and education in 21st century universities will be a highly competitive, international enterprise. When Sir Leszek Borysiewicz gave his seventh and final address to the University of

Cambridge, he cited the four pillars that make the University of Cambridge so successful.

> Our ability to deliver excellence in education…. Our ability to deliver excellence in research…. The collegiate nature of the University…. And our commitment to being a truly global university.[3]

These pillars are, of course, interconnected. Delivering excellence in education and research depends upon universities developing a global perspective and working collegially across discipline boundaries. The issue at stake is how we facilitate the emergence of a global collaborative culture without losing the core disciplinary strengths that have underpinned academic performance on the journey thus far.

Brick Walls and Barricades on the Road to Multi-Disciplinary Integration

Western societies are coming to grips with the fact that the current paradigms for supporting basic research, while contributing to the science base, have failed to meaningfully engage society's stakeholders and generate outcomes that are socially valued. As a consequence of this trend, the research currently funded by most national competitive grant schemes is tending to focus on prestige at the expense of impact. Measures of excellence and esteem have been largely generated by an élite publication system that favours large disciplines with high levels of potential citations. High quality publications identified using this system, with its impact factors and citation indices, have been found to provide a useful analytical framework in terms of transparency as well as intellectual and institutional differentiation. In addition, such readily quantifiable metrics have created an internal mini-industry involving the construction of league tables for the purpose of domestic and international comparisons and providing new indicators for identifying world-class research excellence at the aggregate level.[4]

Non-English speaking nations, small specialized areas of research and highly applied research are disadvantaged by this system.[5] The impact factor and some of the indices it has spawned, such as the h-index, have been roundly criticised as measures of excellence, because they are having an unintended negative impact on the global research culture. Namely, the focus has encouraged safe, "me-too" science where discipline, sector and epistemological fluidity is discouraged and researchers are encouraged to inhabit the most densely populated areas of the scientific landscape in order to enhance the frequency with which their research will be cited. Most disturbing of all is that it is a system that can be gamed to generate higher impacts for publications, scientists and institutions than warranted. As pointed out by Bruce Albers, "this impact factor mania makes no sense" because it has become an end in itself.[6] As a result, there is now a clarion call from the battlements of government to steer research in a different direction: a destination that is not measured in terms of citation indices or impact factors but one that is measured in terms of its impact on society. In Australia this movement has taken form in the guise of the complimentary Medical Research Future Fund (MRFF) and Biomedical Translation Fund (BTF) The MRFF has as its aim: "Through strategic investment, to transform health and medical research and innovation to improve lives, build the economy and contribute to health system sustainability".[7] At its core the MRFF is an applied research agenda that is designed to improve the quality and efficiency of the health service and to commercialise health research outcomes. In order to deliver on this consumer driven research agenda, the MRFF policy statement refers to the need for international, interdisciplinary collaborations involving new disruptive technologies, including the digitisation of patient records and large database linkage. Likewise the BTF, a key initiative under the National Innovation and Science Agenda, "seeks to open up the research pipeline by investing in the commercialisation of the outcomes of health and medical research" through its operation as a for-profit co-investment venture capital fund where private investment is matched with contributions from the Australian Government.[8]

In their excellent book on the emerging economic strength of cities in the rustbelts of America, Antoine Van Agtmael and Fred Bakker emphasise that university-led regional renewal is characterised by a capacity to take on complex multidisciplinary projects that would be beyond the reach of any single individual or organisation.[9] They also highlight the ability of such successful enterprises to operate as a complex collaborative ecosystem with universities at their core and typically involving established companies, start-ups, local government departments and healthcare institutions.

These entities are also commonly de-siloed such that the walls between academia, industry and the public sector as well as the sharp demarcation lines between academic disciplines have been torn down.

The problem with the current approach towards funding research in developed countries is that it remains very discipline specific and favours those who have learned how to think to $450k aliquots — the size of the average NHMRC project grant in Australia.[10] Successful players in this game have learned how to convert their grant funding into metrics that the system values (i.e. publications in high impact factor peer reviewed journals) that enhance the applicant's track record to the point that another project grant is funded — and so the cycle continues. The problem with this approach is that such basic research, while incrementally advancing the science base, has very little direct impact on society at large. Without that impact academics will not be granted the social licence they require to spend taxpayers' money on their research.

In order for the system to gain the support that it needs from society at large, it is important that our basic research agenda is supplemented with programmes that are orientated towards the interests of society's stakeholders and can be evaluated in terms of metrics that society can understand — not publications but jobs, economic growth, patient-waiting times, the cost of delivering public services, etc. In other words, practical outcomes that politicians, public servants, captains of industry and the footsoldiers of community can appreciate and support. As Ian Chubb, the former Chief Scientist of Australia, put it in his 2015 address to the Press Club:

> Science serves our community, is supported by our community and is essential to our community. And acceptance by the community of what scientists do is a critical part of how we build the future we want, rather than drifting along until one just happens along.[11]

Society in general will only ever accept what researchers do, if the outcomes of their labours are measured in terms of social and economic impact. In turn, conducting research that has the desired level of societal influence depends on scientists working alongside industry and service providers to identify problems that have such complexity, scale and relevance for society's stakeholders that the outcomes of the research will be applauded and supported by the community at large.

In order to be effective in this regard, it is essential that we operate as a borderless innovative ecosystem. This applies to the relationships between universities and the stakeholders in government, the health service and industry but also to the universities themselves. Faculties must learn how to combine their intellectual assets in order to solve the major problems engaging society and develop an integrated language, administrative framework and physical infrastructure that facilitates rather than discourages such interactions. In many ways health and medicine constitute an ideal nucleation point in the development of such an open collaborative approach, as crystallized in the concept of "Convergence".

Convergence

Convergence involves the bringing together of technologies and understanding in the natural sciences (such as mathematics, biology, chemistry and physics) and engineering to address the grand challenges being faced by the world today and particularly, the intricate problems encountered in delivering effective healthcare to an ageing global population. Encouragingly, convergence science is already being used to solve some of the major problems faced by society in the form of ageing, cancer, metabolic disease and complex neurological conditions such as dementia. This approach is also having an impact on areas outside of health and is being employed as a general strategy for restructuring of universities and bridging the discipline divide. For example, Yale University in Connecticut and the Weizmann Institute of Science, Israel, have incentivised young scientists to collaborate across discipline borders by providing seed funding to those who propose novel, inter-disciplinary, trans-institutional projects. Additional convergence strategies include the creation of recreational spaces that promote inter-disciplinary interactions such as the Engineering Genius Bar at MIT, or the creation of joint seminar series such as the James and Catherine Patten seminar series at the University of Colorado which bridges the biology/engineering divide. Annual retreats have also been introduced where staff with backgrounds in health and medicine, engineering and the natural sciences can present and workshop their ideas in an inter-disciplinary environment, such as the the Future of Health convergence workshop recently held in Washington DC.[12]

A number of universities have also used the principles of convergence in developing their institutional infrastructure including Monash University's Institute of Medical Engineering, Harvard's Wyss Institute for Biologically Inspired Engineering and Georgia Tech's Parker H. Petit Institute for Bioengineering and Bioscience. The Department of Engineering at the University of Cambridge has also created major focus areas in biological engineering, biomedical engineering and healthcare engineering. All of these institutions, and more, have created foci of research and education excellence based upon the concept of convergence with health and medicine as the unifying theme. However, no university to date has used this principle as a basis for reshaping an entire institution in partnership with its inter-sectoral partners in service provision and industry.

In seeking to bring such change about, university leadership will inevitably face difficulties in creating a convergence ecosystem that respects the traditional culture of investigator and laboratory autonomy while providing an environment in which multidisciplinary activity is supported. Universities contemplating a convergence agenda might also experience reservations because the established national funding agencies are traditionally very discipline orientated and have not yet evolved mechanisms for encouraging interdisciplinary activity, certainly not at scale. Globally, this will be a difficult territory to negotiate because basic science and medicine are funded by different national organisations in most advanced economies. Thus in Australia the funding of basic research is led by the ARC at the exclusion of health, which is supported by the NHMRC. In the UK a similar separation exists between the BBSRC and the MRC while the US has the NSF and NIH. If we are to effectively drive a convergence agenda, collaboration between national funding bodies through inter-agency agreements to tackle key problems of relevance to society will be critical. The US has led the way in this context with such initiatives as the National Robotics (NSF, NASA, NIH, USDA, DOD and DOE) and the BRAIN initiatives (NIH, NSF, DARPA, FDA and I-ARPA). Internationally, inter-agency agreements to support research addressing issues of global significance would also help drive the convergence agenda, such as the NIH-NHMRC initiative in Indigenous Health and Wellbeing. It will also be important to build international partnerships with industry to facilitate whole-of-university, interdisciplinary responses to commercial problems utilising the entire range of intellectual firepower locked up behind faculty walls. Convergence can also encouraged at the institutional and international levels by providing graduate students and postdoctoral fellows with the flexibility they need to cross faculty and institutional boundaries in the pursuit of their research objectives. However, perhaps the greatest single contribution to the convergence agenda can be made by the universities themselves — in terms of the way they are structured as well as the scale and societal relevance of their research agendas. This is particularly important for regional univer-cities, where the academic institution has a role, not just in delivering tertiary education to the local population, but also as a catalyst for regional development. In this context, Faculties of Health and Medicine have particular significance in promoting an inter-disciplinary convergence culture that, through their partnerships with local health services, government and industry, can drive the innovatory changes that will enhance both the quality and efficiency of healthcare delivery within the local community.

Shaping the University of Newcastle

The University of Newcastle is using the principles of convergence in a realignment exercise involving its faculties. Some potential strategies that might be followed in this context are listed below:

Governance

- Develop a STEMM (Science, Technology, Engineering, Maths and Medicine) enterprise within which the Faculties of Engineering and Built Environment, Health and Medicine, and Science reside. The overarching mission of the collaborative STEMM enterprise will be to achieve a borderless, integrated multidisciplinary approach to education and research that will encourage innovation and stimulate growth.
- Encourage the Faculties of Business and Law and Education and Arts to develop a collaborative culture that mirrors the STEMM enterprise

and also facilitates interdisciplinary collaboration. In Newcastle this has taken the form of a CABLE (Creative Arts, Business, Law and Education) Enterprise. Within the convergence agenda, there will be significant opportunities for collaboration across the STEMM and CABLE Enterprises in areas such public health/social science and economics/health.

Education and Research Activity

- Restructure research activities around significant societal challenges. At the University of Newcastle this has involved the creation of cross-disciplinary Global Impact Clusters in such key areas such as Energy and Resources, Better Health, Healthcare and Treatment, Future Industries and Strong Cities, Communities and Regions. The general concept is that such clusters horizontally integrate research across faculty boundaries, constituting the weft in the university's fabric, in contrast to the vertical warp comprising the structures (faculties, schools and disciplines) that are used to deliver and accredit the curriculum and maintain a sense of professional identity.
- Encourage the development of interdisciplinary under- and post-graduate educational programmes covering such areas bioengineering, biomaterial science, bioinformatics, health economics, etc. that are flexible and stackable and can be individually tailored to meet the specific requirements of individual students.
- Encourage a trans-disciplinary postgraduate research environment involving teams of supervisors from different disciplines, and projects that cross disciplinary boundaries. One example of this shift in emphasis comes from our recently introduced Masters degree in Bioinnovation and Design. Masters by Research degrees traditionally involve incremental research projects that are an extension of the supervisor's own esoteric research interests. Such theses fill our library shelves and yet ultimately, they have very little impact. We hope to transform this landscape by presenting our Masters students with research problems that have sufficient complexity, scale and relevance to merit the creation of a multidisciplinary team to effect their resolution. For example, we might create a team involving students

from physiotherapy, computer science and design in order to create virtual reality therapeutic systems to facilitate the recovery of stroke victims who find it easier to mimic the actions of a digital avatar than to process written or spoken instructions.

- Ensure that across the STEMM and CABLE enterprises there is a focus on the globalisation of our educational and research activities and that this international perspective is incentivised through the provision of travel grants, scholarships, international or student exchanges and facilitated by the creation of trans-institutional partnering agreements at individual (shared PhD supervision or other forms of research collaboration) and institutional levels. In this context it will be critical to leverage research collaborations with the US, UK and EU, along with selected countries in Asia, particularly China, Singapore and Hong Kong. The Federal Government's National Innovation and Science Agenda and the Global Innovation Strategy represent a clear commitment from the Australian Government to the further internationalisation of our research agenda in order to address challenges of global significance.

- Ensure that across the STEMM and CABLE enterprises there is a maintained focus on generating education and research programmes that challenge the nuanced inequities in the experience of health and well-being influenced by socio-economic status, gender, geographic location and cultural background, including Aboriginal and Torres Strait Islander status. A commitment to equity is a key value of the university and it is important that this in maintained, and indeed strengthened, as part of a multidisciplinary, inter-sectoral agenda.

Human Capital

- Develop professional incentives for the development of a convergence ecosystem including professional recognition for interdisciplinary, trans-institutional research and course development at STEMM promotion board level.

- Provide opportunities for service providers to engage in an interdisciplinary research agenda underpinned by training in research methodologies and opportunities to actively contribute to research programmes.

Physical Infrastructure

- Develop and support advanced technical infrastructure platforms that can be readily accessed across discipline boundaries. Until such time as the Australian funding system recognises the overhead cost incurred in conducting research, these facilities should be provided at minimal or no cost to the investigators.

Financial Infrastructure

- Develop STEMM (rather than faculty) KPIs and a STEMM budget model that provides stable, equitable and sustainable funding across the enterprise.
- Secure a diversified research funding model that harnesses the power of philanthropy, as well as engagement with Federal and State Governments, industry and international funding agencies.
- Incentivise interdisciplinary research by providing seed funding and PhD scholarships to support such activity.
- Develop incentives for trans-disciplinary educational programmes by allowing the STEMM enterprise to retain an increased portion of the income from such courses.
- Develop an interdisciplinary innovation ecosystem driven by a spirit of entrepreneurialism, supported by venture capitalists and leading to the development of start-up companies and (re) location of industry to a science park of the type already developed so successfully at MIT and the Universities of Cambridge, Leiden, Dundee, etc. Incentivise this interdisciplinary innovation agenda by permitting the STEMM Enterprise to retain a significant portion of IP (Intellectual property) income.

Conclusions

If institutions such as the University of Newcastle are to continue to develop and act as beacons of inspiration and innovation for the regions they serve, they will have to engage in a new way of working. In the 21st century regional universities will have to be more involved in the economic and social development of their local communities by providing enabling expertise, advanced technology platforms and an entrepreneurial culture. They will have to be tightly networked with regional and national government agencies, local health districts, primary healthcare networks, chambers of commerce and industry, and orchestrate programmes of research and education that are globally engaged yet regionally focused. Addressing research problems that have the desired scale, complexity and impact will necessitate the de-siloing of university structures and the development of a convergence culture around a central health and well-being agenda.

The traditional basic science disciplines such as biology, physics, chemistry and geology are already ghosts in the machine. Their long-term future will depend on the development of a more flexible operational framework and a capacity to work in a team-based interdisciplinary manner. The culture surrounding the natural sciences will also have to change so that an interest in real world problems is not seen as intellectually stultifying. If the natural sciences can overcome this hurdle and combine with engineering and health/medicine to create a new synthesis, combining intellectual rigour, creativity and technological depth across discipline borders to address issues of importance to society's stakeholders, then we have every reason to be optimistic about the future of univer-cities.

Notes

1. <http://www.industry.nsw.gov.au/live-and-work-in-nsw/working-in-nsw/places-to-live-and-work/newcastle>.
2. <https://www.newcastle.edu.au/about-uon/our-university/vision-and-strategic-direction/new-futures-strategic-plan-2016-2025>.
3. <http://www.v-c.admin.cam.ac.uk/professor-sir-leszek-borysiewicz/speeches/global-community>.
4. Robert J.W. Tijssen, Martijn S. Visser, Thed N. van Leeuwen, "Benchmarking international scientific excellence: Are highly cited research papers an appropriate frame of reference?" *Scientometrics* 54, no. 3 (2002), pp. 381–397.
5. Anthony van Raan, Thed N. van Leeuwen, Martijn S. Viseer, "Severe language effect in university rankings: particularly Germany and France are wronged in citation-based rankings", *Scientometrics* 88, no. 2 (2011), pp. 495–498.

6. Bruce Alberts, "Impact factor distortions", *Science* 340, (2013), pp. 787.

7. <http://health.gov.au/internet/main/publishing.nsf/Content/mrff/$FILE/Australian%20 Medical%20Research%20and%20Innovation%20Strategy%202016.pdf>.

8. <www.innovation.gov.au/page/biomedical-translation-fund>.

9. Antoine van Agtmael and Fred Bakker, *The Smartest Places on Earth: Why Rustbelts are the Emerging Hotspots of Global Innovation* (New York: Public Affairs, 2016).

10. <https://www.nhmrc.gov.au/grants-funding/outcomes-funding-rounds>.

11. <http://www.chiefscientist.gov.au/2015/03/keynote-address-to-the-national-press-club-for-science-meets-parliament-2/>.

12. <www.convergencerevolution.net/2016-report/>.

About the Authors

R. John Aitken is Laureate Professor and Pro Vice-Chancellor, Faculty of Health and Medicine, University of Newcastle, Australia.

H. Le Gresley is Executive Officer, PVC Unit Health and Medicine, University of Newcastle, Australia.

embryology before his untimely death, climbing Mont Blanc, aged 30. Adam Sedgwick's nephew and namesake, also Fellow of Trinity from 1880, worked on animal morphology, published a great textbook and many articles in the famed 1911 edition of the *Encyclopaedia Britannica*. The physical manifestation of the rising importance of the sciences was the development of the New Museums and Downing sites. All the sciences had new buildings — laboratories, lecture rooms and museums — before the outbreak of World War I.

Change required new resources. The wealth of the Colleges and the University was very much committed to existing purposes — often in the form of tightly drawn trusts that could not be untangled. Those promoting reform recognised this fact, as Henslow had for his ambitions for the Botanic Garden in the 1830s. The wealthier colleges were able to find money to support intellectual initiatives — Trinity College was particularly active in this respect: indeed, at the end of the century the College achieved a leading position within Cambridge (its great rival, St John's, experiencing for a time financial difficulties) by electing many brilliant young scientists to its Fellowship and providing their laboratory needs. Others were not slow in coming forward. William Cavendish, the 7th Duke of Devonshire and Chancellor of the University from 1861–1891, was determined to follow in the footsteps of his predecessor, Prince Albert, in promoting reform across the board: the University had to modernise its curriculum in the manner of German universities and push ahead with the sciences. He gave money for the laboratory that bears his name, on condition that other funds to cover recurrent staffing and other running costs were raised to match his generosity. The Duke's contribution sat alongside countless other private donations and bequests, and from a general public campaign for funds mounted by the University at the end of the 19th century.

By the second decade of the 20th century national policy began to take account of higher education and research and to provide public funding for it. The matter was contentious, for although local taxation and the financial support of local businesses had already played a part in developing the civic universities and colleges of higher education, there was much debate about how national public funds could be passed to universities without incurring political interference or state control. An ingenious solution was brokered whereby a free-standing non-political body — the University Grants Committee — was set up to receive funds from the Treasury which the Committee in turn distributed between institutions of higher education on academic criteria alone.

Cambridge, with considerable heart-searching and some vociferous internal opposition, contemplated the prospect of receiving public money as grant-in-aid. But it took an external initiative to bring it about. In 1922 another Royal Commission devised ways and means of putting public money into the two ancient English universities, overcoming the fact that they were independent legal charitable corporations. Oxford and Cambridge attracted a good deal of public criticism being thought rich, privileged, and socially exclusive, and therefore inappropriate recipients of taxpayers' money. Many within Cambridge feared that acceptance of any public funding would lead to external influences that would destroy its independence. But many recognised that the University needed more money and that it was reasonable for the public purse to contribute a share. Constant vigilance was urged with regard to the amounts on offer, the purposes for which they were given, and the small print of the terms and conditions that would come with the cash. The University never depended absolutely on public funding, and, indeed, as the 20th century progressed and the amounts involved became so much greater, it became more difficult to establish just exactly how much the University drew from government funding since beside direct annual subvention grants for research were channelled through many different agencies and for so many specific purposes. But once the principle of supplying state funding to what was legally a privileged independent corporation had been conceded, and mechanisms devised to protect the interests of all parties involved, there was no turning back: the government of the day, in one manifestation or another, had become a stakeholder in the future of the University.

The flurry of activity brought other tensions as the University entered a new and more complex world. While the disciplines that determined teaching became more clear-cut and prescriptive, research and scholarship thrived notably as it either crossed or ignored disciplinary boundaries. Given the challenges of organisation, management, and finance, academics perforce sought to defend existing arrangements, while at the

same time wrestled with finding ways of escaping them. There was undeni-
ably competition for resources, to gain credence for "new" subjects, and
to claim for their specialities both prestige and utility. Since money and
personalities were involved academic life became increasingly politicised.
It was not always possible to find a way forward by pure reason.

The Colleges grew their numbers (and therefore their scope and
income increased) and the University expanded its role, very slowly
emerging as a central authority juggling many independent or semi-
independent institutions and trusts in a strange species of federal, or
federalising, organisation. The Colleges varied enormously in size and
wealth, leading to inequalities and tensions of every kind. The University,
which before the end of the 19th century was very much an exiguous
body — still with next to no free income that it could spend on scholarly
initiatives, and limited ability to exercise any overall direction of academic
affairs. Until well into the 20th century the University hardly had an
administrative existence: the Chancellor was an absent figurehead, the
Vice Chancellor was a Head of House and only presided over formal
meetings: he had no executive authority. The Registrary maintained lists
of names, keeping a record of matriculations and degrees awarded.
He was conveniently housed in a grand office in the Pitt Building where
the University Press printed the lists off and provided a team of boys on
bicycles to deliver notices of University business to the Colleges. Not
until 1928 did the Registrary have an Assistant and the support of a
Treasurer. Retiring from that post, John Neville Keynes (father of the
economist John Maynard Keynes) reflected on the great increase in
University business since his appointment in 1910. At a dinner given in
his honour he pointed out that the need to manage relationships outside
the University, particularly with the government, would no doubt mean
further development of the administrative service. He was right, and from
that time the University grew its central staff and took a progressively
active lead in developing both undergraduate and research activity.

The process was a canny mixture of evolution and the impact of a
variety of new external stimuli. Change came about in response to several
otherwise unrelated events. The major developments of the 19th century — the
growth of towns, industries, the need for a skilled workforce and the
growth of the professions, led to a demand for more education and for

more higher education in particular. These deep-seated shifts in society gathered hectic pace in the 20th century, forced on by the severe shocks occasioned by that century's two great wars. And since the mid-century, the pace of technological and economic change has quickened further. The Cambridge of today is essentially a result of radical transformations brought about in the past half century.

The University's distinction rests on tradition (often excessively regarded), but this should not obscure just how fundamentally its culture and institutions have adapted and responded to societal pressures. Cambridge has more than doubled its student numbers every thirty years, and rebalanced its efforts in a massive way towards research: in very broad terms, in the 1950s the split between educational spending (i.e. undergraduate teaching) and spending on research was 75/25 — a proportion that now, with hugely enhanced resources, is reversed. The University diversified its curriculum and raised its standards. It broadened its social intake and prepared its graduates for a vastly greater variety of employment: the oarsmen in the first Oxford/ Cambridge boat race in 1829 became clergymen; such a calling is rare among today's crews.

Enterprising dons encouraged research: promoting the PhD became a major concern from the 1950s, and from the 1990s there was a massive expansion of taught Masters' courses. The traditional MA (Cantab) was, and is, not an academic qualification: it is not awarded for further study after a BA degree but signals a promotion to a more senior position within the legal corporation. Historically, it carried with it a right to participate in its government. But in the latter part of the 20th century, following a pattern established elsewhere, old Diploma courses were re-tooled and became new Masters degrees awarded for advanced study. The old Bachelor of Law was brought into line for what it was — a Master of Law degree. Entirely new postgraduate courses were developed — some to prepare students for research, many more as practical professional qualifications. A further dramatic development from the 1990s was the creation of postdoctoral research work, usually funded by short-term contracts and lying outside the regular (permanent) teaching establishments. In many and various ways the University, therefore, was pushed to think about itself and its purposes — to reform its governance, to be aware of its social responsibilities, and to take account, albeit uncomfortably, of external political pressures.

These themes can be well illustrated by returning to the topic of medical education. Sir George Paget had promoted medical sciences at undergraduate, pre-clinical, level as options within the Natural Sciences Tripos. He had supported research in the medical disciplines, and he had persuaded the University to set up a Diploma in Public Health (1875). But his attempts to place Cambridge as a major player within the medical profession had failed. This was partly because the local hospital was small and received patients from a limited hinterland. Cambridge was a market town in an agricultural county with few interesting diseases. By comparison, London with its huge resident population and its exposure to the germs of the world was a much better bet for those wishing to enter the profession. Training in the London hospitals was the long-established route for the would-be medical man.

Co-operation across medicine was bedevilled by political sensitivities. The profession was sharply divided in a trades-union way between surgeons and physicians, barely able to speak to each other and ensconced in their separate Royal Colleges (indeed, one of the few times they worked together was to lobby against the grant of a Royal Charter to the College of General Practitioners). Within Cambridge, petty jealousies bedevilled relations between the University and the medical doctors. The University refused MA degrees (conferring senior membership in its body) to surgeons and physicians working at Addenbrooke's on the grounds that it was not fitting to let mere professional men (almost in some eyes just tradesmen) have a say in the government of the University. The Trustees of the hospital retaliated by refusing to let the University professors have access to beds and patients. After a tussle, and on condition that the University met the costs, Paget's successor in the Regius Chair, Sir Clifford Allbutt (particularly renown for work on mental health) was eventually allowed into the hospital. However, Allbutt was himself opposed to the development of clinical education in Cambridge and during his tenure of office (1892–1925) medical education stagnated and student numbers declined, not to recover until the 1930s.

Cambridge continued to score on the research front. After World War I, Sir Hugh Anderson, the physiologist, worked tirelessly to raise funds for buildings and to establish new research posts. Anderson was an extraordinary figure in Cambridge at the time. Besides his scientific distinction (he was elected a Fellow of the Royal Society in 1907) he was Master of Gonville and Caius College (1912–28), a college with a decidedly medical tinge to its history, having been re-founded by the Elizabethan physician Dr John Caius and boasting among its alumni William Harvey, the discoverer of how blood circulates through the body. Anderson was a great wheeler-dealer within Cambridge, navigating academic politics with a skill few others could emulate. Among other things, he established excellent relations with the Rockefeller Foundation that led first to major benefactions for medicine and then made possible the construction of a new University Library.

The development of Cambridge medicine benefited from government decisions. The town of Cambridge was a county headquarters. Following a public enquiry in 1944, it was decided to establish in Cambridge a hospital to serve an extensive region, going beyond the county boundaries. Then the introduction of the National Health Service in 1948 set the course for ever-increasing resources to be poured into healthcare. The earlier limitations on the successful development were lifted if things could be brought together. A separate (pre-clinical) Medical Sciences Tripos came into being in 1966 with the first students graduating in 1969, but they still went overwhelmingly to London (or Oxford, or elsewhere) to qualify for practice. But in 1969 another Royal Commission recommended that a clinical school be established in the University. It was a controversial decision and it took until 1976 before the school opened.

There were widespread anxieties that the clinical school would flood Cambridge with non-Cambridge people: indeed, there were unseemly spats about the way in which senior medical staff, nearly all non-Cambridge graduates, had the temerity to wear their "foreign" doctoral gowns at official University events — a clear violation of the University Statues governing academic dress. A matter, the reform of which, gave much innocent fun within the University for the next thirty years. More seriously, the anxiety stemmed from the fact that a medical school would constitute such a large part of the University, and be so great a consumer of its resources. It would come to dominate the place at the expense of other subjects and disciplines. This was a fear common to other universities where it was believed that academic priorities were distorted by medicine's voracious appetite. Already by the mid-20th century it was clear that medicine was expensive, it had many stakeholders, and it was a major operation to manage conflicting interests. Negotiations about funding, about patient care, about research, and about its application, involved interactions with government at both local and national levels, charities, hospital management, and big international businesses. Making such arrangements inevitably involved time and skill, and a degree of top-down political management that was unwelcome to an institution which was culturally so wedded to running its own affairs and that lived by the shibboleth of "academic freedom".

Since the mid-20th century the Cambridge region has become one of the largest centres of health sciences and medical research in Europe. On the southern edge of the city a bio-medical campus is being developed which includes within its compass the regional hospital complex, the University's Clinical School, the Medical Research Council's Laboratory of Molecular Biology and the research wings of the international pharmaceutical companies GlaxoSmithKline and AstraZeneca. There is a cluster of research units and centres sponsored by charitable bodies such as the British Heart Foundation, Cancer Research UK, the Li Kashing Foundation, the Wellcome Trust, the Wolfson Foundation, and many others. All this is a far cry from Henry VIII's Regius Professorship or John Addenbrooke's gift of £4,500 made in 1719 to endow a hospital for the town. Some themes run through clear, but essential elements bringing about the mix of town and gown, of learning and benefactions, have come about from unexpected forces generated from outside.

The magnet has been the multiplicity of research emerging from the University. The discoveries of the late 19th and early 20th centuries made Cambridge famous and whatever critical voices were raised (as they still are) against unfair privilege there was no doubt that on both educational and research fronts the University had become truly professional in what it was doing. Other research groups, some government funded, some not, began to gravitate to Cambridge. In 1948, the Agricultural Research Council bought property at Babraham to the south-west of Cambridge to research animal husbandry: over the next half century it would re-orient its activity several times and become closer to the University. Its origins were research in very practical areas of animal husbandry — a matter of vital concern in the 1940s and 1950s as the country struggled to feed itself. But by the mid-1980s, linking up with other groups across the country, it became an Institute of Animal Physiology and Genetics. By 1994 it had changed direction again and, still funded largely but not wholly by a government-backed research council, it turned to study molecular mechanisms that underlay normal cell processes and functions. By the turn of the millennium it had ceased all work with direct relevance to agriculture, but its scientists had picked up a number of Nobel prizes along the way. The Babraham Institute became an independent charitable organisation dedicated to fundamental research, seeking funding from many quarters, including from its own company, Babraham Institute Enterprises Ltd that secured a return from the exploitation of the Institute's intellectual property rights. Some of those working there were Fellows of Colleges; some of the University's doctoral students were based at and supervised in the Babraham Institute.

Molecular biology provides a good entrée into understanding complex changes. One of the great discoveries of the 20th century was the description of the molecular structure of DNA — the Double Helix. The definitive paper on the subject, by Francis Crick and James Watson, was published in the journal *Nature* in April 1953. Later, along with Maurice Wilkins, they were to share the Nobel Prize in medicine for their work. But the discovery did not come about as the result of effort in a single laboratory or from one group. It drew on many disciplinary backgrounds and intellectual traditions. Crick was a British scientist taking his first degree at University College, London. World War II interrupted his advanced study with the result he came to the Cavendish to be supervised by Max Perutz. Perutz was Austrian born and had taken his degrees in Vienna before arriving in Cambridge. His own work was in the field of X-ray crystallography. The Director of the Cavendish, Sir Laurence Bragg (who came of impeccable Cambridge lineage), supported Perutz in establishing a molecular biology research unit in the physics laboratory but funded by the Medical Research Council. James Watson was American, taking his first degree from Chicago and studying for a PhD in Indiana. He then began postdoctoral work in Copenhagen and it was from there that he migrated to Cambridge. But this was not all. Other people in other universities were also doing work relevant to the crucial breakthrough. Rosalind Franklin who had read Natural Sciences at Cambridge had gone on to do chemical research relating to coal and, after a spell in Paris, went to King's College, London where she engaged in the study of X-ray defraction. Franklin worked, not entirely happily, with Sir John Randall and Maurice Wilkins. She accumulated and interpreted vital data for reports presented to the Medical Research Council that proved essential to the Crick and Watson discovery. Wilkins, who was to take a share in the credit for the discovery, was a New Zealander and a physicist who did undergraduate work in Cambridge but whose doctoral experience was at Birmingham University before following his supervisor to St Andrews and then making the move to King's College, London.

Although some scientists (including some Cambridge physiologists) did not think that molecular biology had a future, the revelation of the molecular structure of DNA unleashed an avalanche of further research. It has driven developments in medicine, healthcare, and, as the findings came to be more fully understood and applied, to the pharmaceutical industry turning small companies making pills and potions into powerful international economic and social forces.

Since the 1950s, Cambridge, its ancient university and its medieval market town, has been transformed. It has grown in size and complexity beyond belief. It exists now as a renowned educational and research hub, in which medicine plays a significant, but not the only, part. The development has come about with and without a plan. It has been propelled by interests within the University and just as vitally, by forces from without. Many of what in retrospect have been the most important decisions have been the most hotly contested. Understanding what makes successful univer-cities is not straightforward. These thriving places come about, almost serendipitously, from a mix of many ingredients. They need concentrations of large numbers of highly educated and curious people — so the physical environment matters. The cities will be rich in culture and offer a good quality of life — so the arts, humanities, music, sport and recreational facilities all matter, too (it is no surprise that the Eagle Pub in Benet Street where Crick and Watson sat and drank claims some responsibility for the discovery of the Double Helix). The univer-city is not isolated — it will welcome incoming populations with different ethnic, religious and educational backgrounds, and it will send its own people out to experience the world beyond the parish. It will be a place of tolerance and enlightenment, but also a place of passion and controversy. Here also is a constant balancing of management and anarchy; room for intellectual initiative and where not everything has to succeed. It needs accumulated wealth, or to have access to resources as needed. It will be widely networked, and will, above all, be a place of communication and exchange. The univer-city is a complex being and not simply evolved. It is, in the end, a fragile human creation, requiring constant attention to flourish.

About the Author

Gordon Johnson was a Deputy Vice-Chancellor of Cambridge University (2002–2010) and past President of Wolfson College, Cambridge (1993–2010). He has served two terms as President of the Royal Asiatic Society, ending 2018.

CHAPTER FOUR

MEETING SOCIETAL CHALLENGES THROUGH MEDICAL EDUCATION AND RESEARCH: LKCMEDICINE, NTU-ICL SINGAPORE

BERTIL ANDERSSON

Introduction

Over the last decade, Singapore's continued population growth and the anticipated medical demands of a rapidly ageing population have become key factors in the case for increasing the supply of trained medical doctors in the country. Projections made by the Ministries of Health and Manpower in 2007 predicted demand would continue to outpace supply and it soon became evident that Yong Loo Lin School of Medicine and Duke-NUS Graduate Medical School had only a very limited capacity to support the projected growth and overcome attrition to the private sector. It was then concluded that establishing a new medical school would be the key to resolving the national shortage of trained doctors. The initial intent to establish Singapore's second medical school was first conceived in 2001, during which Nanyang Technological University (NTU) was identified as a potential host for the next medical school but it was nearly a decade later that NTU finally gained its medical school. However, realisation of this initial vision took close to a decade to materialise, as NTU continued to embark on an exercise to further develop and expand its research profile in biomedical sciences, natural sciences, engineering, humanities, arts and social sciences. NTU, a new university established in 1991 primarily as an engineering-based institute, is today a more comprehensive research university continuing its strong technological focus.

The Singapore Government's decision in 2006 to grant autonomy to the universities heralded an era of significant restructure and rapid advancement for NTU. Following the conferral of its autonomous status, one of the immediate institutional changes at NTU was the introduction of the college system, which saw the reorganisation of the twelve schools into four Colleges (Engineering; Business; Humanities; Arts and Social Sciences; and Science). Over the course of my appointment as NTU Provost in 2007 during the leadership of then President Su Guaning, we oversaw the introduction of several key measures aimed at enhancing the University's research and academic excellence. This included the institution of a rigorous Promotion and Tenure system which resulted in a retroactive review of all tenured faculty and the subsequent release of approximately one quarter of the faculty population from existing tenure. This presented NTU with a unique opportunity to reposition itself strategically and engage in recruitment efforts for world-class academics from prime institutions and promising young career researchers of the highest international calibre across various research domains to come to Singapore. In addition, the faculty recomposition also released additional-capital resources which were then redirected towards key investments in campus development and research infrastructure. Likewise, significant investments were simultaneously directed towards curriculum reform, culminating in a comprehensive revamp of both content and delivery and the incorporation of the newest digital technologies for the latter. NTU's growth over the last decade and its unique rapid rise in world esteem have been reflected both in global university ranking league tables as well as its leading position in the region for research impact. Ranked 11th(QS World University Rankings) and 1st(QS Top 50 under 50 2016) as well as 1st in the region for normalised research citation impact in Asia, NTU today offers a wide range of undergraduate and postgraduate programmes to the diverse community of 33,200 students on campus in the west of Singapore.

Founded in 2009, the Lee Kong Chian School of Medicine (LKC Medicine) is a unique ongoing close partnership between NTU and Imperial College London (ICL). The school was established on the basis of fortifying Singapore's healthcare capacity and built upon NTU's broadened academic portfolio over the course of the last decade. Its development has also played an important role in casting pertinent questions to shape the country's long-range roadmap for healthcare delivery and re-examine the alignment of competencies among the existing medical schools. LKC Medicine's development has provided an opportunity for the introduction of the latest pedagogic approaches, especially using new technologies, implementation of a tailored educational agenda for local context as well as advancing solutions for the healthcare challenges of the future. In this chapter, I present an overview of the contextual circumstances, motivational factors and the challenges confronted by both NTU and ICL over the course of establishing LKCMedicine. Through this, the chapter seeks to provide value and insights from the lessons learned for university administrators who may be involved in future plans to establish a medical school. LKCMedicine was so named after becoming a beneficiary of a S$150m donation from the Lee Foundation, in recognition of local philanthropist the late Tan Sri Dato Lee Kong Chian, a key figure in the post-war development of Singapore.

Context and Development of the Medical Eco-system and Education in Singapore

In a 2007 memorandum addressed to the Committee on the Expansion of the University Sector in Singapore (CEUS), statistics provided by the Ministries of Health and Manpower indicated that the projected population increase coupled with demographical changes in the ageing population would lead to a resource shortage and growing strain on the existing healthcare resources in the coming decades. Based on the statistical analysis, it was concluded that Singapore would be required to double the number of doctors by 2020. In terms of output, this translated to increasing the local supply of trained doctors from the current output of 300 to 600 per year. The memorandum concluded that Singapore's then capacity as served by the NUS-Yong Loo Lin Medical School and Duke-NUS Graduate Medical School did not possess the adequate capacity to meet the projected demand as outlined by the Ministries, signifying the need to re-examine the case for establishing Singapore's third medical school.

The year 2007 was the second time the idea was mooted, with the first proposal tabled in December 2001. At the time, it was concluded that NTU required an expanded academic base to better support the research and education requirements of a medical school. Since that time, NTU had taken strenuous efforts to put in place a new College Structure, and created new Schools in Science and Engineering, of which the School of Biological Sciences was the most significant in this regard, cementing its new position as one of the two major higher education institutions in Singapore. Thus, the case for NTU to be a natural host for the country's third Medical School was self-evident.

In an effort to comprehensively evaluate NTU's academic and resource capabilities to support the proposed medical school and following on from NTU's initial proposal, the Provost was commissioned to produce a feasibility and scoping study which he undertook together with Professor Jan Carlstedt-Duke, former Dean of Research at the Karolinska Institutet in Stockholm. In this study conducted in 2008, Professor Carlstedt-Duke identified several schools across NTU working in areas relevant to medical science and in ongoing collaboration with hospitals and clinical research labs. These efforts were undertaken by more than 300 ongoing medically-relevant projects and faculty involvement from the Schools of Biological Sciences, Chemical and Biomedical Engineering, Materials Sciences and Engineering, Physical and Mathematical Sciences, Computer Engineering, Electrical and Electronic Engineering and Humanities and Social Sciences.

Establishing Singapore's Third Medical School

Based on the findings of the feasibility study, a compelling case was put forward for NTU to become host for the medical school. This undertaking eventually set the course for a series of key decisions that would shape the education and research strategy of LKCMedicine. Following the release of the feasibility study findings, NTU's proposal for the new Medical School was submitted for consideration in early 2009. The proposal outlined a response to the contextual challenges of Singapore's healthcare needs as well as proposed outcomes that sought to bridge the gaps in current local practice. The proposal would also go on to provide key recommendations to shape the design and composition of LKCMedicine's management framework, faculty recruitment strategy, pedagogic approach and curriculum content. Strong governmental support notwithstanding, establishing the medical school remained a significant undertaking that required a careful assessment of both the university's resources and the healthcare needs of the community it sought to serve. It was also recognised that the new medical school would lead to a series of beneficial impacts such as to enhance NTU's research activity as well as serving the community through provision of supply and access to better trained doctors and quality healthcare services. The proposal identified the need to further develop community-based medicine initiatives and proposed a programme designed to respond to the needs of the healthcare system of the future and to establish wider practice of doctors working in multi-professional teams. These planning efforts also had to take into consideration that the new medical school would be acting in concert with the Yong Loo Lin School of Medicine, NUS, Duke-NUS Graduate Medical School and the Singapore Ministry of Health's clinical transformation strategy. In addition, the study also recommended establishing an affiliation with a clinical partner as a priority, as well as the need to create interfacing platforms between the proposed Medical School and existing NTU faculty and school. Finally, another key recommendation in the feasibility study suggested seeking out partnerships and sustained engagement with leading medical research and education institutions to further boost the capacity and assist in the quality assurance processes at LKC Medicine. This would eventually lead to the formation of a partnership between Imperial College London (ICL) and NTU.

The Imperial College Partnership

One of LKCMedicine's defining hallmarks is its partnership with Imperial College London (ICL), which witnessed the latter venturing in an unprecedented landmark collaboration to establish a joint medical school abroad. In the early stages of the evaluation process, NTU identified a series of potential international academic and research partners (University of Sydney, Australia; Warwick University, UK; Imperial College London, UK; and the Karolinska Institutet, Stockholm, Sweden) in which ICL rapidly emerged as a strong frontrunner. There was general consensus among the NTU leadership that ICL's leading expertise in engineering and technology, shared research profile and strong integrated platforms to promote interfacing between engineering and medicine research, was similar and would work to complement NTU's research profile and efforts. These attributes were further supported by an existing alliance between NTU and Imperial College built on strong, long-standing collaborations across education and research based on mutual academic esteem. In addition to the academic rationale, ICL also possessed the institutional credibility and academic prestige that resonated with the Singaporean community. Once identified as a strong potential partner, talks between the two universities intensified, finally culminating in a joint agreement in May 2009 and a joint announcement in August 2009 to formally establish LKCMedicine. The decision was also made for LKCMedicine to be established as an autonomous school of NTU, with formalized affiliations to the two universities. The roles of Professor Sir Keith O'Nions, Rector of Imperial College and Pro-Rector, Professor Mary Ritter were critical in the success of the partnership negotiations.

Over the course of the discussions, one of the major challenges that emerged was the way in which the decision-making framework could be designed to ensure an equal partnership across governance and administrative decisions. This eventually led to establishing a Governing Board, which would formally institute joint decision-making and play an important function to ensure that existing quality benchmarks and standards were upheld. Comprising senior representatives from both NTU and ICL, each partner was accorded equal weight in decision-making with the power of veto with respect to academic matters. The reserve matters were jointly identified and agreed upon by both partners and relate to important issues such as governance and administration, faculty recruitment, research matters and curriculum among others. This governance framework proved to be an integral feature of the partnership between the two universities, providing a systematic method to take into account strategic restraints of either partner in the event of key decisions. The Chairman of A*STAR, Mr Lim Chuan Poh, coincidentally a Fellow of Imperial College like myself, and a Member of the NTU Board of Trustees, became Chairman of the LKCMedicine Board and this guidance was especially important. The series of attributes, including his influence in the negotiations and membership of the NTU Board of Trustees, made him the perfect candidate for the role.

Fig. 4.1 Experimental Medicine Building, NTU Yunnan Garden Campus.

Fig. 4.2 LKCMedicine White Coat Ceremony at Nanyang Auditorium, 17 August 2015.

Fig. 4.3   Toh Kian Chui Annex, Novena Campus.

Fig. 4.4   Clinical Sciences Building, Novena Campus.

Fig. 4.5 LKCMedicine Tree Planting Ceremony with Professor Sir Keith O'Nions at Novena Campus, 14 August 2014.

Fig. 4.6 Tan Sri Dato Dr Lee Kong Chian.

Fig. 4.7   Group photo with Deputy Chairman of Lee Foundation, Dr Lee Seng Tee (first row, leftmost), Minister for Health Mr Gan Kim Yong (first row, fifth from left), and then Minister for Education Mr Heng Swee Keat (first row, fifth from right) following the Groundbreaking Ceremony at Mandalay Road, 28 May 2012.

Fig. 4.8 Foundation Stone Laying Ceremony of the Experimental Sciences Building and Clinical Sciences Building, NTU Yunnan Garden Campus, 8 January 2015.

This engagement and representation of ICL leadership was also a critical feature of the composition of LKCMedicine's academic leadership. Professor Stephen Smith, then Principal of ICL's Faculty of Medicine was recruited to serve as Founding Dean of LKCMedicine. His appointment was followed by a series of joint senior appointments from ICL including Professor Jenny Higham as LKCMedicine Senior Vice Dean responsible for curriculum development. Succeeding the Founding Dean, Professor Dermot Kelleher, was instrumental in consolidating the success of the joint enterprise. This senior representation in governance and administrative arrangements was crucial in ensuring that the school received the necessary expertise and advice.

Curriculum Design and Research

The design of LKCMedicine's curriculum entailed the consideration of several key factors, which among others include delivery methods, learning materials, and technology capacities. Unencumbered by tradition and given a strong mandate for innovation, LKCMedicine's curriculum was envisaged to distinguish itself from the current offerings around the world by providing a strong grounding in community-based medicine while employing pioneering pedagogical approaches and the latest e-learning technologies. At the heart of LKCMedicine's educational mission is the successful training of high quality doctors who are adapted to respond to future medical challenges. In view of this, LKCMedicine's Curriculum Development Team worked closely with the ICL curriculum team to adapt the latter's existing curriculum within the context of Singapore with a focus on self-directed learning. The new curriculum was jointly developed over a period of four years and making use of a pedagogic shift towards team-based learning. This team-based learning pedagogic approach remains a distinguishing feature of LKCMedicine's curriculum, heavily incorporating the use of information technology and electronic tablets for delivery and assessment. As the first undergraduate medical school to completely replace classroom lectures with pre-recorded lessons, the move to adopt team-based learning was chosen due to its interactive and collaborative nature and the learning strategy's emphasis on comprehension and application. It was also made possible by NTU's prior investments in IT infrastructure and enhanced by the NTU Board of Trustees to ring fence a budget of S$20 million to further support e-learning investments across the university.

A major discussion point that emerged early in the planning stages, was the limitations of the existing clinical capacity to support the new Medical School, presenting a paradoxical situation with the projected shortage of doctors. As such, one of the key aspects of LKC Medicine's curriculum is its affiliation with Tan Tock Seng Hospital and Singapore's National Healthcare Group to provide its undergraduate students with early extensive exposure to patients and clinical care conditions. With the curriculum's emphasis on patient-centred care, the clinical education arrangements seek to expose students to the whole pathway of care and encourage deeper understanding of patients' needs within a holistic framework. The various components in the learning curricula combine to create a transformative learning experience designed to produce thinking, collaborative and empathetic doctors essential to an evolving and challenging healthcare delivery landscape. As an example of novel approaches to enhance these qualities is the long-term patient project where pairs of students follow a patient with a chronic disease during Years 1 and 2 with regular contact with the family, following the clinical and social implications of the disease. This approach is a crucial component of the curriculum, providing a service-learning experience for the students, and serves to facilitate collaborative teamwork and simulate patient-centred care. In contrast to existing Medical Schools, LKCMedicine exposes students to patients at a very early stage in their learning. Students not only meet "real" patients but the school has invested in "mock" consulting areas, where students practice on actor-patients under close observation.

In addition to clinical education and training and in line with the Humboldtian notion of linking research to education, LKCMedicine is equally committed to pursuing the development of its clinical and translational research programmes. LKCMedicine's research strategy straddles across four key thematic areas (metabolic disorders, neuroscience and mental health, infection and immunity and dermatology and skin biology) in population health with a strong focus on addressing the issues and healthcare challenges of the community. LKCMedicine's research strategy also represents a significant opportunity to leverage the research strengths at NTU and generate greater inter-disciplinary collaborative opportunities between medicine and engineering. To this end, the dual campus model with the Experimental Medicine Building located at NTU's Yunnan Garden Campus and adjacent to the School of Biological Sciences served to promote opportunities for interaction and convergence to better drive basic medical science research efforts. This was further advanced by the establishment of a virtual institute, the Nanyang Institute in Health and Medicine (NITHM) that acted in an interdisciplinary function across all Colleges and schools to enhance medically-related research across the University. Thus, the two academic partners mirror each other in having medical schools within predominantly engineering institutions. In addition to NITHM, the Medical School is a key component of the Nanyang Integrated Medical, Biological and Environmental Life Sciences (NIMBELS) cluster bringing together life and biomedical sciences to form a coherent strategic whole.

Outcomes of the Medical School, Opportunities and Challenges

Over the course of bringing LKCMedicine's blueprint to life, the management and implementation team has encountered their share of challenges as documented in this section. Since the enrolment of its first cohort of students in 2013, the steady state student cohort has seen subsequent enlargements as manpower projections for medical professionals continue to rise. This is further compounded by the significant constraints posed by scarcity of manpower and tensions in adapting ICL content for the local context and delivery. One of the key lessons that emerged from these tensions was the need to coordinate and build a dedicated staff team in curriculum development to ensure quality of education remains uncompromised. Fortunately, these pressures were partially eased by the emergence of positive developments in the healthcare delivery landscape, such as a growing base of clinical partners and consequently a larger pool of clinical educators to draw from. Furthermore, information communication technologies (ICT) have played a significant role in curriculum delivery, and its rapid development continues to present vast opportunities for transformative changes and innovation in both future content and delivery. LKCMedicine's new pedagogic delivery also presented ICL with an opportunity to refine its curriculum delivery having previously sought to introduce an IT-enhanced pedagogy with limited success. The successful implementation of LKCMedicine's ICT enhanced curriculum encouraged ICL to renew its efforts and re-export the revamped pedagogic approach back to its classrooms in London. LKCMedicine has also met with tremendous success in attracting outstanding and engaged students, forming a highly competent student body set to have a positive impact as future advocates for civic engagement through medicine. However, the rising costs of a medical education continues to pose as a challenge to access and may pose serious implications on the supply and diversity of doctors in the future.

In research, LKCMedicine continues to face important challenges going forward. The first ongoing challenge is to ensure the framework conditions and mechanisms are sustained to optimise and encourage ongoing academic interaction between LKCMedicine and rest of NTU. In a bid to promote greater interaction between LKCMedicine and other schools and major research institutes, NTU has sought to incorporate transdisciplinary structures and research institutes that provide both a joint platform for research and unique capabilities for translation of basic medical research into technologies. To this end, NITHM and NIMBELS continue to play an important role in creating strategies to address collaborative gaps and facilitate cooperation between LKCMedicine and the rest of NTU.

LKCMedicine's recruitment efforts were not without challenges which saw the school stretched to provide faculty and clinical educators in the early stages of what has been a uniquely rapid set-up phase. The school addressed the challenges by embarking on a strategy to leverage ICL as a resource of academic experience and joint faculty appointments, which was effective in serving to ease and abate the burden to a certain degree. The joint appointments were also key to fostering and sustaining the academic ties and relationships between the two universities. Despite the challenge of being a new medical school, LKCMedicine was also successful in recruiting leading international academics which helped to propel the rapid development of strong research competencies and augment the existing research clusters and capacity. With the key resources in place, LKCMedicine is becoming a stable, sustainable and forefront medical school within the global medical community.

The events that have unfolded over the course of establishing LKC Medicine have played an instrumental role in strengthening the school's ability to contend with the challenges. The overarching lesson to be drawn from the LKCMedicine's experience, however, is the successful adoption of a strong collaborative approach across various aspects of governance, education, research and funding. The management's ability to effectively gain support while maintaining a degree of autonomy from their stakeholders in government and their clinical partners have put them in good stead to accomplish their research and education missions. As noted previously, the consensus to establish a clear, equal and effective management structure to address issues and conflicts has played a substantial role in supporting the successful delivery of the school's educational and research outcomes. At time of writing, LKCMedicine is about to graduate its first cohort of doctors for Singapore. While the challenges may vary as a result of circumstantial and contextual differences, this chapter attempts to offer some insights into the approaches adopted by LKCMedicine in overcoming its major hurdles that could be adapted by university administrators when developing future blueprints for a medical school and answering social imperatives.

The partnership between NTU and ICL reaches far beyond the traditional confines of typical research collaborations, forming instead a deeply integrated joint institution from which students graduate with both the accreditation of NTU and ICL. Distinctly positioned to provide future doctors with the most comprehensive education and training, LKC Medicine's formation has also led to the creation of one of the world's most far-reaching partnerships in education.

Acknowledgements

I am indebted to Ms Richie Chen who has assisted me in writing the account of LKCMedicine. I also want to thank Professor Jan Carlstedt-Duke and Mr Tony Mayer for their valuable comments.

Photo credits: LKCMedicine.

About the Author

Bertil Andersson is President, Nanyang Technological University, Singapore (2011–2017).

CHAPTER FIVE

UNIVER-CITY OF ZURICH: AN EVOLUTIONARY-MEDICAL PERSPECTIVE

FRANK RÜHLI AND MACIEJ HENNEBERG

Switzerland has a long academic tradition and Zurich is its major hub, with the Swiss Institute of Technology (ETHZ) and the University of Zurich (UZH), both leading academic institutions. Medical sciences are the prime part of the University of Zurich. The University Hospital in Zurich (USZ) is a separate institution providing medical care to patients and teaching/researching clinical medicine.

The aim of this chapter* is to highlight the unique history and the current and future challenges of the UZH, with a particular focus on the medical disciplines and especially the Institute of Evolutionary Medicine. The description of the establishment of the discipline of evolutionary medicine at the Medical Faculty of the UZH may serve as a model for the ongoing challenging transition in science and academia in general.

The Academic Situation in Zurich

Switzerland is a small country, well known for its political and financial stability and its centuries of tradition of democratic, bottom-up govern-ance. Zurich is the economic capital of Switzerland and its largest city. Typical local "cultural principles" historically derived include Protestantism and a modest, neutral, sustainable yet innovative behaviour. Within the city of Zurich, education and healthcare are the second and third most important branches of industry, after finance.

In the central area of Zurich the major higher educational institu-tions, the ETHZ and UZH, are located. Also, one of the largest Swiss

---

*This chapter represents the author's personal view only and is not the official position of the UZH or the University of Adelaide.

hospital, the University Hospital is situated in the very same area, with its oldest records dating back to 1204. The University of Zurich — Universitas Turicensis — that is the major institution discussed here, was founded in 1833, yet built upon educational institutions dating back to 1525. It is a full university with a total of seven faculties and some 25,000 students. The UZH is the very first European university established through a democratic government, not by the church or a head of state. Consequently it runs under constant public control, especially in terms of budget and legal framework. The main budget is awarded every year after in-depth discussions by the local, cantonal parliament.

The UZH defines itself as a leading university, both in research and teaching: for example, twelve Nobel prizes have been awarded to members of the UZH. Also, the UZH is a member of the League of European Research Universities.

Medical Sciences at the UZH include the Medical Faculty, the only Swiss Veterinary Faculty (a joint faculty of the Universities of Zurich and Berne) and tracks such as biomedicine in the Science Faculty. The Medical Faculty was one of the four founding faculties (besides Theology, Law and Philosophy). The Medical Faculty UZH is the largest Swiss faculty (currently a total of ~ 2,000 students). It counts for roughly a third of the UZH budget with an annual total of ca. 300 million CHF. It includes dentistry and chiropractic medicine. A dedicated MD-PhD programme exists, and also a strong inter-action with the Life Sciences Zurich Graduate School. Medicine is supported by various top-down UZH initiatives, e.g. by University Research Priority programmes (URPP) and clinical research priority programmes. Overall, the UZH medical faculty ranks number five within continental Europe and number 33 worldwide (Academic Ranking of World Universities 2016).

The Case of an Emerging Academic Field: Evolutionary Medicine

Evolutionary medicine is a novel field of medical science created by inte-grating principles of evolutionary biology with medical research and teaching. Since the 1990s it has been an emerging academic concept with a major boost in the last few years, particularly due to the establishment of large academic centres in the US (e.g. Arizona State University) and Europe (e.g. University of Zurich).

In 2014 a new institute, the Institute of Evolutionary Medicine, was founded as part of the Medical Faculty at the UZH. The motto of the institute is "Learning from the past for the present and the future". Its vision reads as follows: "We are a leading international and globally connected research, teaching and service institute which is part of the medical faculty at the University of Zurich. We analyse ancient biological material and associated data to better understand modern human health issues and diseases. Due to specialist scientific expertise, excellent infrastructure and state-of-the-art methodologies, we are able to work on various interdisciplinary research questions in the context of the field of Evolutionary Medicine." (www.iem.uzh.ch)

The Institute is unique worldwide and is part of a top-down funded field at the UZH, in particular by being part of a URPP called "Evolution in action". The Institute's setting is mostly interdisciplinary, e.g. it bridges the Medical and Science faculties. It consists currently of four different groups, ancient biomolecular, evolutionary morphology and adaptation, paleopathology and mummy studies and museum of medicine and medical collection. The latter is a part of the former Institute for the History of Medicine, which was dissolved in 2014 and partially incorporated into the IEM. The medical collection is one of the largest of its kind in Europe. The planned Medical Museum shall be a window towards medical research (historic, current and future) and a venue for potential donors. The Institute consists of some 50 academic members (including post-graduate students) and roughly half of the Institute's brutto budget originates from third-party funding. Further information about the setting and current research and teaching outlines of the Institute can be found at <www.iem.uzh.ch>.

The impact and role model of the establishment and successful running of this Institute is multifarious. It is an excellent example of the emerging trend of interdisciplinary research and teaching. By being increasingly incorporated into the curricula of various faculties such as Social Sciences (Archeology students) or Science (biology students) it has increasing transfaculty recognition. Most importantly, it encourages "critical thinking" of medical students by teaching through elective courses. Evolutionary Medicine is a crucial component for shaping effective future health policy strategies.

Major challenges for the establishment of this new institute at the Medical Faculty were the lack of collegial knowledge about this emerging field itself, the constant lack of space for the number of institute employees roughly doubling every 1.5 years and finally uncertainties in establishing additional senior positions due to multiple local factors. With strong leadership, well-defined internal procedures and transparent internal and external communication, the establishment of the Institute and the field itself was achieved to a high degree in the last two years. A specific focus is laid on local clinical collaborations to further promote its awareness and acceptance. Although the described development of the emerging research field and subsequent establishment of such a unique institute occurred in the second decade of the 21st century, it followed the pattern in which the first European academic institutions were established in the 11th and 12th centuries — a group of scholars interested in expanding and teaching their knowledge strove to be recognized and achieved their goal. This was a bottom-up initiative rather than a top-down managerial decision imposed on academics.

The Future of UZH Medicine

To maintain the high international reputation of the Medical Faculty a number of multiple governance and research initiatives have been launched as an ongoing process:

Hochschulmedizin Zürich (Academic Medicine Zurich) is an initiative to promote interdisciplinary research and education at the interface of basic research and clinical medicine. This includes the three main academic players in Zurich: the ETHZ, the UZH and the USZ.

Another initiative is the so-called Dachstrategie Universitäre Medizin Zürich (Overarching Strategy of the University Medicine Zurich) with the idea of creating adjusted governance, more clusters and space-wise connected research. As part of this initiative a "Vision 2026" will be developed. For example, novel clinical research is promoted in collaboration with the University Hospital Zurich to boost innovation in translational medicine, to establish Zurich as a major healthcare provider with new supply concepts, information technology and innovative medical curricula.

Univer-City: Hochschulmasterplan Zürich (Higher Education Masterplan Zurich)

Another major challenge is the future physical expansion of the UZH within downtown Zurich, highlighting the problems of interdependence of urban planning and academic needs. Since the major expansion of the academic facilities in the early 19th century, the city and its surroundings have grown enormously, thus future space expansions become a major issue for the UZH. The need for investing in properties is estimated to be about the double in 2030 in comparison to the year 2000. To overcome at least some of these shortcomings, a joint effort has been made by the Canton of Zurich, the city of Zurich, and the three academic institutions ETHZ, UZH and USZ to renovate and expand their facilities in downtown Zurich. One goal of the UZH is to concentrate its properties into two locations from currently four major locations. One major obstacle is the fact that large areas of the planned major downtown campus are under Heritage protection. Furthermore, in a re-shaped central downtown campus one also expects green areas among these many new buildings, which further restricts its spatial planning and expansion. However, the development of such a reshaped downtown campus also provides new opportunities for the academic people and for the general public. The interconnection of research and everyday life is most essential in a modern democracy. Only if taxpayers understand and subsequently fully support the importance of sustainable funding of its centres of excellence the higher academic institutions can prosper. In Zurich specifically, the local anchoring is crucial due to its democratic control.

Challenges for the Academic Hub Zurich

In general, like many other places, Zurich has seen a substantial increase of number of students, with an increase by some 200% at the UZH within the last 40 years (from ca. 8k to 24k). Also, particularly due to the Bologna reform, the number of curricula has increased substantially. Future challenges for the medical education at UZH are new curricula being developed in neighbouring academic institutions. These at least partially have been triggered by federal (financially beneficial) initiatives to promote more medical study places. In general, a strategic framework of the teaching options — named "Bologna 2020" — will address the pitfalls of the European-wide Bologna reform.

Furthermore, the above-mentioned space restrictions and also political pressure to cut the public part of university budgets (or at least cut an increase of budgets) are major complications. Another issue might be the question to what extent a Swiss university is facing not only a European but also global competition and at the same time to what extent it has to meet local and regional constraints. This may be reflected in the slow speed of decisions by democratic bodies or other political requirements such as inter-cantonal agreements on funding (ca. 10% of the UZH budget) and student access. Furthermore, like in many places, particularly in Switzerland the unique status of universities fades away. New Universities of Applied Sciences have been established and compete for students, funding and even research topics.

Similarities of the Three Levels: IEM — UZH Medicine — Univer-City Zurich

There are several core challenges, which can be found as main disruptive factors at all levels, at the single Institute (IEM), the Faculty (Medical Faculty) and the university in general (UZH). These are intellectual challenges such as new emerging technologies, big data sets or general trend of digitalization. These hurdles can be addressed by flexibility and operative openness at the respective institutions. There are also challenges by a fast-changing environment, represented by alterations in funding sources (a general shift from public towards private funding), global competition, and trends in society (e.g. research ethics, transparency). The self-positioning is most important: what are the main strategic goals, outcome measures and how can the operational procedures be optimised.

Thus, at each level, most effective strong management with optimised processes is needed. At the University level there is often a call for stronger leadership, more strategic freedom and more professionalism for managerial positions. To what extent this clashes with traditional, well established cultures of academic freedom and bottom-up governance supporting individual creativity and trust in academic excellence goes beyond the scope of this article but is in the author's opinion a most decisive issue to be discussed in the future.

Obviously various levels also differ substantially from each other the IEM mostly serves in research and teaching where service activities are negligible while the university in general has a broader scope and mission and the Medical Faculty faces additional problems specific to its responsibility for human health.

Universities are complex multidisciplinary institutions with a multitude of functions linking them to the world, the country and the local community. Despite many faults in their organisational structures, physical accommodation, funding and management, universities not only perform their core functions of preserving, developing and spreading knowledge but also expand their activities without strict lines of management being defined. Universities are evolving entities where various parts interact in complex ways preserving the core of the academic pursuit of untainted knowledge.

Conclusions

Medicine at UZH usually ranks among the top ten within Europe, and life sciences (Medicine, Veterinary Medicine, and Science Faculty combined) count for approximately half of the UZH budget. In order to promote even further research, such as innovative clinical research in collaboration with the University Hospital Zurich, there is an ongoing process of multiple governance initiatives, with some having already been successfully launched. Another major challenge is the future expansion of the UZH campus within central Zurich, highlighting the problematic interdependence of urban planning and academic needs. The recently created Institute of Evolutionary Medicine serves as a model on how to establish an emerging interdisciplinary research and teaching field. The Institute is unique worldwide as it is part of the Medical Faculty but has much well established collaboration internationally in other than medicine research communities. The lack of space and the challenge on how to best position itself within a globally competitive setting are common denominators at all levels: the presented Institute, the UZH Medical Faculty and Zurich academia in general.

To summarize, the Univer-City of Zurich serves as an excellent example of a tradition-steeped academic hub — particularly in the medical fields — yet one that is facing key opportunities and challenges, both in a local setting and a globalized market. In future, academic collaborations at all levels are crucial; diversity and flexibility must be core values.

Acknowledgement

The authors acknowledge funding from the Mäxi Foundation and the University of Zurich.

About the Authors

Frank Rühli is Director, Institute of Evolutionary Medicine, University of Zurich, Switzerland.

Maciej Henneberg is Professor of Anthropology and Comparative Anatomy, University of Adelaide, Australia and Academic Guest at the IEM.

PART II

UNIVER-CITIES 2013 UPDATES: BERKELEY, OTTAWA, HONG KONG

CHAPTER SIX

UNIVERSITY OF CALIFORNIA, BERKELEY IN THE BAY REGION: THE PRESENT AND FUTURE OF A PUBLIC RESEARCH UNIVERSITY

EMILY B. MARTHINSEN AND JOHN J. PARMAN

In 2013, in concert with UC Berkeley Professor Richard Bender, we looked ahead to 2050 and imagined Berkeley, city and campus, as a univer-city. We noted that the future of the University of California at Berkeley would be closely tied to the future of the Bay Region and of California. We posited two scenarios — "Berkeley Small" and "Berkeley Large" — and then described a third alternative, "Berkeley Slow" that reimagined "the way students, faculty, and staff interact and the places and spaces, real and virtual, where collegial interaction occurs". We were particularly interested in how the university and the city could leverage and reinforce the best of each.

What do we now see happening at the university, in Berkeley, and in the Bay Region? And how does this affect campus planning and the changing physical location and character of the campus environment? In the four years since our last presentation, the Bay Region itself has become an ever-more intentional univer-city. As univer-cities develop, individualistic notions of distinct colleges and universities change. This was illustrated just two months ago with the announcement that Mark Zuckerberg and his wife Patricia Chan were establishing a US$3 billion health research effort connecting three of the region's powerhouse universities: UC Berkeley, UC San Francisco and Stanford.

Does the independent physical campus, for a college or university still matter? We think, emphatically, that it does. We are clearly, however, in a time of transition and experimentation for higher education. Rather than the development of new and distinct colleges and universities (and campuses for them), we are beginning to see a kind of eco-system of higher education: the univer-city as a regional hub for learning, research and innovation of all kinds. The Zuckerberg/Chan gift reflects this. Instead of entirely new campuses, institutions are becoming closely linked networks. Physical campuses remain important and in place; but connections among all components of the "higher education sector" are enriched. Administrative, political, and cultural boundaries limiting academic relationships between institutions break down. Shared enterprise becomes common and the differences between public and private universities less important as activities, resources, and initiatives develop organically among them.

Opportunity and Austerity

Experiments in organizing, delivering, and innovating higher education have shaped long- and short-term decisions made by colleges and universities begun in the dotcom era. Opportunities presented by distance learning, privatization, and civic, institutional, and business partnerships have all affected the shape and form of higher education today. None of these experiments has produced a viable new model, so defining the future of a public research university remains a challenge.

Yet we have learned a few things from these attempts. For example:

The physical campus matters: Although the distinction between town and gown no longer holds — scholarship and instruction in partnership with private and public interests is commonplace — the campus' "sense of place" gives these activities identity. Serendipitous interactions no longer require people to cross physical paths; and profound communities can develop over great distances without physical presence. At the same time, though, the importance of the physical environment of campuses has grown and its value as part of our cities has increased. The campus is a setting for civic education and experiment; it provides amenities; and, for many people, an education in design of environments — built and natural. The need to apply new thinking about higher education to campuses in order to transform them makes campus planning more complex, but it also points squarely at the future.

Austerity is the other driver of change: Ironically, many of the experiments that Berkeley and other public universities have carried out were motivated by the strictures of austerity budgets and mindsets. Both colleges and universities — and their physical campuses — reflect the time and context of their origins. Abraham Lincoln created the great public universities of the United States in 1862. Despite the existential threat to the Union in that first year of the American Civil War, with the Confederate army in ascendance, President Lincoln and the US Congress authorised the establishment of land-grant universities in support of the country's future economic growth. Thanks to Lincoln's foresight, these colleges and universities — located outside the cities and focused on agriculture, forestry, and mining — proved to be the drivers of much of the post-Civil War economy, especially in the American West.

Not unlike the Civil War period, public higher education in most of the US today is facing challenging circumstances. Ours is a time of austerity. Ironically, it is an austerity amid plenty. By 2016, California had recovered from recession and a four-year drought, supplanting France as the fifth largest economy in the world. That achievement is tempered by deficits in housing, transit, infrastructure, environmental management, and public investment — including higher education. While austerity can spur innovation, it can also lead to inequity, misdirection, and false economies. Every decision is a balancing act.

The percentage of state funding for the University of California, Berkeley has decreased from 50% thirty years ago to 14% today. Student tuition and fees, just 17% of total revenue in 2008, is now about 30%, forcing us to confront the question: is "public" higher education now providing a private rather than a community benefit? The response to this question drives policy debate and decision-making on issues from student debt to enrolment growth to research agendas to every kind of capital investment. Because the stakes are so high — not only preserving but also strengthening the public mission and role of universities — understanding new and changing relationships of cities and universities is critical to society's future well-being.

In the 150 years since the first federal legislations, public colleges and universities have grown to encompass a much larger portfolio: instruction, service and research in a wide range of disciplines, providing access opportunities for increasingly diverse populations. Public colleges and universities support the most advanced research, both basic and applied, leading the way in solving global problems and enhancing lives, through

Science and Technology as well as through the Social Sciences and the Arts. Importantly, public colleges and universities educate students as citizens underscoring the critical connection — in fact, the integration — between these institutions and their political/social/cultural and economic environments. The physical campus itself plays a significant role, and important towns and cities have grown and developed around them.

Back to the Future

If, over the past 10 years or so, the enthusiastic embrace by colleges and universities of various futures has proved illusory — MOOC's are perhaps the most well-known example — the University of California has seen larger bets underperform, as with UC Merced, or falter, as with the Berkeley Global Campus.

Planning for a 10th University of California campus in the Central Valley began in the late 1980s. There is no question that the vision — political, educational, and physical — looked back to best practices learned from mid-20th century public university campuses. A high profile, comprehensive, and political site-selection process led eventually to the development of the UC Merced Campus on its current site, a 2,000 acre parcel of land about eight miles from the historic centre of Merced, the seat of Merced County in the San Joaquin Valley. A more-or-less conventional campus, albeit with advanced sustainable features, was planned and partially implemented at the site. Care was taken to create a campus community with thoughtfully designed buildings and common spaces. However, development of the bricks-and-mortar campus slowed as state-funded capital investment became increasingly difficult in our stressed budget climate. A number of approaches to campus development have been explored in the past five years; and, after a multi-year competitive process, the University of California has just announced the latest initiative: the UC Merced 2020 Project.

At the time the current site was selected, Berkeley Professor Richard Bender put forward an alternative proposal. Rather than developing a self-contained campus, he suggested using the rail corridor that connects Merced and other Central Valley towns and cities, distributing the 10th campus' facilities in their transit-accessible downtowns. The proposal anticipated the eco-systems that many of today's univer-cities are creating: settings for higher education that integrate with their communities economically, socially and culturally.

Interestingly, the cost of new construction at the campus site — and, likely, but harder to measure, the more appealing character of the historic downtown — has led UC Merced to locate a number of its academic programmes and administrative activities downtown, adapting and reusing historic buildings as well as constructing new ones. Downtown Merced has become a lively centre for the arts, with the campus and the community sharing performance venues, cafés, stores, and public spaces. A parallel UC Merced 2020 Project seeks to recreate a downtown experience on the self-contained campus by partnering with the private sector. Renderings show active, mixed-use spaces along a main street. A legacy of the vision that placed the campus out of town, its lack of synergy with downtown Merced may stretch its development out beyond 2020.

The Berkeley Global Campus was a more recent initiative of the former Berkeley Chancellor, Nicholas Dirks, to create a separate, five-million-square-foot campus as a focus of federal and joint university/corporate R&D investment. Initially prompted by the expansion plans of the Lawrence Berkeley National Laboratory, the Global Campus went through a multi-year planning effort that included competitive site selection, conventional master planning, a lengthy community engagement process and consultation with many, many potential partners — academic, real estate, industry — in the US and abroad.

The Berkeley initiative had a counterpart in Cornell Tech in New York City, a partnership of Cornell University and the Technion–Israel Institute of Technology. Launched by then-New York City Mayor Michael Bloomberg through an international competition that attracted competing proposals from Stanford and other institutions, Cornell Tech is now a reality in New York's Chelsea neighbourhood, and its new campus on Roosevelt Island is under construction.

The Berkeley Global Campus, however, did not fare so well. In the summer of 2016, Chancellor Dirks announced that for the time being its development as a campus was on hold. The concept — that real estate developers, foreign universities and private industry would invest in the development of a new bricks-and-mortar campus in that location — proved unfounded. In hindsight, the expediency-driven choice of a university-owned property as the site reflected the worst of austerity thinking. Its effective collapse provides a valuable opportunity to recalibrate.

As the innovation guru Edward De Bono notes, "Good ideas often emerge from bad ones." It can also be helpful, in looking for those good ideas, to ask where the bad ideas came from.

Unpacking the Competition

The strong interest that the Berkeley Global Campus initially attracted reflected the sense from potential bidders that it would either relate to the historic UC Berkeley Campus — taking sites in the downtown district, for example — or would be sufficiently accessible by transit that proximity would not be an issue. The potential of a five-million-square-foot building programme was of course the bigger draw, but a good location, even without an immediate commitment to build, would still be promising to developers.

When Chancellor Dirks and his advisers chose Richmond Field Station, their competition devolved to architects. Five local and national firms submitted designs. Following the competition, the international firm BIG was hired by a donor to provide a sixth scheme. While the local team tried in earnest to address the site's numerous environmental challenges, none of the competing firms challenged the site itself.

Richmond Field Station, originally a military installation from World War II, is really only accessible from the UC Berkeley Campus by car. Transit access may eventually be provided as part of an extension of the Bay Area Rapid Transit (BART) system to San Rafael in Marin County, crossing the Richmond Bridge. The site adjoins residential and other waterfront development, so a station serving both would make sense. Its development is unlikely to take place in the next 20 years, given competing priorities for transit.

Yet Richmond Field Station was chosen, first because UC Berkeley owned it and second because it could accommodate the full five-million-square-foot building programme. The "expediency" of the choice, made to keep the idea alive in the face of Lawrence Berkeley National Laboratories' withdrawn commitment, doomed the Berkeley

Global Campus concept, but so did the decision to develop a single new campus.

A Precedent: UCSF Mission Bay

In opting for a single campus to house its consolidated building pro-gramme, UC Berkeley was likely influenced by UC San Francisco's Research Campus in Mission Bay. Like the Berkeley Global Campus, UCSF Mission Bay began as a competition, inviting world-class architecture firms to submit plans. Unlike the Berkeley Global Campus, Mission Bay was a Redevelopment Area and former railyard owned by Catellus, previously the real estate arm of the Southern Pacific Railway. In planning since the 1970s, the project was stalled. The then San Francisco Mayor Willie Brown and the city's business leaders joined forces in 1997, in part to keep UCSF's medical research facilities from migrating to a competing site in Brisbane, a largely industrial city south of San Francisco. By giving UCSF a substantial site for its Research Campus, Catellus (and San Francisco) gained a way to get construction started and attract the region's biotech industry as office/lab building tenants.

It worked. Today, the UCSF Research Campus is adjoined by private-sector office buildings focused on the biotech and tech industries. A new hospital, jointly developed by UCSF and the City of San Francisco, is in operation to the south. On paper, this success story seems like a good model. In reality, it is mostly inapplicable, and not just because of the dif-ferences in the two sites. Mission Bay reflects 1990s-style planning, in which different uses are kept within their respective precincts. Nominally mixed use, the mix it achieves is more suburban rather urban. Density is allocated in "ground-scraper" blocks of offices, labs, and, to the north, housing. Today, a development like this would aim for a richer, denser mix.

That desire for urbanity is reflected in working and living styles that favour mobility and make the boundaries between organisations and activities more porous than they used to be. While tech giants like Apple cling to secrecy, their competitors are opening up, locating closer to where their talent lives and collocating R&D with the start-ups they help incubate and accelerate. This trend, which started in the tech industry, has spread to biotech. It has also spurred new partnerships with universities.

Alternative Models of Accommodation

These shifts have not eliminated the need for large-scale accommodation in the biotech and tech industries in the Bay Region, but new strategies have emerged that range beyond (and possibly challenge) the two models on which the Berkeley Global Campus drew. One strategy is the vertical campus, which in San Francisco is best exemplified by Salesforce. After almost building a new mid-rise campus in Mission Bay, this fast-growing tech company chose instead to lease space in downtown San Francisco's transit corridor, becoming the anchor tenant in the new Transbay Tower, the city's tallest building. When completed, the tower will adjoin the redeveloped Transbay Terminal, a transit hub that will eventually connect the local and regional transit network with a high-speed intercity rail system.

Salesforce's decision to locate along downtown San Francisco's regional transit corridor points to the importance of mobility for today's biotech and tech employees. Mobility means two things: shorter commutes, if possible, between work and home; and the ability to work from different locations during the work-day and work-week. The Bay Region suffers from chronic shortages of "close in" housing that even well-paid biotech and tech employees can afford, and from decades of underinvestment in transit. To compensate, employees use mobility to avoid rush hour commuting and to get individual work done that is easier outside the conventional workplace than within it. The workplace proper becomes mainly a place for teamwork. But the rise of startups and the incubators and accelerators that accompany them has made larger biotech and tech companies look hard at those settings in terms of fostering innovation.

Co-working spaces, maker spaces, and other settings are proliferating in the Bay Region and elsewhere to support entrepreneurial activity in these fields and help them scale. They are now a category of street-front occupancy that is replacing traditional large footprint retail tenants like bookstores. They are also taking space upstairs, posing an alternative to conventional leasing for growing businesses.

Both these models are relevant to the Bay Region's research universities as they consider their future.

The Bay Region Today and in 2050

Let's stop briefly to consider the Bay Region itself. It has an economy the size of the Netherlands and is a huge factor in California's position as an economy bigger than France and Brazil. The region is wealthy, but it lacks an effective regional government. (Los Angeles, in contrast, is a city and county that embraces and governs most of its metropolitan area.) While there are regional authorities with clout, investment in transit has lagged and housing development is largely left to the market. Neither the state, which came close to a Greece-like default in the wake of the 2008 "Great Recession", nor the federal government, which takes more tax dollars from California than it gives back, have filled the gap.

The Bay Region's wealth literally reflects the presence and prowess of its research universities. Berkeley and UCSF together spurred the region's biotech sector, one of the larger clusters in the US. Stanford spawned Silicon Valley and is closely tied to its growth and reinvention. Ensuring that the Bay Region remains a world centre for basic and applied research in science and technology is a widely shared goal. Despite the lack of adequate investment, the Bay Region has an exceptionally good armature for future growth that can support the historic ties between its flagship research universities and the current and emerging sectors that will maintain and extend the region's importance as a global research centre. The transit corridors and urban centres that will sustain this growth are already in place. What remains is to bring them to contemporary standards of capacity and performance while preserving the qualities that make the Bay Region so attractive as a destination: the presence of nature and the quality of life.

The urban centres in question include: Berkeley–Oakland–Fremont (UC Berkeley); San Francisco–Peninsula (UCSF, Stanford); and the Silicon Valley "arc" anchored by downtown San Jose (but connected by cross-bay rapid transit links between Palo Alto and Fremont, and between San Mateo and Hayward benefiting UC Berkeley and Stanford).

Secondary corridors, like Concord–Walnut Creek–San Ramon and Berkeley–San Rafael, will create new urban centres at the region's edge that relate to adjoining counties to the north and east. Similarly, Silicon Valley's current arc will by 2050 link by intercity rail to Santa Cruz and Monterey to the south.

These urban centres will carry the bulk of new growth, which will be closely linked to transit access and the availability of housing, amenities, and services. Most important, they will be *urban*, with sufficient urbanity to compete with older centres in the region as attractive places to live and work. Their urban densities will enable the Bay Region to maintain the growth boundaries that preserve its open spaces for agriculture, recreation, and nature (including flood control and wildlife preservation).

Research Universities and Their Regions

Looking to 2050, we foresee a shift from "univer-cities" to metropolises like the Bay Region that build on the innovating power of basic and applied research that universities provide their economies. These regions will actively support their universities, public and private, as core institutions. Whether they are public or private will be less important than their public identity as being partners with their regions in a shared, symbiotic future. Reflecting a collective vision will help the universities transcend old rivalries and fulfill their role as enlightened stewards of their regions' human capital.

Despite its size and wealth, the Bay Region and its three universities are competing on the national and world stages. To maintain the region's drawing power as a leading centre for advanced research in the sciences and technology, its three flagship research universities are stronger as a cooperative whole than as competing parts. Their main strengths as institutions are also complementary: Berkeley on pure science and biotech; UCSF on biotech and medical research; and Stanford on applied science, technology, and medical research. In relation to the regional armature outlined previously, each institution relates to a different but adjoining urban centre and transit corridor. Expanding within it and then using the armature to promote collaboration is the one strategy that will allow three institutions to leverage the region's future growth.

Looking ahead, it is not difficult to imagine the form this will take. UC Berkeley will extend south along the East Bay, finding common ground with Stanford in the high-tech manufacturing corridor centred in Fremont. UC San Francisco will overlap UC Berkeley and Stanford in the areas of medical and biotech research, with its Mission Bay Campus as a hub. Stanford will tie more closely with Silicon Valley and the South Bay, while building new ties to the biotech and tech hubs in San Francisco. Faster transit and denser transit-linked development will bring the three institutions much closer together, creating greater synergy among research teams and more effective use of talent and resources. The goal will be for researchers on all three campuses to have ready access to the others for lectures and collaboration.

As longtime observers of the region, we are confident this sanguine view of the future prospects of its flagship research universities is justified. It is also appropriate that the two public universities join forces with the private one to support the region's continuing prosperity from their different standpoints. Berkeley and UCSF are steeped in a long tradition of research with public benefit, while Stanford has been about applying the research for economic benefit. The complementary and overlapping nature of their roles blurs the distinctions in positive and creative ways, we believe, that will benefit all three.

The Land Grant College at Mid-century

By 2050, almost two centuries will have passed since Abraham Lincoln signed the legislation which set up the Land Grant College system. This became the network of public research universities that Berkeley anchors in California. Austerity, now accentuated by a hostile administration in Washington DC, gains perspective when Berkeley's long and distinguished history as a research institution is considered.

The willingness of the Bay Region's technology entrepreneurs to fund research in the Sciences and Medicine reflects their estimation of this legacy and their confidence that it will endure. As California asserts itself as an economic force literally built on the breakthrough research of its leading universities, the condition of its flagship public research university will strengthen. While the current moment in US politics finds these institutions portrayed almost as the enemies of a new order proud of its ignorance, the stewards of the US economy are clearer on the vital role they play. Yet this is not enough. To regain the ground they have lost, these institutions need to revive the public mission that spurred their founding.

While Berkeley and UCSF will benefit from making common cause with Stanford to heighten the region's standing as a global research centre, Berkeley especially is and will always be a public research university whose reason for being is to train the next generation of leaders in the Arts, Sciences, and professions. It is a "people's university" in a way that Stanford is not. At the same time, Berkeley's roots as a land grant college obligate it to support California's economy "on the ground", establishing ties to its communities to sustain its long-term growth in the face of the natural and man-made issues that hinder it. In short, Berkeley exists to apply its research for the communal good, not simply to exploit it economically.

The breach between America's great public research universities and their populist critics reflects the loss of this felt connection. Facing austerity, Berkeley has flirted with becoming "almost" a private university, foregoing its history. Seen as élite and unaffordable, it risks alienating the public on which it depends for political support. This is where we are, and Berkeley is fortunate not to have lost that support within California itself.

Austerity is always relative. When choices are to be made about where to allocate investment, the clear benefits of one over another come to the fore. The land grant colleges proved their worth historically by propelling the US economy forward, transcending agriculture — their initial focus — by embracing and supporting development in a wider sense. They helped America envision its future, state by state. That role is every bit as crucial today as it was in the midst of a Civil War. In many ways, we are at that juncture again — two diverging views of our prospects, one of which ignores history and devalues science. Helping to lead the country out of this wilderness is why Lincoln enacted them, so that responsibility is clear. When we look ahead to mid-century, we see institutions that have found their voice and purpose once again, envisioning a country that is unafraid to be a beacon for knowledge and its application. California, always at the forefront, will shine all the brighter for this recommitment to its public, communal role. Berkeley, one of America's great public research universities, will be there, *fiat lux*.

Acknowledgement

This paper has benefited from the advice and counsel of Professor Richard Bender of the University of California, Berkeley.

About the Authors

Emily Bachman Marthinsen is Campus Architect. Until December 2017, she was an Assistant Vice-Chancellor at UC Berkeley.

John J. Parman is a Senior Associate at Gensler, a global design consultancy.

CHAPTER SEVEN

AN ARCHITECTURE OF LIGHT: OTTAWA, THE CITY OF LIGHT

ROSEANN O'REILLY RUNTE

Louis XIV, *le roi soleil*, the Sun King's urban design and renewal projects and architectural and costume design choices were largely responsible for the success of France and its capital city, Paris.

All cities, at the beginning of the 18th century were completely dark at night. The streets were unsafe, frequented by robbers. People generally stayed at home after sundown. That all changed when Louis XIV ordered street lamps to be installed throughout Paris. People came from across the Channel and Europe to witness the marvelous City of Light. Shops stayed open after dark; residents and visitors spent evenings shopping, seeking entertainment and dining experiences. Business flourished. More than two centuries later, tourists the world over still flock to the City of Light.

Illuminating the streets was not Louis' only achievement in urban design. Great cathedrals, like Notre Dame de Paris, were invisible from the exterior as homes and shops had been built around them, using the existing walls of the cathedral to economize on construction material. The structures hiding the cathedrals were removed, creating spacious avenues, giving Parisians views of monuments and lending the city a distinctive character. Bridges were nearly impassable because shops and houses had also been built along the sides. Roads became grand avenues and were opened to traffic and great plans for circulation, like the Place de l'Etoile, were adopted. Fountains were constructed around the city, providing clean and easily accessible well water for the inhabitants. They were placed in the centre of public squares, convenient for gatherings. Paris is celebrated still today for its beauty, gracious squares, and impressive layout. As dark streets were opened and monuments unveiled, the City of Light earned its reputation in the daylight hours as well.

Versailles is famous for its lavish halls and gardens, which brought to Paris the nobles who lived in the provinces as well as the ambassadors of other nations. The great mirrors in the hall were strategically located. They were of extraordinary dimensions for the time. Very few craftsmen could produce large panes of glass or mirrors like those at Versailles. Indeed Louis had to bring these artists from Venice. The size and impressive play of light from the mirrors provided Louis XIV an appropriate setting from which he could shine. France's power and influence on the world stage were magnified and multiplied by this structure and the mirrors, which reflected the glory of the Sun King.

Portraits of *le roi soleil* show him in full regalia, his robes studded with thousands of diamonds. These precious stones were brought from India and Louis started a new, high-fashion fad, which very nearly depleted the Indian mines. The diamonds shone with light and spoke of authority, power and glamour. Over the course of the century, Paris became the city of fashion, a commercial hub, a centre of power — both national and international.

Known as the Enlightenment, the *siècle des lumières*, 18th century France was a time that celebrated the arts, philosophy and science. It was a period when great ideas were hotly debated in the public, when Voltaire, Rousseau, Diderot, and d'Alembert led hosts of others in contemplating the meaning of life and ways to improve it. From discovering ever smaller cells in organisms, to speculating on the origin of the universe, to proposing universal education and writing an encyclopedia, to creating new springs for coaches (making travel more efficient), to promoting smallpox vaccinations, scientists and philosophers' ideas illuminated the minds of the century. The light they shone for France was the metaphoric capstone of the glittering jewel created by the interplay of light and reflection, wealth, and power.

The City of Bright

In the chapter "Carleton University: The Architecture of Knowledge and the Knowledge of Architecture" in Volume II of this univer-cities series, it was proposed that cities supporting universities as hubs of knowledge, connected around the world, would become the cities of Light, Might and Bright — the homes to knowledge, economic strength and innovation.

If that formula were applied to the City of Ottawa, the capital of Canada, it would indeed be apt. What better way for a nation's capital to be known? Ottawa: the City of Bright: bright minds, bright ideas, a bright future for Canada. Certainly, this would reflect the reality. Ottawa has the highest per capita number of PhDs in Canada. It ranks first in Canada in the number of scientists and engineers and they hold more patents than any other city in Canada. In this, Ottawa ranks second in North America, just behind San José, California. The city has the most educated workforce in Canada with over 50% of its employees holding a post-secondary degree. Ranked first among 61 global cities in the "creative class", Ottawa is home to two universities and two community colleges that play a vital role in this achievement.

In 1893, a few years prior to his election as Prime Minister, Sir Wilfrid Laurier delivered a speech in which he presented his vision for Ottawa: "…to make the City of Ottawa as attractive as possibly could be, and to make it the centre of intellectual development of this country".

The City of Ottawa has engaged seriously in urban planning over the years. Rules were put in place ensuring clear views of the capital buildings from every angle. Along with height restrictions, these limits to growth were relaxed over the years. A green belt surrounding the urban area was established to encourage density but developments just hopped over the green belt and suburban communities were established and continue to flourish at the expense of a longer commute and less core growth. Building styles have been described as formalistic and functional, Romantic and Picturesque, Gothic, Neo-Gothic, Lowertown cottage, Second Empire, and Italianate with some southwestern Adobe sprinkled in for good measure. With a number of neighbourhoods, each with a distinctive character, the city offers a charming variety of locations in which to live, work, and play, according to the *Invest Ottawa* website. Indeed, the city therein described, boasts of the presence of many embassies, 1,700 knowledge-based companies, 44 federal labs, an airport, conference centre, a low cost of living, 70 golf courses, seven sailing clubs, seven ski resorts, 246 skating rinks and 7.8 kilometres of skating on the Canal, 14 museums, 90 festivals, 600 kilometres of bike trails, three sports teams, beaches …. and of course talent, which includes the four post-secondary institutions and the $320 million they contribute in research annually to the local economy.

The City of Ottawa is currently concentrating on a Light Rail Transit project that is both massive and extremely important to the long-term sustainability of the city. Students will be beneficiaries as they can purchase transit passes at a reduced rate. The additional mobility offered them by the project will enable more students to commute from home or to find perhaps less expensive accommodation to rent, albeit at a greater distance from the university campuses. It will also enhance the ability of the four institutions to collaborate, to work with business, government and industry in the region, enabling students to complete internships with greater ease while improving faculty commute times. Bringing people together is definitely a way to foster creative exchanges! There is, however, another way to bring the universities together and that is, through urban design.

A Model for Campus Design and Architecture

Spaces may enable or hinder people in the accomplishment of their work. They may inspire or depress. They may encourage certain kinds of work. For example, for those who require quiet and concentration, an open design with a heavy flow of traffic would not be appropriate. Spaces may energise through the use of light and colour. They may distract as well. They may reinforce hierarchies and silos.

Universities and colleges today seek to be global, interconnected, interdisciplinary, flexible, and welcoming. When one looks at most campuses one sees buildings, which are designed for research and others for teaching. This is inefficient and discourages faculty from bringing students to labs, and students from visiting labs, emphasising two separate functions when they should enhance each other. You also see buildings or wings dedicated to departments. This means that faculty and students must make an effort to visit and exchange information and ideas. Universities can attempt to remediate this problem by creating spaces where faculty can come together informally but the results will be completely random unless the new spaces are accompanied by programming which draws people together. Luncheon speakers, discussion groups, blue-sky exercises, all deliberately offer the opportunity to bring scholars together around a theme. Universities can reorganise and reconfigure spaces. This has often been done with great success but also at considerable expense. Remodeling old buildings makes them sustainable but shuffling the residents may present a challenge. Virginia Commonwealth University in Richmond, Virginia, built a new engineering building a few years ago. While each floor was designated for the traditional departments of engineering (mechanical, electrical, etc.), the Department of Computer Engineering was located on a vertical grid with several offices in each of the traditional departments which were laid out horizontally. This made the programme both interdisciplinary and unique (and the faculty among the fittest). New buildings can be designed as interdisciplinary hubs such as the System of Systems building at Old Dominion University or the Health Science/Health Science Policy building at Carleton University.

Dynamic workspaces like teaching facilities designed for change and flexibility will receive maximum use and serve future needs. They will create an environment where people will want to work, to remain. They will make work a pleasure. The new Discovery Centre at Carleton University is an excellent example of just such a place. The air fairly buzzes with energy and the hum of ideas being shared. The furniture is entirely mobile, on wheels, and is reconfigured many times a day as students come together on different projects. Large computer screens provide international connections of the highest quality. Three-D printers, designed and built by students, computers dedicated to graphic design and three dimensional digital production, bright colours, light and vast expanses of window enchant students in such numbers that they reserve seats as they would in a concert hall.

Welcoming spaces are thus defined as bright, open, flexible, and technologically smart. Global spaces are defined by the international connectivity and the incentives provided through scholarships or project awards which emphasize global issues and teamwork among students across national borders. Global spaces are operationalized by awareness and accommodation of cultural differences, for example by the provision of a variety of seating arrangements.

A Tale of Two Neighbours

The University of Ottawa and Carleton University are, on the one hand, like the two anchors at either end of a shopping mall and, on the other, like two planets whose orbits intersect at times. The universities share courses and resources as well as cross-town rivalry. Both institutions are unique and complementary. From the start, Carleton and Ottawa Universities have had distinct and very different missions and constituencies. This individuality has been encouraged by provincial mandates to avoid unnecessary duplication among post-secondary institutions. On the other hand, the need to collaborate and share resources for economic reasons and a joint desire for excellence, has led the two universities to share some 28 graduate programmes and to allow undergraduate students to take courses at either institution. The result is an extraordinary resource for the city and the nation as there is a great breadth of programming at a reasonable cost. In addition the two institutions together rank second in Ontario for research productivity, an achievement which comes from the extraordinary work done in joint facilities, in government labs, by teams working in one university or the other, and by individual faculty members working together.

Architecturally and geographically, the two institutions are also quite distinct. The University of Ottawa is embedded in the downtown core and is spread over several locations while Carleton is located on a peninsula within the city but removed from the city centre. The older of the two institutions, the University of Ottawa's early architecture reflects its 19th-century roots. Over the years, neoclassical buildings like Tabaret Hall gave character to the campus, while modernist, and post-modern buildings have more recently been added. Carleton's buildings were originally more modest in concept but recent additions and renovations have opened the campus to the river and canal views through the use of glass and have brought the buildings closer together to create an urban street front while maintaining attractive interior quads. Each campus serves the academic community well and each location has certain advantages, which contribute to the distinctiveness of the two institutions.

The two campuses are less than 10 kilometres apart: too far for rapid pedestrian access (with the possible exception of speed skaters on the Canal in winter) and yet, close enough to allow for the sharing of courses and research with adequate allowances in scheduling. The two campus communities are of sufficient size and difference that joining them completely would be nearly impossible (to consider the obvious: that would be one very-long pedestrian walkway!). In addition, there is a linguistic impediment: Ottawa is bilingual and Carleton is unilingual. The universities do belong to consortia for purchasing to reduce costs and at each level, administrators, faculty, staff and students share experiences and ways to operate. Presidents meet regularly as do Vice-Presidents, Deans, Chairs, and Directors. Some faculty have joint appointments (the Joint Chair in Women's Studies, for example) and some teach on both campuses. Some programmes share teaching (an illustration would be Latin courses which alternate between campuses). Other programmes have developed purposely in different areas of expertise so that they do not compete but complement each other. Thus, the savings of sharing have, for the most part, been realised.

The universities can, however, be drawn more closely together and, through this newly created proximity, help Ottawa achieve Sir Wilfrid Laurier's dream of being *the* intellectual capital of Canada, Canada's City of Bright. There are several ways to accomplish this goal and all might proceed simultaneously.

First, there is the creation of a corridor between the two institutions, along Bank and Preston Streets, a corridor like the Village in New York, featuring Internet cafés, art galleries, lofts for young entrepreneurs, perhaps the municipal library. The City of Ottawa recently turned one segment of this area into a large recreational site with parks and sports facilities, a farmers' market, informal restaurants and bars, a movie theatre, some shops and an upscale grocery. This was a most significant project and is extremely successful. It will contribute to the appeal of the streetscape, which should now include attractions for high tech aficionados and the arts community. This would place the two universities in a prominent spotlight and underscore the value attached to this aspect of life in Ottawa. Not only is the City a fine site to work and play but an excellent place to study and network.

The second connection would be invisible but would be a network. A cloud should join the two institutions and the surrounding neighbourhood, especially this corridor.

The third connection would be practical. Carleton University has started a regional council on economic development, which includes all post-secondary institutions in Eastern Ontario, representatives of business, industry, the city governments and economic development councils. This is the first time that all universities have been included in the discussion of economic development. In reports published to date, communities have regarded the universities as excellent consumers and stable employers. They must, however, be seen as partners and innovators. This changes the architecture of the perceived landscape on which the universities were static and assigns them an active role, reflective of their capacity and their vibrant communities, which are part of the whole.

When Richard Florida wrote about successful cities, he included the importance of an industry unique to the area and entertainment and sporting facilities, which would be attractive to those working in the area. New York is known for banking — and great theatre; Los Angeles for the film industry — and great sports and entertainment; Austin for high tech — and country music.

Ottawa should be known as the knowledge capital. All the parts are present: universities, colleges, an educated workforce and lovely sporting facilities and countryside along with museums and the National Arts Centre. This can all be brought together, celebrated and made known (attracting more of the same) by working on the space joining the two universities — the metaphorical Avenue of Ideas!

Northrop Frye wrote that Canada's first European settlers built communities which turned their backs on nature, facing either inward as if to escape the vast and dangerous wilderness or eastward (toward the Atlantic Ocean) in memory of lands forsaken. Canada's capital features buildings on a grand scale which rise up on the cliffs over the rapids of the Ottawa River in defence of a great nation. The economic backbone of the city was wood — forests floating down river to be milled and turned into the homes and businesses of the cities of North America and the world. The Rideau Canal was built to ensure transportation security. Today success is not to be obtained by circling the wagons and looking inward.

We need to create networks extending virtually around the world. We need to create an environment hospitable to the knowledge workers who are the backbone of the economy today. Unlike the forests, which take generations to replenish, the intelligent people who inhabit this smart City of Bright are growing in number every year as the universities expand and continue to flourish. We need to look at the universities not simply as a resource but as the drivers of economic, social and cultural welfare — the most important ingredient in the recipe for sustainability. Ottawa possesses that which others seek!

Louis XIV created the reason for scientists and philosophers to visit and live in Paris. We now have the means in sight to make Ottawa known as the national centre for ideas. This would be something of which all Canadians would be proud. It would be the same kind of leadership Canada could demonstrate in the world. In the past, some of Ottawa's best designs were altered by people who simply built homes where they wished and by skyscrapers, which grew taller than the Parliament Buildings. The result has been a warm and friendly collection of accidental neighbourhoods where people are proud to live and look out upon the Parliament Buildings, which are still visible both from the ground and the 25 floors!

A design *by* the people — not *for* the people — would herald a new era of appreciation and support for higher education. It would afford a place of importance to ideas and knowledge. It would be connected virtually to the world but also cast a welcoming beam to the peoples of the world who value wisdom, support dialogue, diversity, and wish to share the benefits of education by giving the universities a place of prominence and easy access. Ottawa's light must no longer be hidden under the proverbial barrel. It is time for the city to shine its beams across the country and around the world.

About the Author

Roseann O'Reilly Runte is President and CEO, The Canada Foundation for Innovation, Ottawa, Ontario Canada.

CHAPTER EIGHT

RE-INVENTING THE UNIVERSITY OF HONG KONG IN BOTH MORTAR AND SPIRIT: BUILDING THE CENTENNIAL CAMPUS

JOHN MALPAS

Introduction

The University of Hong Kong (HKU) was founded in 1911 from the pre-existing Hong Kong College of Medicine, and is the oldest tertiary education institution in the territory. In 2017, the University comprised 10 academic faculties occupying three campus sites on Hong Kong Island. The Main Campus, located in Mid-Levels, is 160,000 square metres of hillside land on the Peak, and hosts the Main Building, the University's oldest structure. This listed heritage building was constructed between 1910 and 1912 in the post-renaissance style from red brick and granite, and is the iconic structure of the University. Just 4.5 kilometres south of the Main Campus is the medical campus which includes the Lee Ka Shing Faculty of Medicine, Queen Mary Hospital and a number of research facilities. The Faculty of Dentistry is situated at the Prince Philip Dental Hospital in Sai Ying Pun, 1.5 kilometres to the northeast of the Main Campus.

Although originating on an open but steep hillside, the Main Campus was soon surrounded on three sides by dense urban development, but still retained a southern border with the protected greenery of Lung Fu Shan Country Park. Successive phases of construction, particularly in the 1970s and 80s resulted in a campus crowded with high-rise blocks and very little open space, to the extent that it became virtually impossible to develop any new facility without replacing older blocks. Nevertheless, the Main Campus was one of the few areas in the densely populated Western

District of Hong Kong which was, and still is, used for relaxation and recreation by both the university community and the local community. It has been estimated that there are as many as 25,000 visitors to the University every year, many of whom undertake morning exercise on the campus grounds.

The Millennium Campus

HKU developed during the 1990s as a research intensive institution, with a growing number of academic and support staff and postgraduate students, and increasing internationalisation at all levels. The growth of the physical facility was, however, unable to keep pace with the population increase since it was governed by the UGC's "Kaiser formula" for government-funded space, which tended to look at historical figures for student numbers and research rather than the potential of future development. Given the resultant space shortfall, the university Accommodation Committee commissioned an independent consultant to advise what the requirements of the institution might be given its size and complexity, and how any disparity might be rectified. The report of the consultant calculated, by comparison with other world-leading research-led universities of similar staff and student numbers, that HKU was short by approximately 100,000 covered square metres. Clearly it was impossible to provide such an increase within the confines of the Main Campus, and to solve the problem the consultant suggested the possible expansion onto an adjacent plot of land to the west of the main estate. This area, however, had been occupied by the Eliot facilities of the Water Supplies Department for more than 60 years, including fresh and salt water reservoirs, and pumping and filtration plants that served much of the Peak and Western District of Hong Kong Island. Nevertheless, the consultant's report formed the basis of the Millennium Campus concept, a rudimentary expansion plan that foresaw a one-third addition to the area of the Main Campus. In the first years of the new millennium, it was difficult to envisage how such a development might be funded but, given the unlikelihood of any alternative, preliminary discussions with the Water Services Department were initiated with a view to sharing the site.

2012 Curriculum Reform

It is not often in the history of a university that opportunities are offered that stimulate major changes in curriculum and programmes. Such changes were to be pan- institutional and accompanied by the resources to build additional physical facilities to support these academic advancements. Such, however, was a major challenge to the University of Hong Kong in the six years leading up to its centenary in 2011–12.

In 2004, the Education and Manpower Bureau (EMB) of the Hong Kong Government made proposals to change the secondary school and university undergraduate education system from 3-2-2-3 years to 3-3-4 years, extending the normative university programme by one year at the expense of a year in senior high school. The government formally announced this new academic structure together with a new senior secondary curriculum in 2005, and the first intake of students to the new four-year university programmes was to be 2012. The new senior secondary (NSS) curriculum included four core subjects (Chinese Language, English Language, Mathematics and Liberal Studies), two to three electives from 20 NSS subjects and/or a wide range of courses in more career-oriented studies, and other learning experiences. In addition to fundamental changes in curriculum, there were to be drastic changes in the public examinations including components of school-based assessment.

These changes at secondary level clearly had consequences for the universities, not only in curriculum but perhaps more significantly, in the increase of the number of undergraduate students on their campuses. In the case of HKU this would amount to an extra 4,000+ individuals. These extra students, together with the additional new teaching staff, would clearly necessitate more facilities at the universities. Hence the government made funding available through the University Grants Committee (UGC) for large scale campus expansions.

HKU took this once in a lifetime opportunity to significantly revise its undergraduate curriculum by making it more student-centred, introducing a common core for all students, adding more language and elective courses, and additional flexibility in choosing major and minor subjects of study. Greater emphasis was to be placed on co-curricular activities to

provide for HKU's concept of "whole-person education". All these features together presented a challenge in designing appropriate learning
facilities which would have to be multi-faceted, flexible, in close proximity
to each other (to minimise travel time between classes) but not crowded,
well-supported with IT, and pleasant to work in. The University saw this
as an opportunity to re-invent itself in bricks and mortar as well as in
spirit, and began by revisiting the Millennium Campus plan as a basis for
its expansion.

The Design of the Centennial Campus

When the government-led, territory-wide educational reforms were
announced, The University of Hong Kong embarked upon major developments that would not only add new space to the campus but also upgrade
much of the existing space. This was to be accomplished with government
funding in support of the new university four-year undergraduate programme, and private funding raised through donations and gifts, to support additional space. Very early in the process a Project Group was
formed under the chairmanship of the Pro Vice Chancellor (Infrastructure),
consisting of a number of academic members of the university's
Accommodation Committee (which is responsible for overall space and
facilities management of the institution) and representatives of the
Estates Office, Finance and Enterprise Office, Registry, Development and
Alumni Affairs Office, and Communications and Public Affairs Office. The
main responsibilities of the Project Group were to oversee the general
direction and management of design and construction, including finances,
and to maintain liaison with end-users. Detailed design was to be over-
seen by a Core Implementation Group working closely with project
engineers and architects. Since the opening of the new facilities were to
fortuitously coincide with the celebration of the University's first one
hundred years in 2011–12, this was soon referred to as the "Centennial
Campus Project".

One of the first meetings of the Project Group in Spring 2005
established a number of key principles which would govern the design
of the Centennial Campus. These Planning Principles were intended to
represent HKU's vision of being the core of a "University District",

which would inspire and enrich the lives of those who live in the neighbourhood, as well as those who learn, work and visit the campus. They were:

1. **The University is a learning community:** *The ever-changing University landscape should support the intellectual curiosity, social well-being and spiritual life of all its residents and visitors.*
2. **The University should aim for a unified campus:** *Each physical change to the University estate — building, open space, neighbourhood — should enrich and harmonise with the whole community, and if possible the campus should be physically integrated.*
3. **Respect for the environment and heritage:** *Given the unique natural environment surrounding the University, the institution should seek a sustainable future which respects and cherishes its history, culture and natural setting.*
4. **There should be open and respected processes of stakeholder communication:** *As a leading public institution and an integral part of Hong Kong, the University would invite all those who have an interest in its future to share their views during the design and construction processes.*

With these principles in mind, a competition was held for the detailed design of a campus masterplan that envisaged an eventual overall addition of 100,000 square metres of covered space, with as much as half of this on the new site to the west of the Main Campus. The competition was open to major Hong Kong architectural firms, each together with an international partner with global experience of innovative campus design. A shortlist of four partnerships was finally reduced to the competition winners, Wong and Ouyang from Hong Kong together with Sasaki Associates from California. Given the principles established by the Project Group, this team proposed the goals of their masterplan as: creating a campus with a sense of place expressive of HKU's mission and strategic principles; building on the heritage of the existing campus buildings and landscape; introducing a framework that unified the campus to create a clear sense of space; rendering the campus more understandable and easier to navigate; establishing a strong linkage to the community; providing the setting for a vibrant learning community; and facilitating implementation along the principles of sustainability.

The Project Group further determined that, as a **learning community,** a major portion of the new campus would be occupied by facilities for a number of academic faculties, as well as areas which could be used by all members of the institution, particularly students. Given the predicted amount of available new space, it was decided to bring the Faculties of Arts, Social Sciences and Law into closer proximity to one another to further encourage synergy between them. These three Faculties would be provided with much needed modernised facilities with between one-third and one-half total space increase for each. Moving them would also free up areas of the Main Campus for subsequent redevelopment for others. It was pointed out that, given their proud histories, it was also important that they retained their own identities as separate academic units, e.g. in distinct buildings. However, as part of the drive towards greater efficiency in space usage, most of the larger teaching spaces were to be combined and managed centrally as a set of common classrooms, although seminar and tutorial rooms, and specialised laboratories would continue to be managed at faculty and department level.

The concept of a **unified campus** was a central feature of the Wong and Ouyang masterplan. Because the main estate of the University developed east-west along a steep hillside on the northern slopes of The Peak, the old campus had no recognisable main datum, and building entrances were to be found at multiple levels, linked by stairways. This arrangement proved confusing to newcomers to the campus, making it difficult and tiring to find direct routes to specific buildings. The architects realised the necessity of linking the new westward extension of the campus to the already existing facilities by a main, constant level thoroughfare and extended this concept throughout the combined campuses as a core aspect of their design. This 500 metre-long feature was to become the major pedestrian spine to the campus, linking many of its buildings and key open spaces, and was named "University Street". (See Fig. 8.1)

In terms of design details, it was felt that some conformity of new buildings with aspects and appearance of the historic buildings on the Main Campus would be appropriate, whilst at the same time providing

Fig. 8.1 The University Street.

modern, 21st century structures. For this reason the new campus was centred around three academic courtyards which mimicked those found in the 100 year-old Main Building, and the curtain walls of the new buildings were finished with terra cotta panels to resemble the red brick finish of the older parts of the university. A new lily pond was added to the furthest westward extension of the Centennial Campus to complement a much-loved key feature of the Main Campus.

Respect for the natural environment and the heritage of the site was considered to be of prime importance by the Project Group and was reflected in a multitude of their decisions. Significantly, the new site was itself immediately adjacent to the Lung Fu Shan country park. It seemed initially that slopes would have to be cut and a large number of trees felled to provide adequate space for access and re-provisioning of water facilities. This was avoided by the simple but novel solution of tunnelling below the parkland to provide two expansive caverns in which to relocate new saltwater reservoirs, thus preserving the hillside and its natural vegetation. Furthermore, the original saltwater reservoir was a large sub-surface feature in the middle of the building site and could itself be re-utilised as part of the podium of the Centennial Campus. Tunnelling was carried out by the most environmentally sensitive, non-explosive excavation methodology and the caverns became the first of their kind to be used in this way in Hong Kong. The few trees that were removed from the site were either transplanted or replaced as part of the 500 new trees planted elsewhere on the estate. The roofs of new fresh water reservoirs built immediately behind the Centennial Campus were also planted as gardens, adding much needed green area to a previously crowded campus.

There were three listed historical buildings on site, the Grade II Senior Staff Quarters of the Eliot water supplies facility (Fig. 8.2), and the Grade III workmen's quarters and filtration plant. All three were preserved and the former two refurbished to become part of the University. Both the Senior Staff Quarters and the less salubrious workmen's quarters lie adjacent to the new western entrance to the campus and have

Fig. 8.2 Former Senior Staff Quarters of Eliot water treatment facility, home to the University Press.

been transformed into the headquarters of the University Press and a University Visitor's Centre respectively.

With the MTR's westward extension of the Island Line happening at the same time as campus development, it was possible for the University to have its own station on the rail network. The University of Hong Kong station is directly linked to the Main and Centennial Campuses by high-speed elevators which lift directly to University Street resulting in much easier pedestrian access and therefore a significant reduction in vehicular traffic. Such has been the success of the railway link that serious thought is now being given to pedestrianising additional parts of the campus. Together with the extensive greening with grassed courtyards, green roofs, tree planting and garden areas, this will eventually make the biggest visible change to the previously congested estate.

A whole variety of sustainability features were incorporated into the new buildings. Many of these have been designed to reduce consumption of power and to better save water, and were considered to have a pay-back period of no more than eight years. Others were designed to be experimental and to offer opportunities to demonstrate new technologies. In this way the concept of having "buildings that teach" was realised.

These sustainability features include: waste heat recovery and heat recovery wheel systems; night air purging; optimisation of cooling tower control; chilled water storage system, a novel displacement AC design for classrooms, PV panels and solar heating of water; wind turbines (see Fig. 8.3); rainwater and grey water recovery systems; food-waste composters; and lift regenerative power. To demonstrate their effectiveness, an Environmental Monitoring System has been installed, with LED screens placed at key points on campus. Developed in layers of increasing detail, this real-time, interactive display system provides extraordinary access to information about the campus' and buildings' environmental performance such as power usage and production, and water consumption.

The emphasis placed upon the importance of environmental protection in the design, but also in the construction of Centennial Campus (such as monitoring of construction traffic, minimising noise and dust generation, and sourcing of building materials where possible from sustainable sources), was recognised by a number of local and international

Fig. 8.3   Wind turbines on roof of Run Run Shaw Tower.

awards including HKBEAM Platinum and LEED Platinum status. (See Figs. 8.4 and 8.5)

During both the design and construction phases, the University considered it most important to maintain an **open and respected communication process** with all stakeholders. In so far as the end-users, staff and students, were concerned, regular meetings were held with the Core Implementation Group to ascertain their wishes and aspirations, and to receive comments on design details. A series of bulletin boards was set up campus-wide to provide regular news updates on progress. Many end-users became members of working groups which dealt with specific aspects of both the new campus and upgraded facilities on the Main Campus, including: teaching and learning spaces; amenities; landscaping; heritage; IT and electronic communications; art and decoration; furnishing and signage; and sustainability features.

At the earliest stages of the project in 2005, consultation sessions were held with staff and students on the four design principles and in 2006 the four shortlisted masterplan designs from architectural consortia were widely exhibited both inside and outside the University. Views on

Fig. 8.4   Centennial Campus (right), and Main Campus (left), viewed from the north.

Fig. 8.5   Centennial Campus viewed from the west.

these proposals were fed into the decision-making process for the winning design. This selected masterplan formed the focus of extensive consultation with the local community throughout 2007. Six public forums and workshops, two District Council meetings and more than 50 other meetings with student, alumni and community and neighbourhood groups were held, and appropriate modifications made to the detailed design of the Centennial Campus during 2008.

Key Features of the Centennial Campus

The Centennial Campus is made up of three 8–10 storey tower blocks on top of an extensive 4 storey podium centred around three academic courtyards, and provides a total of 43,000 square metres of covered academic space. The three courtyards provide shade and shelter from hot and humid weather, and induced breezes encourage students and faculty members to sit outdoors, offering opportunities for personal interaction to facilitate a dynamic learning community. The two largest towers, the Jockey Club Tower and the Run Run Shaw Tower house the Faculty of Social Sciences and Faculty of Arts respectively, with the smaller Cheng Yu Tung Tower at the west end of campus hosting the Faculty of Law. These blocks are made up of predominantly office accommodation, research laboratories and specialist teaching areas. All roof areas are planted and can be used as accessible outdoor spaces.

The heart of the new campus is the Chi Wah Learning Commons (Fig. 8.6). Located in the podium and spread over two whole floors, this 6,000 square metres of space represents a revolutionary change of learning experience in the 21st century — from teacher-oriented to student-oriented learning. Like the university library, the Learning Commons is a space for study, discussion, information access and learning assistance. But it is much more than a library. It is a collection of flexible, formal and relaxed, private and group, silent and noisy learning spaces. While there are quiet areas for study, there are ample areas for eating, drinking, group discussion and the use of AV facilities. Users can gain access to library materials through digital resources, and study and conduct research in a comfortable setting. This highly collaborative and interactive space can accommodate up to 1,600 students, and parts of it are open 24 hours a day, seven days per week.

Fig. 8.6   Chi Wah Learning Commons.

Much of the rest of the podium is taken up by class and seminar rooms. There are more than eighty of these varying in capacity from 20 to 900+ persons, providing a total of 6,150 seats. They vary in style from tiered lecture theatres with fixed seating, to flat-floored rooms with moveable partitions and furniture. Flexibility and variability of teaching and learning spaces is a key feature of the campus and a number of "innovative" classrooms have been built to suit a variety of pedagogical practices.

The original underground saltwater reservoir that occupied the site has been converted to a large 900-seat auditorium built as a box-in-box structure allowing for superb acoustics. This "Grand Hall" is fitted with a retractable stage area and excellent backstage facilities, and has played host to a multitude of very successful public concerts since opening in 2012. It has thus been instrumental in furthering interaction between the University and the community. (See Fig. 8.7)

Fig. 8.7 The Grand Hall.

Successful Completion of the Centennial Campus

The building of the Centennial Campus faced many challenges. The site chosen for construction was originally already occupied by a complex infrastructure providing essential water supplies to a large part of Hong Kong Island. This water supply could not be interrupted at any stage, even for the shortest period of time. New water storage facilities had to be built and the site prepared before development of the buildings could commence. The site was also a difficult one to deal with geotechnically, the hillside being prone to landslides during the summer wet season. These preliminaries to construction were originally estimated to take at least 5 to 7 years. Together with a construction period estimated at a further 3 years, the overall required time was simply not available given the campus had to be ready for use at the start of the 2012–13 academic year.

Beginning in March 2007, with little interruption for bad weather, the re-provisioning of the water supply facilities was, in fact, accomplished in 2.5 years using a design-and-build methodology. Construction of the Centennial Campus buildings began in October 2009 and the occupation permit was obtained in December 2011. This allowed the users to move in between May and September 2012. Perhaps more surprisingly, the overall cost of the project was maintained within the original estimate of HK$3 billion, a budget set by the University Council in 2006.

The University of Hong Kong has enjoyed a renaissance at the beginning of the 21st century. The Centennial Campus has become its new iconic feature, enjoyed by students and staff and visited by many admirers both local and international. Furthermore, it has brought an exciting and invigorating environment to a 100 year-old university that befits its status as a world renowned institution.

Photo credits: University of Hong Kong.

About the Author

John Malpas is Professor Emeritus and former Pro-Vice-Chancellor and Vice-President, University of Hong Kong (2000–2013).

PART III

ECOSYSTEMS OF GLOBALISING UNIVER-CITIES: STRATEGIC AND EVOLVING IMPLICATIONS

CHAPTER NINE

SAFE WATER FOR THE DEVELOPING WORLD: RHETORIC AND REALITY

ASIT K. BISWAS AND CECILIA TORTAJADA

"To deny people their human rights is to challenge their very humanity."

Nelson Mandela

Introduction and Background

Since the very dawn of history, water has always been noted as one of the fundamental requirements for human and ecosystems survival. Many early civilisations developed near major rivers like the Nile, Tigris-Euphrates, Indus and Yellow River. In earlier times, major clusters of human population were few and scattered, and the ranges of human activities were limited. Water was plentiful, especially compared to its total demand, and of reasonably good quality. Accordingly, water was not a major consideration, unless there were prolonged droughts or severe floods.

As the population increased over the centuries, and the range and extent of human economic and commercial activities expanded, especially after the Industrial Revolution, available water sources came under increasing pressure, both in terms of quantity and quality.

The global population and associated economic activities increased significantly during the post-1955 period. This, plus continuing poor water management in nearly all countries meant that the world was using not only steadily increasing quantities of water for all purposes but also more and more wastewater that was being discharged into the environment with limited or no treatment. By the late 1960s, continuing indiscriminate discharges of inadequately treated wastewaters into rivers, lakes, groundwater and coastal seas had seriously deteriorated their qualities and ecosystems.

By the early 1970s, many water bodies in Western countries were seriously polluted, endangering human health and the environment. Major rivers like the Trent in England, the Rhine in Europe and numerous others in Japan, United States and Canada were severely contaminated. In the United States, the water quality of the Cuyahoga River had become so bad that it was officially declared to be a fire hazard (Ohio History Connection, n.d.). Major lakes, like the Great Lakes between Canada and the United States and Lake Biwa in Japan, were undergoing serious eutrophication due to phosphate and nitrate discharges from agricultural and domestic runoffs. Groundwater was becoming increasingly polluted by domestic, industrial and agricultural wastewaters. Significant increases in red tides were observed in coastal areas due to discharges of inadequately treated wastewaters.

These developments meant that the global water demands for various uses were advancing while concurrently the amount of water available for various uses was declining because of increasing levels of contaminations.

Between the late 1950s and early 1970s, the health costs of water pollution in the industrialised countries became a serious social and political issue. The Minamata disease was officially discovered in Minamata City, Japan, in 1956, due to discharge of wastewaters containing methyl-mercury from the chemical plant, Chisso Co. Ltd. This disease resulted in 1,043 deaths, and several thousand others were affected.

Similarly in 1968, the Japanese Ministry of Health and Welfare officially declared *Itai-Itai* disease (it hurts-it hurts) because of the cries of intolerable pain of the stricken victims. The disease was caused by chronic cadmium poisoning due to inadequately treated wastewater discharges from the Kamioka Zinc Mine owned by Mitsui Mining & Smelting Co Ltd in Toyama Prefecture.

Poor domestic wastewater treatment practices led to the seventh cholera pandemic which started in 1961, in Sulawesi, Indonesia (Hu *et al.*, 2016). It then spread to the Korean peninsula, Southeast Asia, Indian sub-continent, Middle East and North Africa. Thus, by the early 1970s, the world became increasingly aware of the importance of good quality water

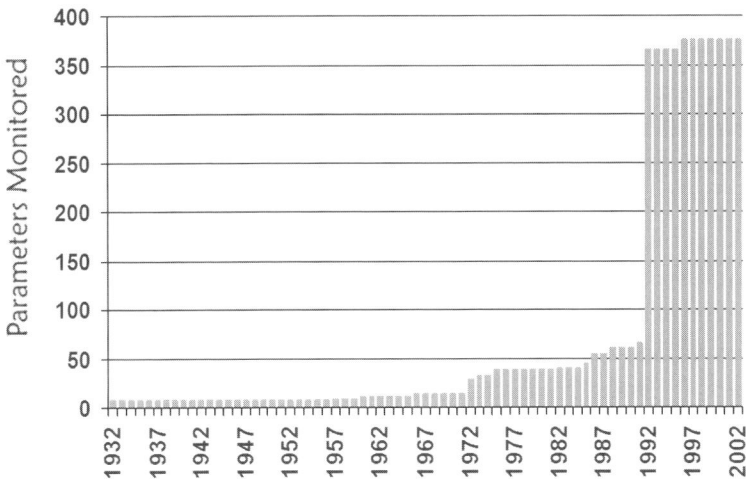

Fig. 9.1   Number of water quality parameters monitored, Ottawa 1932–2002.
Source: Biswas, 2007.

for human consumption. This realisation that good water quality is important because of human health and environmental considerations led to
the monitoring of a increasingly larger number of water quality parameters in the industrialised countries. Figure 9.1 shows how the number of
parameters monitored for the city of Ottawa, Canada, exploded during
the 1972–2002 period (Biswas, 2007). An overwhelming majority of cities
in the industrialised world shows similar monitoring trends from 1972.

Water: Basic Human Need or Human Right

Since the early 1970s, the International Labour Office (ILO) has been
working on a basic human needs approach. It published a report entitled
Employment, Growth and Basic Needs: A One World Problem (ILO, 1977). This
report identified five basic human needs: food and water, clothing, housing,
education and public transportation. One can of course argue whether
these are the most essential basic human needs or there are others. The
report also noted that the basic requirement for life is food and water.

If all the resolutions and declarations that have been adopted by the
United Nations since 1970 are analysed, it will indicate that these have

regularly vacillated between declaring water as a basic human need and human right. In fact, these two terms have often been used interchangeably in the various UN declarations and resolutions, without any clear understanding of either the two concepts, or their implementation requirements. The general approach during the 1970s and 1980s was basically inconsistent.

In November 2002, the Committee on Economic, Social and Cultural Rights that was established by the United Nations to oversee the implementation of the Covenant on Economic, Social and Cultural Rights presented a document (General Comment No. 15) during its 29th Session in Geneva, 11–29 November 2002. This document reinterpreted Articles 11 and 12 of the Covenant, and concluded that under this Covenant water can be considered to be a human right. In addition, some other international agreements can also be interpreted to promoting this view. Under Article 11, the General Comment noted:

> The adequacy to water should not be treated narrowly, by mere reference to volumetric quantities and technologies. Water should be treated as a social and cultural good and not primarily as an economic good. The manner of the realization of the right to water must also be sustainable, ensuring that the right can be realized by present and future generations.

In retrospect, the discussions on water as a human right were kept alive during the 2002–10 period primarily by human rights professionals (in contrast to water professionals) and activist NGOs who were against water pricing and private sector involvement in the water sector.

James Wolfensohn, a former President of the World Bank, noted in 2005, that to some governments who constituted the Bank's shareholders, "the very mention of the words human rights is inflammatory language" Wolfensohn, 2005: 454. The problem was also complex because the word "rights" often had different meanings to different constituencies. Furthermore, understanding and interpretation of rights varied widely between different interest groups.

Discussions on water as a human right have focused almost exclusively on domestic water use, which accounts for only about 10% of total global water use. Other types of water uses like for agriculture, energy production and generation, industry and nature have been mostly missing from this debate.

Any objective analysis will indicate that the possibility of a treaty-based approach to establish water as a human right was, for all practical purposes, near zero, at least for the first few decades of the 21st century. Thus, to make further progress, in 2010, during the 64th General Assembly of the United Nations, Bolivia introduced a resolution that would recognise human rights to water and sanitation. The voting for the resolution indicated the complexity and acceptability of the issue. Voting in favour were 122 countries, none against, 41 countries abstained, and 29 countries were absent. Among the important countries that abstained were Australia, Austria, Canada, Denmark, Israel, Japan, Netherlands, Korea, Sweden, Turkey, United Kingdom and United States.

It should be noted that nearly all the countries that abstained felt obliged to explain why they had abstained. Each country started their statement by confirming that they strongly support the idea that every human being should have access to clean water and sanitation. Most pointed out what they were doing to achieve this goal.

Thus, United States said safe and accessible water supplies furthered the realisation of some other human rights. However, the resolution described right to water and sanitation in a way not reflected in existing international law since there is no right to water and sanitation in an international legal sense. Australia pointed out that when new human rights are recognised, consensus is essential. This, regrettably, was not the case for the resolution. United Kingdom abstained due to both substance and procedure. There was insufficient legal basis for declaring or recognising water or sanitation as a freestanding human right, nor was there evidence that they existed in customary law. Other countries put forward similar reasons for abstaining.

In our view, given the current geopolitical landscape, acceptance of water and sanitation as a freestanding treaty-based human right is not possible in the foreseeable future. Furthermore, General Assembly resolutions are simply advisory in nature and not binding as those by the UN Security Council. Even Security Council resolutions are often flouted by many countries because of lack of enforcement clout.

The fact that not a single country opposed the General Assembly resolution indicates every country agrees that access to clean water and sanitation are desirable goals. Equally, 70 countries that did not support by abstaining or by not being present meant that there was no consensus on this new derived right. The absence of consensus was specifically stressed by countries like Australia, Canada, France, Norway, United Kingdom and United States as one of the reasons for abstaining.

Countries that voted for the resolution also expressed some reservations. Colombia pointed out that the resolution established "an unsuitable precedent" in human rights matters. It noted that its Constitutional Court had noted that protecting the right to drinking water was not appropriate in situations where human life was not dependent. States were obliged only to ensure delivery of public services. Singapore, another country that voted in favour, said that discussions on the right to access to clean water and adequate sanitation should continue. However, the scope and obligations of the nation states needs to be clarified. Argentina, which also supported the resolution, explained that main human rights treaties were pillars of the country's legal order. The relevance of access to clean drinking water had been recognised by many of its legal instruments (Pope Francis, 2017). However, it is the main responsibility of the states to ensure its citizens had access to safe drinking water and sanitation.

An objective analysis of the General Assembly debate indicates that every country supported the view that all human beings should have access to safe water and good wastewater collection and treatment. Thus, the main issue hinges around not whether access to clean water is desirable but rather how to achieve this goal.

An important concern for some of the abstaining countries was that they were not sure what are likely to be the legal implications if they accepted this new right. Some countries were concerned that they may be sued by their citizens for compensations since they may not be able to meet the obligations for decades. Others were concerned that adopting this right may mean provision of clean water and proper wastewater treatments free or at highly subsidized rates which they cannot afford. There is no question many countries are unlikely to subscribe to this concept until their responsibilities and accountabilities are clarified (Biswas, 2007).

It is also important to note the distinction between two types of human rights: civil and political rights and economic, social and cultural rights. The implementation requirements for these two types of rights are very different. Civil and political rights can be endowed upon individuals by ensuring that the governments do not interfere with them. These rights generally do not require appreciable budget to be granted, nor do they need major institutional realignments to be properly enjoyed. They are comparatively easy and economic to implement, given the necessary political will.

In contrast, economic, social and cultural rights, including access to clean water and proper sanitation, will require active interventions and appropriate machineries at all levels of government. This will mean formulation of national, regional and/or municipal policies, and then ensuring functional institutions exist so that these rights can be enforced. Appropriate budgets should be available in a timely manner, and also in perpetuity to the institutions responsible for implementing these rights.

Thus, implementation of an economic, social and cultural right like access to clean water and sanitation will not be cost-free. On the contrary, its implementation will require very substantial financial resources in perpetuity as well as adequate technical, managerial and administrative capacities and continued strong political support. Since water supply and sanitation are municipal responsibilities, it will require direct support and involvement of all levels of governments. This is seldom easy. For such an enabling environment to develop in any country, it will be necessary for the citizens to demand this right continuously and vociferously. Equally they must be willing to pay the costs of the necessary services directly to the utilities and/or indirectly through taxes. Unless this enabling environment is assured, progress is likely to be slow in ensuring universal access to safe drinking water (Biswas, 2007).

Challenges to Implement Safe Drinking Water as Human Right

To ensure that every person has access to safe drinking water and proper sanitation, there are many important myths and challenges that must be taken care of. Only the major challenges will be discussed here.

What Is Safe Water?

It is essential to decide what is meant by "safe" water and "proper" sanitation. It is then necessary to decide how much water is needed by each person to lead a healthy life, both in terms of quality and quantity. Thereafter, it will be necessary to consider financial requirements and presence of functional institutions with necessary managerial, technical and administrative capacities.

The most important issue in this context is what is meant by "safe" water and "proper" sanitation. Sadly, an honest and objective discussion of such a fundamental issue has been conspicuous by its absence over the past four decades. A brief historical background is necessary to understand how we have arrived at the present unsatisfactory situation.

Even though access to clean water and proper sanitation was known to be an important development issue, surprisingly this concern was not reflected in the national and international political agenda till about the mid-1970s. It was first discussed seriously during the United Nations Conference on Human Settlements, in Vancouver, in 1976 (Biswas, 1978; UN, 1976). The Conference was concerned with the fact that in developing countries "nearly two-thirds of the population do not have reasonable access to safe and an ample water supply". It requested in recommendation C.12 "urgent" actions in terms of:

- "programmes with realistic standards for quality and quantity to provide water for urban areas";
- "reduce inequities in service and access to water";
- "promote efficient use and reuse of water"; and
- "take measures to protect water supply sources from pollution".

The Vancouver Declaration considered water to be a basic human need. The concept that water is a human right was not raised (Biswas, 2007). The Vancouver resolution on water was picked up by the United Nations Water Conference, in Mar del Plata, Argentina, in 1977 (UN, 1977). Discussions during this Conference vacilitated between water as a basic need and as a human right. In Resolution 1, it stated: "All people … … … have the right to have access to drinking water in quantities and of a quality equal to their basic needs" (Biswas, 1978).

It then went on to recommend that "the decade 1980–1990 should be designated the international drinking water supply and sanitation decade". It suggested that the countries should "establish standards of quality and quantity that are consistent with the public health, economic and social policies of Governments", and also, importantly, "that those standards are observed".

Like the 2010 resolution on water as a human right, the Vancouver and the Mar del Plata Action Plans were approved by the UN General Assembly. However, unlike the water as a human right these two were approved with significantly fewer countries abstaining or not being present.

It should be emphasised that in all the discussions leading to and during the UN Water Conference the requirements for drinking water was clear: it must be **safe** to drink without any potential adverse health impacts and must be easily accessible.

Regrettably, following the Mar del Plata Water Conference, the UN devised a meaningless term "improved" sources of water which really has no practical value. What happened during the post-1980 period is that UN organisations and all the development banks started to use this meaningless term "improved" sources of water extensively, even though it had no real relation to quality. Over the last 35 years, all these organisations have collated data from national governments on access to water. Basically, as long as people receive water, irrespective of their quality, they are assumed to have access to "improved" sources.

If quality and accessibility of water are not considered, then 100% of people in the world always have access to water: otherwise they would not survive. The important issue that has been lost during the past 35 years is that the entire emphasis has been to provide water of any quality to the people of the developing world and then estimating how many people have access to these "improved" sources.

What is even more disheartening is that all the major international organisations like UNICEF, WHO, other UN agencies, World Bank, etc., have used the term "improved" sources of water, "safe" and "clean" water interchangeably. Consider the latest (2015) update on progress on sanitation and drinking water (UNICEF and WHO, no date). The very first paragraph of this report notes "access to safe drinking water". In the second paragraph it mentions "improved drinking water". Throughout this report, "clean", "safe" and "improved sources" of water have been used interchangeably. This has been the standard practice since the early 1980s for all the international organisations. Thus, not surprisingly, an overwhelming majority of the people all over the world now believe "improved" sources of water is actually "clean" or "safe" water (Tortajada and Biswas, 2018).

On 12 March 2012, UN Secretary General, Ban Ki Moon, proudly proclaimed in a message to the Sixth World Water Forum, in Marseille, France, that: "Last week we announced that the world has met the target of reducing by half the proportion of people without sustainable access to **safe** drinking water" (my emphasis). Sadly, nothing is further from the truth (Martínez-Santos, 2017).

The latest update by UNICEF and WHO claims that "only" 685 million people now do not have access to improved or clean sources of drinking water (UNICEF and WHO, no date). They further estimate that in 2015, the following percentages of urban populations in different developing countries had access to "improved" sources of water: Bangladesh 87%, Brazil 100%, Egypt 100%, India 97%, Iran 98%, Malaysia 100%, Mexico 97%, Nepal 91%, and Pakistan 94%. These are impressive figures except for the fact that an overwhelming majority of the citizens in these countries do not dare drink water from the tap because of poor quality.

Let us consider only South Asia, with a population of some 1.7 billion people. Except for a medium-sized town in India, Jamshedpur, people nowhere in South Asia, either in urban or rural areas, have access to clean water that they consider safe to drink. Thus, to say only 685 million people do not have access to safe water is at best an exaggeration and at worst deliberate misinformation to mislead the global debate. In fact, estimates made by the Third World Centre for Water Management indicate that some 3.5 to 4.0 billion people in the world do not have access to water that is safe to drink. This is at least five times more than the WHO-UNICEF estimate.

Currently in all the South Asian countries and an overwhelming majority of the developing world, households do not receive a safe and reliable 24×7 water supply. Accordingly, in order to have acceptable drinking water available, households have to take charge of their own water supply by each becoming a mini water utility. Water is provided by the utilities for about 3 to 5 hours per day. Each household collects water when it is available in an underground tank. It is then pumped to an overhead tank. Thus, even though the supply is intermittent, each household converts this intermittent supply to 24-hour continuous water availability through their own individual efforts.

Since quality of water supplied by utilities in most cities of the developing countries leaves much to be desired, each household has been forced to develop its own process to treat the water received so that it can be made safe to drink. Thus, most households have their own individual treatment processes which are installed and maintained by the private sector.

In addition, the quality of water in many third world cities has progressively deteriorated because both surface and groundwater have been steadily contaminated by known and unknown pollutants from discharge of untreated, or partially treated, domestic and industrial wastewaters.

Over the past decades, the number of middle-class people in the developing world has steadily increased. They are now more literate and also have more access to information compared to previous generations. They are more aware of the potential impact of the poor quality of water on family health and hygiene. They thus make their own arrangements to treat water received from the utilities and make it safe to drink.

A decade or more ago, the quality of water supplied by utilities was reasonable so that households could use simple treatment processes like filters to improve their quality. With steadily declining water quality, along with increasing affluence and literacy, average households in major cities like Delhi are now using sophisticated treatment processes like membranes to get drinking water. Membranes were originally developed for desalination of sea water. Now they have become an integral part of domestic household treatment processes in many cities and even rural areas to make water drinkable. A major problem with membranes is that at household levels they are very inefficient. Membrane treatment produces 60–70% of wastewater which is basically thrown out.

The residents of most Third World cities currently receive free or highly subsidised water which is mostly undrinkable. The supply may be free but the coping costs for converting intermittent to continuous supply, and then make water drinkable are quite significant. This has created a "lose-lose" situation. Water utilities from Delhi to Lagos now do not have financially sustainable models because of low water pricing, while the coping costs of individual households are quite high. Thus, both households and utilities have become long-term sufferers.

Improved Sanitation

The world is facing an equally strange problem with a similar concept of "improved" sanitation which really does not mean much. As it is used now, this simply means availability of toilets without much attention to how wastewater is collected, stored, treated and disposed of in an environmentally acceptable way. For several decades now, developing countries, international organisations and aid agencies have focussed on construction of toilets, with septic tanks and low-cost sanitation for collecting and disposing wastewater. Sadly, "improved" sanitation does not include collection, proper treatment and disposal of wastewater in any sustained fashion.

Consider Patna, capital of Bihar state, India. With over two million people, it is the 18th largest urban agglomeration in the country. Currently, only about one-fifth of households are connected to a sewer system. The rest depend on septic tanks and low-cost sanitation. Its sewage treatment plants, like in most parts of the developing world, suffer from poor operation and maintenance practices. Thus, wastewater quality, even after treatment, leaves much to be desired. The balance of 80% of its households depends on septic tanks and other low cost sanitation. Because of poor construction and maintenance of hundreds of thousands of individual septic tanks, shallow groundwater is becoming increasingly contaminated with regular discharges of inadequately treated wastewater. Also, septic tanks are cleaned by small and untrained private operators every 2–4 years. They basically suck in the wastes and then dump them in public lands, forests, water bodies or open drains. The city has no standards for these private operators for discharge of such wastes. They basically dispose of waste in ways that are most economical to them. Since the city depends primarily on groundwater, its quality is progressively deteriorating because of such waste-disposal practices.

Because of rapid urbanisation, the Patna Master Plan expects the region to have over six million people by 2031, a three-fold increase in only one and a half decade. Such rapid growth rates will most certainly overwhelm the city finances and management capacities, including construction of new water supply and wastewater management facilities and their proper maintenance.

There are two major problems with the current focus on improved sanitation and not wastewater management. First, cities will be discharging more and more wastewater into the environment without adequate treatment. This will contaminate water bodies that are sources of water to downstream communities. Second, as cities grow, historically their water requirements have increased as well. In the past, they have increased their water availability by tapping additional sources of water further and further away. Currently, other neighbouring urban centres are growing and they are also planning to obtain extra water from the same sources that are often already over-allocated. While this practice has worked reasonably well in the past, it has now become a serious problem. Thus, not only for health and environmental reasons but also because of exhaustion of new sources from which water can be obtained economically, urban centres now must consider treating their wastewater properly in order to reuse it regularly. There are simply no other long-term solutions. Wastewater must now be considered a new source of water as well as energy.

The concept of "improved" sanitation is another meaningless semantic invention. In 2015, it was estimated that 2.4 billion people globally do not use "improved" sanitation (UNICEF and WHO, no date). However, if one considers what is the percentage of people in developing countries that have access to good wastewater treatment and disposal facilities, an objective estimate will be about 15–20%. Thus, for all practical purposes, like "safe" drinking water, UNICEF-WHO estimates of access to sanitation have given the world a very rosy but erroneous picture. The situations are significantly worse than what the UN has estimated and currently accepted globally.

Water Needed per Person per Day

From empirical studies, it is evident that not only quality but also quantity of water used has an important impact on human health (Biswas, 1981). How much water does an individual need per day? There are no easy answers even for basic survival, let alone for a healthy life. There is also a major difference between what is needed and how much is actually used. Water needs for basic survival depend on various factors, including body size, physiology, climate, type of work being conducted and hygiene. Normally, for basic survival, daily water needs could be 4–6 litres.

Survival needs are very different from health needs which are significantly higher. Information on the minimum amount of water needed to maintain good health under different conditions is scarce. Some indications can be obtained from a ten-year study carried out in Singapore between 1960 and 1970. This attempted to correlate domestic water use in terms of waterborne diseases in Singapore hospitals. It indicated that as per capita water use went up, disease rates declined. However, there did not appear to be much improvement beyond daily use of 75 litres per person. This could be considered the "social minimum" for the city-state (Biswas, 1981). Current water use in Singapore is 151 litres, twice the "social minimum" amount.

In the absence of similar studies elsewhere, it is difficult to say how much clean water people need for a healthy lifestyle. The recommended daily per capita water requirements are mostly plucked from thin air, without any serious studies. At present, they range from 40–200 litres. The Indian standard BS1172 recommends for communities of more than 100,000 people, it should be 150–200 litres per day. Unquestionably, this is high. The upper figure of 200 litres is more than twice the water required if it is used efficiently. Figure 9.2 shows that in several European

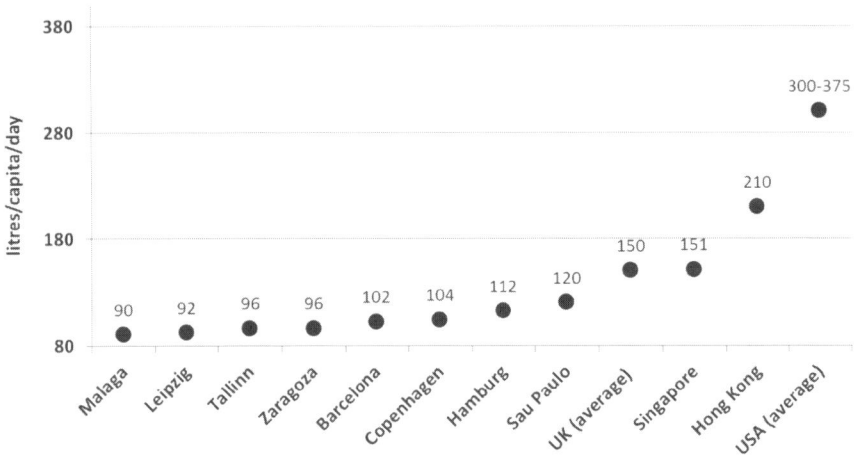

Fig. 9.2 Daily water consumption per capita.

Source: Third World Centre for Water Management.

cities, daily per capita water use is now between 90–100 litres. Such efficient levels of water use allow the inhabitants of these cities not only to have a healthy lifestyle but also to reduce costs. It ensures that less water has to be treated for drinking, which means less wastewater is produced that needs to be treated. Serious reductions in per capita daily use will only be possible through pricing, economic incentives, public awareness, environment ethics and behavioural changes. It will also need strong and sustained political support.

If domestic water use can be brought down to 90–120 litres per capita per day, and wastewater can be properly treated and reused, clean water as a human right can be implemented in even in the most water-stressed cities of the world. Currently, domestic water use accounts for about 10% of global water use. Thus, if water use can be made increasingly efficient, there is absolutely no reason as to why every citizen of the world cannot have enough clean water not only now but also by 2050 when the global population is estimated to be around 9.7 billion.

Equally, with current knowledge, management practices and technologies available there is absolutely no reason why cities of 200,000 people and more cannot have a viable and sustainable financial model which could provide safe water as their right (Biswas *et al.*, 2018). Consumers must be willing to pay for this service directly through tariffs and/or taxes. Right to water does not mean that all human beings can have as much water as they wish, whenever they wish, free. Rights come with responsibilities. Free or highly subsidised water, as the experience from all over the world shows, will never ensure that every person has daily access to 90–110 litres of clean water. Only poor and/or large families, whose water bill exceeds 2% of the household income, should receive targeted subsidies.

Private Sector or Public Sector

Over the past two decades there has been a serious debate as to who should provide water to the people: public or private sector. It has been primarily an ideological debate, with limited practical relevance. Some feel water is a human right, essential for survival and thus should be available to everyone free or at highly subsidized costs.

The fact is, as noted earlier, water is a derived human right and not a treaty-based right. Even for treaty-based human rights like food and health, there are no similar contentious debates as to whether food and health services, including medicines, should be available to everyone free. Water seems to have a mystic of its own where proponents and opponents of public or private sector have been at loggerheads for decades as to what is the best for society. Proponents of private sector claim its involvement will ensure efficient water provisioning. This is not necessarily correct. The world's two most efficient water utilities, Tokyo and Singapore, are managed by the public sector. No private sector has come close to their performance. Equally, a large number of public water utilities are truly inefficient.

Accordingly, which sector provides the best service to society is not a meaningful debate. Instead, the discussion should focus on whatever sector in a specific city can provide clean water reliably and cost-effectively to its entire population, including the poor. The appropriate sector should be allowed to do so. Irrespective of which sector provides the water, it has to be properly priced, with targeted subsidies to the poor, so that the utilities have a viable and sustainable financial model with limited political interferences.

During the post-1990 period, private sector concessions to run water utilities have increased steadily. By 2015, the number of people served by the private sector had increased to well over 1.11 billion (Fig.

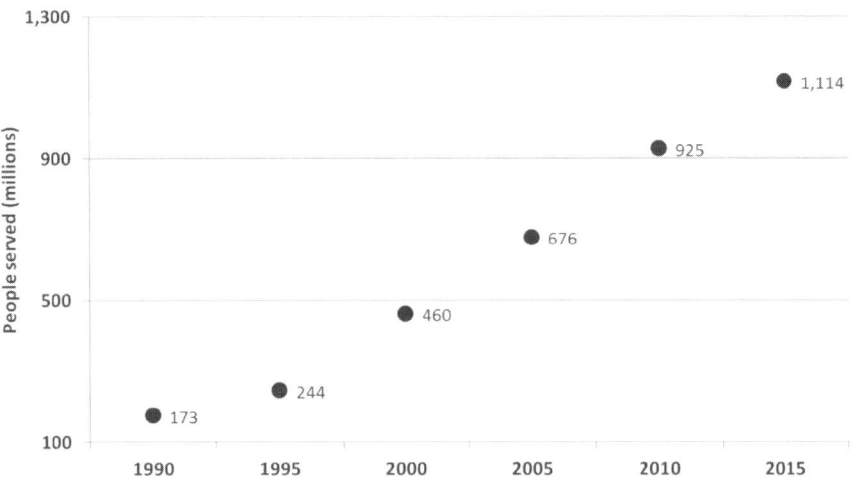

Fig. 9.3   Millions of people served by private sector concessions.

Source: David Lloyd Owen, personal communication, 2016.

9.3). This is not surprising given the poor levels of services from numerous public water utilities where their management, work programme and finances are regularly interfered with by public officials having one eye on the next election. Populist short-term policies are often not the most appropriate for the long-term proper functioning of water utilities.

In addition, governments in most developing countries do not have enough budgets to invest in updating dilapidated water supply and sewer systems, let alone provide for very substantial investments needed to account for new water and sewer systems. The problem is especially serious for sewer systems since they are now totally inadequate to meet the needs of the present population, let alone the escalating demands due to rapid urbanization. Nor do most municipalities have capacities to manage this expansion. For these and many other reasons, private sector concessions for water provisioning are likely to increase steadily during at least the next two decades.

It should also be noted that during the past decades many water utilities have been re-municipalized for a variety of reasons. The number of people affected by re-municipalization is estimated at less than 100 million. Anecdotal evidence from important cases like in Cochabamba, Bolivia, further indicate that these re-municipalized utilities are having considerable difficulty to attract appropriate investment and talents to improve the current levels of poor services.

While virtually all the discussions of private sector involvement have been on the concessions to run water utilities, private sector has been playing increasingly important roles to implement the people's rights to have access to clean water and wastewater management. Over the past decade or so, some enlightened business leaders, like Paul Polman of Unilever and Peter Brabeck-Letmathe of Nestlé, have institutionalized new business policies which have meant that one of their important objectives is to ensure they create long-term value for society. Under this new business philosophy, many multinational and national companies are reducing significantly their water footprints, extensively practising water conservation and recycling. They are assisting their employees and the communities where they manufacture and source their raw materials with availability of clean water and construction of toilets as well as their maintenance.

Nestlé and Unilever are two of the world's largest MNCs. They now have restructured their internal guidelines so that their factories and offices in whatever countries they may be, as well as their suppliers respect and contribute to implementation of human rights to water. They have established due diligence mechanisms like conducting human rights impact assessments of their own activities as well as of their suppliers. These have dramatically increased their impact on the water sector. These two companies, as well as others like Procter & Gamble (P&G) and Coca-Cola, now source ingredients like coffee, tea, cocoa, milk, sea food, spices, sugar, palm oil, and other similar products from many small, medium and large suppliers. They provide direct advice to their farmers on how to manage water properly not only for drinking but also efficient use to reduce water use and contamination (Biswas-Tortajada and Biswas, 2015). Companies like Nestlé have over 8,000 agronomists all over the world who advise the farmers on agricultural issues as well as on water management. Very often, especially in rural areas, these company employees are major and reliable sources of information on water, agriculture and environmental issues (Biswas et al, 2014). These companies further work with independent organizations like UTZ, Rainforest Alliance, Fairtrade and Greenpeace so that products are ethically sourced, water and other environmental conditions are properly managed and human rights are not violated. They have made significant progress during the last decade on improving sustainability of their business practices and contributing to continuing assessments of all types of human rights in their businesses like child labour, slavery, and rights to water and sanitation. All the four companies are giving special attention to water and sanitation needs of schools in communities where they and their suppliers operate. Thus, P&G is providing 10 billion litres of clean water to schools. In India, Nestlé is providing clean water to 127,000 students, and Coca-Cola to some 200,000 students.

It is not only multinational companies that are helping to ensure that people have access to clean water but also many national companies are following their footsteps as well. For example, GNFC has now provided access to clean water to nearly 150,000 people in Gujarat, India.

What is also not appreciated is that many private sector companies like P&G are reducing domestic water use by making increasingly more water-efficient products for use in homes. P&G's goal is to ensure one billion people have access to water-efficient products by 2020. Through product innovation, P&G is reducing the time people spend in showers, thus reducing water consumption. They have further eliminated all phosphate from their detergents to prevent eutrophication of water bodies. Thus, the private sector is playing an increasingly important role in providing access to clean water, sanitation and hygiene, both directly and indirectly. Accordingly, future discussions on implementation of human rights to clean water and sanitation must involve both public and private sector.

Concluding Remarks

No country or sane individual has argued that human beings should not have access to clean drinking water and reliable wastewater management services. Without clean water and efficient wastewater management, people cannot have a good quality of life and a healthy environment to live in and reach their full potential. The issue is thus not whether these should be achieved but rather how they should be achieved as soon as possible in a reliable, cost-effective and equitable manner.

As a first step, it is essential to determine the magnitude and extent of the problems. Most unfortunately, the latest global figure of only 685 million people do not have access to clean water is a gross under-estimate. The real figure is around five times this number.

There is no question that enormous investments will be necessary in terms of construction of new water and wastewater infrastructure replacing older ones, and building up technical, administrative and management capacities of the countries. For urban centres of 200,000 people or more, we now have enough knowledge and technology to formulate a sustainable financial model where all consumers will pay for water and wastewater services that are efficient. Only those households where water bills exceed 1.5 to 2% of household income should receive targeted subsidies.

The decades-long debate whether water-related services should be highly subsidized or even free has not been productive. Domestic water use everywhere must become increasingly efficient. This will ensure not only less clean water has to be produced but also less wastewater will have to be treated. The heated discussions of whether public or private sectors should provide water have been mostly ideological and unproductive. Whoever can provide a reliable, cost-effective and equitable service should be encouraged to do so. Irrespective of whether public or private sector provides the service, consumers will have to pay for it. Otherwise even 50 years from now, people will not have access to clean water and proper wastewater services. The problem cannot be solved by linguistic gymnastic and by creating meaningless terms like "improved" sources of water, as has been attempted in the past.

The safe drinking water problem of the world is solvable. For this to be accomplished, there has to be sustained political will and determination, consistent demands from the people to have clean drinking water, and public and private sectors as well as NGOs to work together. As W. H. Auden has noted: "Thousands have lived without love, and no one without water".

References

Biswas, A. K. (1978). *United Nations Water Conference: Right Paper Summary and Main Documents*. Oxford: Pergamon Press.

Biswas, A. K. (1981). "Water for the Third World". *Foreign Affairs*, 60, no. 1: 148–166.

Biswas, A. K. (2007). "Water as a Human Right in the MENA Region: Challenges and Opportunities". *International Journal of Water Resources Development*, 23, no. 2: 209–225.

Biswas, A. K., C. Tortajada, A. Biswas-Tortajada, Y. K. Joshi, and A. Gupta (2014). *Creating Shared Value: Impacts of Nestle' in Moga, India*. Heidelberg: Springer.

Biswas, A.K., P. Sachdeva, C. Tortajada (2018 forthcoming). *Phnom Penh Water Story*. Singapore: Springer.

Biswas-Tortajada, A. and A. K. Biswas. (2015). *Sustainability in Coffee Production: Creating Shared Value Chains in Colombia*. Abingdon: Routledge.

Hu, D., B. Liu, L. Feng, P. Ding, X. Guo, M. Wang, B. Cao, P.R. Reeves, L. Wang (2016). "Origins of the current seventh cholera pandemic". *Proceedings of the National Academy of Sciences* 113, no. 48: E7730–E7739.

ILO (International Labour Office) (1977). *Employment, Growth and Basic Needs*. New York: Praeger Publishers.

Martínez-Santos, P. (2017). "Does 91% of the world's population really have 'sustainable access to safe drinking water'?" *International Journal of Water Resources Development*, <http://dx.doi.org/10.1080/07900627.2017.1298517>

Ohio History Connection. "Cuyahoga River Fire". <http://www.ohiohistorycentral. org/w/Cuyahoga_River_Fire> last accessed on 9 February 2018.

Pope Francis (2017). "Address of His Holiness Pope Francis". *International Journal of Water Resources Development*, 33, no. 4: 512–513, DOI: 10.1080/ 07900627.2017.1309790

Tortajada, C., A.K. Biswas (2018). "Achieving universal access to water and sanitation in an era of water scarcity," *Current Opinion in Environmental Sustainability*, forthcoming.

UNICEF and WHO (no date). *Progress on Sanitation and Drinking Water: 2015 Update and MDG Assessment.* WHO Press, Geneva, 80 pp.

United Nations (1976). "United Nations Conference on Human Settlements, The Vancouver Declaration on Human Settlements". <http://www.un-documents. net/van-dec.htm> last accessed on 10 January 2018.

United Nations (1977). "Report of the United Nations Water Conference, Mar del Plata", 14–25 March 1977. <https://www.ircwash.org/sites/default/ files/71UN77-161.6.pdf> last accessed on 10 January 2018.

United Nations (28 July 2010). *General Assembly Adopts Resolution Recognizing Access to Clean Water, Sanitation as Human Right.* 64th General Assembly, Plenary, 108th Meeting (AM). Document GA/10967.

United Nations Committee on Economic, Social and Cultural Rights (20 January 2003). *General Comment No. 15: The Right to Water Document* (Arts. 11 and 12 of the Covenant). E/C. 12/2002/11. Office of the High Commissioner for Human Rights, Geneva, p. 4.

Wolfensohn, J.D. (2005). *Voice for the World's Poor: Selected Speeches and Writings of World Bank President James D. Wolfensohn, 1995–2005,* vol. 889, page 454. Washington DC: World Bank.

About the Authors

Asit K. Biswas is Distinguished Visiting Professor at the Lee Kuan Yew School of Public Policy, National University of Singapore.

Cecilia Tortajada is Senior Research Fellow, Institute of Water Policy, Lee Kuan Yew School of Public Policy, National University of Singapore.

CHAPTER TEN

ON STRATEGY FOR DEVELOPING AN INNOVATIVE UNIVERSITY: S-FACTOR, S-GAP AND VECTOR DELTA (δ)

NAM P. SUH

Introduction

Advanced economies need strong research universities. The activities of research universities today affect the future wellbeing of humanity and the world. These universities attract some of the best minds (i.e. students, professors, and researchers) and generate educated human resources to establish and maintain stable, prosperous, and vibrant democratic nations. In addition to generating an educated workforce and future leaders, they advance the knowledge base in science, technology, medicine, biotechnology, economy, transport systems, and many other fields. They also shape the discourse in social sciences, politics, and economics. In addition, they act as incubators and provide homes for technology innovators and future industries. During the last three decades, new relationships among academia, industry, and governments have emerged to involve universities in solving all aspects of societal problems. Universities provide the intellectual fountains that generate and test new ideas. It is easier to have full open debates on disparate and controversial concepts in an academic environment, which provides the long-term stability, progress, and prosperity of society-at-large. Universities have been champions for the free flow of people — professors, researchers, and students — and for thought-provoking ideas. In many countries, universities have provided students with otherwise limited opportunities for upward mobility, which has been important in strengthening democratic society. For these and many other reasons, there is great support for research universities.

During the past six decades, many universities in the world have undergone transformations from purely teaching institutions to research-intensive universities through increased expansion of graduate education and research programmes. The latter seek fundamental knowledge and promote technology innovation. Research universities have attempted to attract specially gifted people from all over the world to their institutions to fill their student ranks, professorships, and research rosters. However, these people tend to favour the better-known research universities in the world. Highly advanced research universities have also attracted more research funds, venture capital, and support of industrial firms because of their reputation and competitiveness. Cities and regions where these research universities are located have attracted capital investments and prospered through the establishment of high technology industries, primarily because of the congregation of outstanding people. Therefore, the race is on to make each research university the most innovative, creative, and productive. Their strive for excellence bodes well for the future of higher education.

Universities have many diverse missions. Central to these missions is the nurturing and education of students as well as providing opportunities for aspiring scholars, and the grooming of future leaders. Some universities do a better job in these tasks than others. Consequently, graduates of competitive universities tend to have more opportunities. Research universities also enhance the culture of technological innovation, the search for fundamental truths in all fields, and enable basic scientific discoveries. All these functions of a research university ultimately contribute to improving the quality of life for all inhabitants of the world. Indeed, the impact made by research universities in creating, discovering, and advancing knowledge through research and education is well recognized in all advanced economies. Because of the important roles of research universities, the quality of universities is of keen interest to prospective students, their parents, funding agencies, and future employers.

Although it cannot be definitively supported by statistical data, the return on investment (ROI) in education and research universities has been substantial. It is most likely that this trend will continue in the future as new knowledge and the people who create new ideas are likely to create new economic engines in many fields for their regions and ultimately for the world. Indeed, exciting things are happening at leading universities in many new fields, as well as in traditional areas of opportunities. For instance, enormous potential exists in established fields such as biotech and medical sciences, information and communications technology, nano-technologies, new materials, artificial intelligence, transportation, energy, water, linguistics, green energy, and energy storage. Even in infrastructure related fields, we need innovations to deal with, for example, the consequences of global warming.

In view of the importance of universities and the strong interest in their quality, several organizations assess and publish relative world-wide university rankings. These rankings are based on two kinds of measures: *quantifiable metrics* and *qualitative measures*. The quantifiable metrics include numerical data on publications, citations, patents, employment of recent graduates, quality of faculty, selectivity of incoming students, financial resources, research funding, and others. On the other hand, the qualitative measures are based on peer reviews, i.e. the opinions of academics and societal leaders about a given university, which is, by its qualitative nature, subjective. Based on these data, these agencies rank universities using unique algorithms. Although some in academic circles dismiss these rankings as frivolous, these rankings nevertheless raise important questions about the responsibility of university administrators in making their institutions more effective and competitive for the sake of their students and the supporters of their institutions.

A few observations about the *top-ranked universities* selected by these ranking agencies may be instructive. First, the top set of universities chosen by many ranking agencies is nearly the same set year after year. The difference in numerical score is small, perhaps within the margin of error. Second, the reputation and known contributions of the top ten universities of the world are clearly discernable without much debate based on their long-standing reputation. However, within any group of 10 or so universities (e.g. those ranked between 45th and 55th), a difference of few points in the numerical score significantly changes their relative rankings. Therefore, the "peer review" — the qualitative part of the assessment — tends to favour well-known universities. If we eliminate the peer review and use only quantitative measures, as was done by Reuters starting in 2015, the list of the "Top Innovative Universities" changes significantly and many well known universities do not make the list. This further supports the fact that the "peer review" favours well-known universities with long histories, i.e. that pedigree matters. Irrespective of the ranking, academicians and academic administrators should be searching for ideas to improve their institutions competitiveness because their students deserve improved education and a more competitive reputation.

Review of Top Ranked Universities by Ranking Organisations

The *Times Higher Education* (THE), a London-based organization, published their top ten highest ranked global universities of 2015–2016 based on their evaluation of teaching, research, knowledge transfer, and international outlook. The top ten universities were then as follows:

California Institute of Technology
University of Oxford
Stanford University
University of Cambridge
MIT
Harvard University
Princeton University
Imperial College London
ETH Zurich
University of Chicago

The names in italics are universities in England, except ETH, which is in Zurich, Switzerland. The rest are all American universities. This list is only slightly different from its 2014 list, which were:

California Institute of Technology
Harvard University
University of Oxford

Stanford University
University of Cambridge
MIT
Princeton University
University of California, Berkeley
Imperial College London & (9) Yale University
University of Chicago

The THE ranked the University of Chicago as 11th because Imperial College and Yale ranked the same 9th place. The important point is that the rank of these top universities hardly changes, although the University of California, Berkeley, did not make the cut in the latest list.

The top 10 highest ranked universities by QS (Quacquarelli Symond, Ltd.), also a London-based ranking organization, is the same as those picked by the *Times Higher Education*, except the order is slightly different as follows:

MIT
Stanford University
Harvard University
University of Cambridge
California Institute of Technology
University of Oxford
University College London
ETH Zurich
Imperial College London
University of Chicago

The universities in italics are again British universities except for ETH Zurich. Again, the same five universities are universities in the United States, but the ordering has changed.

Both the QS and the THE rankings are subjective in that the peer review (i.e. personal views or opinions about specific universities) counts towards the university ranking. A difference of a few points in peer review can drastically change these rankings, especially for lower-ranked universities.

In 2016, Reuters published its 10 *most innovative universities* of the world, which were as follows:

Stanford University
MIT
Harvard University
University of Texas System
University of Washington System
KAIST, Korea
University of Michigan System
University of Pennsylvania
KU Leuven, Belgium
Northwestern University

According to Reuters, the most innovative universities are selected from "the ranks of the educational institutions doing the most to advance science, invent new technologies and help drive the global economy. Unlike other rankings that often rely entirely or in part on subjective surveys, Reuters relies exclusively on empirical data such as patent filings and research paper citations. Our 2016 results show that big break-throughs — even just one highly influential paper or patent — can drive a university way up the list, but when that discovery fades into the past, so does its ranking. According to our findings, consistency is key, with truly innovative institutions putting out groundbreaking work year after year." <http://www.businessinsider.com/the-2016-ranking-of-the-10-most-innovative-universities-in-the-world-2016–9>

In the Reuters ranking of innovative universities that does not include peer reviews, eight of the ten most innovative universities are in the United States. Three of them (Stanford, MIT, and Harvard) also made the top ten QS and THE lists. The sixth most innovative university in this list is KAIST (Korea Advanced Institute of Science and Technology) of Korea. The ninth is the Katholieke Universiteit (KU) Leuven of Belgium. In this list, none of the British universities make the top ten, whereas in the QS and THE rankings that include peer reviews, half of the top ten are British universities. Reuters chose these universities based on the data on academic papers and patent filings from the Intellectual Property & Science division of Thomson Reuters.

These innovative universities are engaged in the innovation of technologies and the development of socio-economic solutions as well as economic development through the creation of new venture firms. They are also incubators of public policies on issues such as long-term solutions for the environment. Stanford claims that all the companies formed by Stanford entrepreneurs generated US$2.7 trillion in annual revenue, which is equivalent to the 10th largest economy in the world. Similarly, MIT claims that as of 2014, MIT alumni have launched 30,200 active companies, employing roughly 4.6 million people, and generating roughly US$1.9 trillion in annual revenues. That revenue total compares favourably with the world's ninth-largest GDP, Russia (US$2.097 trillion), and the 10th-largest, India (US$1.877 trillion). These two universities, MIT and Stanford, have created not only huge wealth for the United States but also brought many tangible and intangible benefits to people in many other countries.

On the Development of Research Universities

The S-Curve: S-Factor, S-Gap, and Vector Delta

If we define the "S-Factor" as the integrated total measure of the quality of a research university, the development of two research universities over a time period may be depicted as shown in Fig 10.1. This figure assumes a linear change of both A and B, which would be the case when each university works hard to improve through productivity increases and quality improvement. However, the basic assumption may not be valid, because the rate of change, i.e. the improvement of all aspects of a university, may be highly non-linear. The development of a university may be more like the change of the wealth of two individuals, one with much more wealth the other as shown in Figure 10.2.

According to French economist, T. Piketty in his book *Capital in the Twenty-First Century (2013)*, "the rate of capital return in developed countries is persistently greater than the rate of economic growth, and that this will cause wealth inequality in the future". His finding from the historical data in France is that wealth produces more wealth faster than the wealth that can be generated through productivity increases and hard work when the rate of return on capital is greater than the rate of economic growth over the long term. Consequently, rich people (or rich

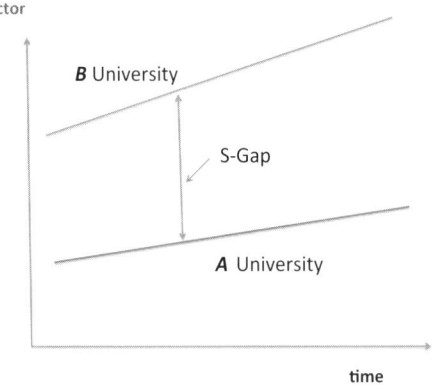

Fig. 10.1   The development of two research universities as a function of time. It shows that university B is developing faster than university A, but both universities are improving linearly as a function of time. The gap between these two universities is denoted as the S-Gap. This change of S-Factor may not be a realistic depiction of what actually happens.

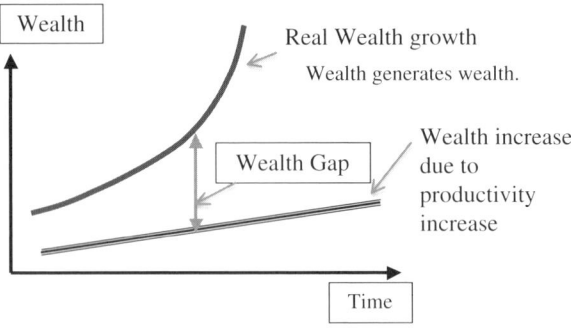

Fig. 10.2   The Piketty curve of wealth growth. The curve on the top shows that the wealthier person gets richer at a much faster rate than the person who tries to accumulate wealth by working harder.

nations) tend to get richer faster because of the wealth that they already possess, i.e. wealth breeds more wealth than just working harder. This finding is schematically shown in Figure 10.2. Similar phenomena may be present in the development of research universities.

A similar phenomenon seems to occur with universities. The universities that are leading in all of their chosen fields have a much greater probability of growing even stronger because of the intellectual, human,

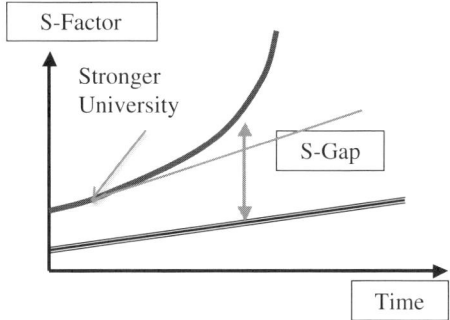

Fig. 10.3 The S-Factor of a university is a composite index of what constitutes the reputation of a university. The lower curve represents a university with a lower S-Factor, which develops more or less linearly with time through hard work, etc. The S-Gap between the wealthier and/or with higher reputation grows by a combination of linear growth and the compound rate due to the existing prior reputation. The S-Gap between these two universities continues to increase unless some drastic actions are taken.

and financial resources that they already have. If we call the aggregation of all the elements that go into strengthening a university the "S-Factor", the growth may be depicted as shown in Figure 10.3. The figure is a composite strength of a university, represented as the S-Factor, as a function of time. The top curve is for a stronger university and the lower curve represents a less well-known university. The stronger university tends to attract better faculty, students, and major financial gifts. Thus, the gap between the two, the "S-Gap", grows as a function of time. The S-Factor is a composite measure made of many elements that make a university great, such as the quality of faculty, students, and staff; the size of the endowment and financial resources; its current reputation; past academic and scholarly achievements; and future prospects. Stronger universities with more "intellectual and financial assets" will grow faster than universities with a low S-Factor. Therefore, the gap between them, the "S-Gap" shown in Figure 10.3, will grow larger with time. For this reason, stronger universities attract more resources and people, which accelerate their growth.

　　The much faster growth (or advance) of the university with a higher S-Factor is due to many possible factors. The contributing root causes of the S-Gap may be the following:

- More competitive students and faculty go to the universities with better reputations and resources.
- Resources (financial gifts, funds, etc.) tend to concentrate at and/or favour richer universities or better-known universities.
- Faster growth of the S-Factor (e.g. outstanding faculty, students, facilities, reputation, etc.) at stronger universities may be due to the existing advantages.
- Safety factor: for students and faculty members considering their choice of a university, joining a successful enterprise may be deemed safer.
- Quality of life may be better at richer institutions.
- More opportunities may exist at a university with a higher S-Factor.

Vector δ

Universities that have a low S-Factor at a given instant in time (indicated by the lower curve) should not stay on their current trajectory if their long-term goal is to become one of the best universities in the world. They must transition to a higher trajectory as indicated by Vector δ in Figure 10.4. Vector δ may take many different forms depending on specific institutional conditions. For example, Vector δ may consist of the addition of a large number of outstanding faculty members, attracting the most

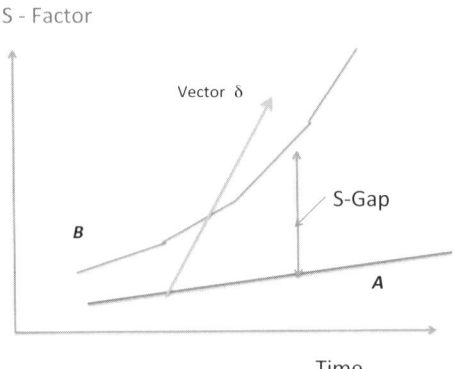

Fig. 10.4   Vector δ to transform University A from its current trajectory to a higher trajectory.

competitive students, generating significant financial resources, making major scientific discoveries, and introducing technological innovations that solve the most important problems of the 21st century. The actions chosen to initiate the transition, i.e. Vector δ, must be achievable goals based on the given conditions of each university. A number of universities (e.g. Arizona State University, Carnegie Mellon University, Georgia Institute of Technology, KAIST, Nanyang Technological University, among others) appear to have gone through transformations to be on a higher trajectory.

Typical characteristics of leading universities often include the following: first, outstanding students and distinguished faculty from all corners of the world want to be at these universities; second, these universities have made major contributions to humanity through major scientific discoveries, technological innovations, and creation of theories of various kinds in all scholarly fields that have changed the way people think; and third, these universities have introduced major educational paradigms that have affected learning and teaching. To create a great university, we must attempt to solve the most profound problems of our era, such as global warming, energy, environment, water, and sustainability. It is easier said than done.

Figure 10.5 shows the impact made by research as a function of the research spectrum, which spans topics from fundamental research to technology innovation. The greatest impact is made by research done at the two ends of the research spectrum, i.e. fundamental research and technology innovation. Yet, most of the research at universities tends to be in the middle of the spectrum, where it is easier to generate results and publish papers. This is because many universities count the number of publications rather than the *impact* made by research as a criterion for promotion and rewards. This is often done because a quantitative measure is much easier to administer than qualitative assessment of the impact made by a faculty member. This is a fundamental flaw at many research universities, because it deprives faculty and students of opportunities for major scholarly and technological contributions by focusing intellectual and financial resources on short-term gains. In reality, the time to generate great ideas and results is not any longer than to work on trivial problems that are hard to publish.

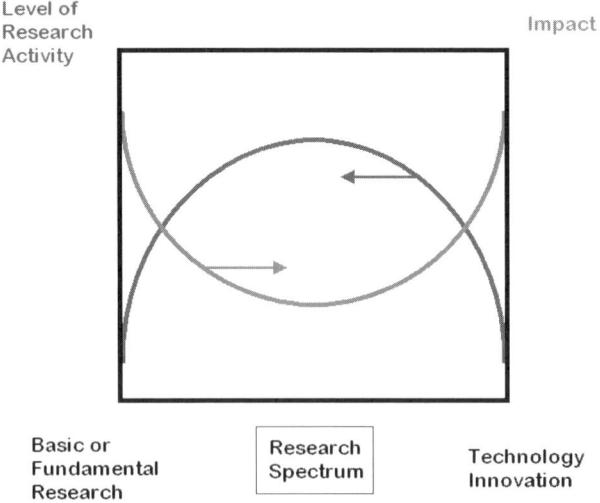

Fig. 10.5   Research spectrum of research done at universities ranges from basic and fundamental research to technology innovation. The level of research indicates the intensity of the research done as a function of research spectrum. Most research is done in the middle of the research spectrum at many universities where the impact (u-shaped curve) made by the research is least. The greatest impact made by research is at either ends of the research spectrum.

Illustration of Vector δ

The KAIST Case

As an illustration of Vector δ, the transformation of KAIST will be briefly reviewed. KAIST was established in 1971 to support the transformation of the Korean economy from labour-intensive businesses (e.g. textiles, apparel, shoe making, etc.) to heavy manufacturing industries for automobiles, steel, ships, electronics, electric power plants, etc. This change was initiated by the Korean Government. To achieve this ambitious goal of industrialisation, Korea needed engineers and scientists with advanced degrees. The Korean Government decided to establish a new university of science and technology, The Korea Advanced Institute of Science (KAIS), that would offer graduate educational programmes in science and engineering rather than investing their scarce resources into then existing universities. It was partially funded by the United States Government through its Agency for

International Development (USAID) with a one-time grant. In 1986, KAIS merged with KIT (Korea Institute of Technology), an undergraduate institution in science and technology, to become KAIST. In 2008, it merged again with a small private university in telecommunications (Information and Communications University, ICU).

From its inception, KAIST was given special support by the Korean Government: tuition-free education, higher salaries for the faculty than the then-prevailing salaries at other universities, governance by an independent of board of trustees (rather than by the government ministry), and military deferment for its students once they enrolled in KAIST and successfully completed their education. Since the government controlled the budget and the board of trustees (with four votes out of 18 in 2013), the government had enormous influence over the operation of KAIST. Some of the brightest students in Korea have attended KAIST from the beginning. Many of KAIST's students are the top graduates of special science high schools, which are also highly selective. KAIST has produced a large number of leading engineers and scientists for Korea. These graduates have played key roles in creating the modern industrialised nation that Korea has become. In 2006, KAIST had about 3,000 undergraduates and 5,800 graduate students (now 4,000 undergraduate and 6,500 graduate students), and 400 faculty members (now about 650 professors). About 10% of all professors in Korea in the field of science and engineering are KAIST graduates. The rapid industrialisation and growth of the Korean economy should be attributed to the outstanding work done by able Korean technologists, scientists, technicians, managers, and educators. KAIST graduates have done their part for Korea's industrialisation and also contributed globally by working in many countries.

It should be noted that the Korean economy in 1980 was in dire shape, because the investment made in heavy industries beginning in 1970 had not yet yielded the financial returns. (Investment in heavy industries takes many years to mature.) Also, the new Korean heavy industries had only limited technical know-how and low productivity in the 1970s. In 1980, a major overhaul of the industrial structure was made to increase the competitiveness of Korean companies. By the mid-1980s, the Korean economy was in high gear, ultimately producing the miracle of the Han River.

When I joined KAIST in 2006 as its president, KAIST was a good school with enormous potential but it had a few structural problems. Some of the problems I identified will be outlined here in order to illustrate how KAIST found a new trajectory, i.e. Vector δ. This is an important step since solutions can only be found when the problems are delineated and identified. These problems are not unique to KAIST, but can be found at many universities throughout the world. Nevertheless, it is useful to highlight the problems to provide an integrated view of the issues that had to be resolved.

In 2006, QS ranked KAIST about 196th in the world, a respectable ranking but not certainly where KAIST should be in light of its outstanding students and faculty. KAIST students have been in the top 1% of high school graduates in Korea, many having attended special science high schools and high schools for gifted students. Then what were the reasons it was ranked so low? Clearly, it was not due to problems that individual students or faculty members had created. They were created by the "system" adopted over the years to operate KAIST. This situation may not be unique to KAIST and some other universities may share similar problems.

The basic problems KAIST had can be attributed to malfunctioning of the "system" with unintended consequences. The following issues with students were delineated. Although the majority of KAIST undergraduate students were excellent and studied hard, a small minority of KAIST students took advantage of the largesse provided by Korean people. For instance, KAIST students did not have to perform at their best to graduate from KAIST, since the system allowed them to re-take the same subject until they received the top grade of A. They could also stay at KAIST longer than four years without graduating, still receiving living expenses and free tuition until they graduated.[1] Because of this policy, there were about 800 extra undergraduate students in facilities designed for 3,000 undergraduate students. Since they were exempt from military service, there was no urgency to finish their study in four years. Some of the students, in some ways, were the victims of the Korean secondary educational system. It is extremely competitive to get into (and stay in) good science high schools and high schools for gifted students. Some of KAIST's incoming students were exhausted by the time they graduated from high school. The system did not bring out the best in KAIST students because it did not give them the opportunity to work to their utmost individual capability. These and other problems had to be dealt with to transform KAIST into a merit-based system with intellectual freedom to pursue whatever activity and study the students chose to pursue.

The KAIST graduate school has about 6,500 students, about the same number of students as MIT. The number of graduate students is about 50% larger than the undergraduate programmes at both institutions. However, the number of faculty members at KAIST was much smaller than MIT. (The KAIST faculty was about 40% of the size of the MIT faculty.) Students at KAIST were excellent. However, some doctoral students spent ten years to get a PhD because of the rule that stipulated that doctoral candidates had to have a paper published before they could get their degree. Unfortunately, sometimes, even an excellent paper takes a long time to be accepted and published by a reputable journal. This system persisted, in part because most of the KAIST students received a government stipend administered by KAIST. Therefore, there was no financial burden on the part of either the student or the supervising professor, regardless of the length of their residency at KAIST.[2] Furthermore, since KAIST counted the number of publications rather than quality of the papers and/or innovations for promotion and graduation, many students were working on topics that were similar to those published in the past.

Some aspects of the system for faculty were also lax. Once someone was hired as a faculty member, it was equivalent to getting a lifetime appointment, i.e. almost everyone received tenure. At the same time, even really outstanding faculty members had to wait for their turn for promotion. It was a de-facto seniority-based system, although this was not a part of the formal regulations. The emphasis was on the number of publications rather than the impact made by their research. Since each faculty member supervised a large number of graduate students (whom they did not have to support financially except for those receiving research assistantships) and since all masters and doctoral candidates had to write theses based on research, the number of papers published per faculty was the same as those of world's leading universities in the US, but the impact made by these papers (measured by the number of citations) was much less. In some cases, it was because the papers were refinements of previous papers rather than exploring bold new ideas. Also, the hiring process was not truly objective. It favoured those who were doing work that was similar to the work of others, rather than hiring candidates who had a unique academic background. Almost everything, e.g. lab space, was distributed equally among all professors, regardless of individual needs. Few professors collaborated with other professors in research. Even the most capable and ambitious professors were not able to use their full capability because the system did not recognize and reward exceptional contributions. Their international participation with leading scholars in other countries was limited to a few professors. Thus, the faculty were not competing and collaborating with the best brains of the world. Since the government controlled the size of the faculty, the number of students, budget, physical facilities, etc., there were many problems. For instance, the faculty size was fixed at about 400 and the median age of the faculty was 55 with few professors in their 30s and 40s. In comparison, the size of the faculty at MIT is about 1,000. Since the retirement age was 65, faculty members could not do much once they reach the age of 60, because the system cut back the support for faculty members over 60. By 2006, the buildings and facilities that were built in 1986 had deteriorated for lack of maintenance. Students could not perform research at night and on weekends because the management shut down the heat during the winter. The number of women professors and the international students were miniscule. Instruction was conducted in Korean, sometimes using books translated from English, which limited the global competitiveness of the students. Although this practice can be rationalized from Korean perspectives, this was not consistent with the fact that Korean economy had depended on global trade and overseas markets, and that KAIST graduates were often working for global companies that require proficiency in English. Furthermore, most incoming freshmen were reasonably proficient in English, since many learned it when they were in secondary school.

The Vector δ to change the trajectory of KAIST, which was implemented beginning in 2006, consisted of the following:

1. Decided to increase the faculty size to 700 from 400 unilaterally even without government support. By 2013, the faculty size increased to 630.

2. Adopted a merit-based system for faculty promotion and tenure. Created a super faculty rank of "Distinguished Professor" to reward exceptional faculty members.

3. Evaluated contributions by the impact made in research and teaching, replacing the number of publications.

4. KAIST decided to undertake major research projects to solve global problems of the 21st century in energy, environment, water, and sustainability (EEWS).

5. Created major inter-disciplinary units called KAIST Institutes (KI) by having professors with the same interest share space regardless of their departmental affiliation. Built a large new building that was specifically designed to promote collaboration.

6. A new teaching and learning system was introduced (Education 3.0) where formal lectures were reduced or eliminated and discussion-based teaching through discussion among students with faculty members was favoured to provide the overall guidance and control the contents of the course.

7. Hired faculty members only based on their qualification rather than allocating a fixed number of faculty positions to various departments (a quota system), i.e. departments were allowed to hire as many highly qualified faculty members as they could find. The president of KAIST interviewed all final candidates before the formal offer of employment was made.

8. Adopted English as the language of instruction.

9. Changed the governance system to the department head system, where the department head was responsible for the department decisions on salary, space, and promotion rather than making decisions based on majority faculty vote. The department head controlled the faculty salary based on KAIST-wide policies.

10. Adopted an asymmetric decision-making system. Under this system, the department head could make an affirmative decision on promotion, etc., and then try to get the concurrence of the dean if the dean's approval is needed. If the department head had made a negative decision, the dean and the upper administration could not reverse the department head's decision. The upper administration could render a negative decision, but could not interfere with the

decision made by the department head. The philosophy behind this policy is to empower the department head and let the person who knows more about an issue make the right decision.

11. Increased the number of non-Korean faculty members and international students.

12. Sought an increase in government support.

13. Increased the donations from the private sector.

14. Built 14 new buildings to accommodate increased faculty and student size.

15. Increased the number of undergraduates from 3,000 to 4,000 to increase the number of highly qualified applicants to the KAIST graduate schools.

16. Admission to the KAIST undergraduate programme was based on interviews and high school grades, replacing the written entrance examination.

17. To provide opportunities for students from rural, farming, and fishing villages, 150 students out of 1,000 freshmen were selected for admission purely based the recommendation of the principal of high schools, who were asked to recommend only one student from each school.

18. Increased the number of women faculty and students.

19. Actively promoted international collaboration.

20. Replaced the quantity-based system to a quality-based system in promotion and tenure.

21. Undergraduates who did not finish their degree in four years had to pay tuition.

22. Graduate students who did not finish their PhD in ten years had to pay tuition.

The ranking of KAIST moved up over the following years when these changes were implemented successfully. As stated earlier, by 2016, KAIST ranked 6th among Reuter's most innovative universities in the world. This ranking reflects the fact that KAIST professors and students became much more internationally competitive and influential through their achievements. KAIST professors have won recognitions in international forums and competitions. For example, they won first place at the US Department of Defense competition in robotics. KAIST students obtained easy access to graduate schools in other countries when they chose to study abroad, since the language is no longer a barrier in English-speaking countries. The EEWS programme yielded many major techno-logical innovations such as On-Line Electric Vehicles (OLEVs). OLEVs receive heavy electric power wirelessly from an underground cable, thus eliminating the internal combustion engines from automobiles, buses, etc. KAIST also created the Mobile Harbor (MH). This innovation eliminates the need to build large expensive harbours that damage coastal areas by unloading containers from large ships using a special transport that can easily operate in confined spaces. Also the biological and health sciences became strong by recruiting bright researchers and professors from all corners of the world. The addition of 350 more young professors, increasing the faculty size to 630 by 2013, rejuvenated the faculty rank tremendously.

As Newton's laws state, there is always a "reaction" to any change. This was also the case at KAIST. The Vector δ was implemented at KAIST, although some senior professors, especially those active in the Faculty Association opposed many of these measures. The most resisted changes were teaching in English, the merit-based salary system, and the department head system. There were several reasons for the quick adoption of the new policies, despite the opposition of the Faculty Association. First, the changes were implemented in a relatively short time. Second, the Korean press and people supported the changes. Third, the rapid progress being made under the new system was visible to almost everyone. Finally, the 350 new younger professors who joined the KAIST faculty under the new policies had done outstanding work in research and teaching, and strongly supported these changes.

In retrospect, the behaviour of the KAIST Faculty Association under the leadership of some senior professors was not any worse than the behaviour of those who had lost their privileges. Similar things happened at the US National Science Foundation and at MIT. It must be a human reaction when suddenly one's comfortable life is disturbed by someone's actions, regardless of the long-term benefit of such actions to each indi-vidual member of the community, the organization, and ultimately, the nation. Self-interest appears to be the most powerful force that often dictates human instant behaviour. It is sometimes irrational, but it is also perfectly understandable. After all, we are all human beings with our own travails and egos. It is the role of universities to educate people to overcome these negative traits of human being, i.e. for the long-term progress of humanity.

The MIT Case

For four years, I had the privilege of observing engineering research and education conducted at American universities from the vantage of the US National Science Foundation (NSF) as a presidential appointee in charge of engineering. At the time, our goal at NSF was to fulfill the mission of NSF as defined in the NSF Act of 1950 (amended), i.e. to promote advances in science and engineering; provide health, prosperity, and welfare; and secure national defense. We tried to fulfill the original mission of NSF by strengthening the US competitiveness.[3] Although NSF funded some of the best researchers in the country, a large fraction of research funds were granted to well-established senior researchers/professors who were solving similar problems in many different ways under the banner of engineering science rather than working on urgent or new problems so as to advance the engineering field, strengthen the competitiveness of the United States through innovation, and/or solve critical problems of the 21st century. We created many new programmes to support engineering research in fields that lacked the science base (such as design and manufacturing), emerging technologies (e.g. opto-electronics, MEMS, etc.), and critical technologies related to, for example, infrastructure. Another major initiative was the creation of Engineering Research Centers (ERC) to promote interdisciplinary research in universities and in collaboration with industrial firms. We also shifted more funds to support young researchers rather than supporting primarily well-established senior researchers.[4] These changes, including the establishment of the National Earthquake Research Center at the University of New York at Buffalo rather than at one of California' universities, have made me rather unpopular with a certain segment of the higher educational establishments in the United States. However, the University of New York at Buffalo submitted a stronger proposal and the review committee was convinced that the taxpayers money would be better spent there.

One thing I learned was that many grantees did a wonderful job trying to achieve their original research goals, but once the grant money was exhausted, some universities went back to their old system, abandoning the goal of transforming engineering research and education. Based on this experience, I came to the conclusion that it would be difficult to influence the American higher educational system from outside. To make a real change at universities, one has to transform it at the department level from inside the university.

A few years after I returned to MIT from NSF, I was asked to be the Head of the Department of Mechanical Engineering in 1991. I took this job, rather than the presidency of a university, thinking that if the best-ranked department in the field of mechanical engineering changes its direction and programmes, other universities would follow, thus affecting the direction of engineering education and research in the United States, and perhaps even in the world.

My concern with the engineering research in the United States at the time was that after making major progress in many engineering fields after World War II, engineering schools were not working on new problems and issues of the 21st century. Instead, too many professors were solving similar problems many times over, making small incremental improvements rather than spending more time at the two ends of the research spectrum shown in Figure 10.5. By the end of my term at NSF, I realized that the transformation of universities must be attempted from inside a university. The job of being the head of the highest ranked mechanical engineering department in the country was a unique opportunity to achieve this task. Since my professional life had evolved around people who had enormous influence on the development of mechanical engineering at MIT and elsewhere, I thought that I knew how the department could really become great through transformation, which might also help other engineering schools.

The MIT Department of Mechanical Engineering had been the highest ranked department of its kind in the United States, and perhaps one of the best in the world as well. Its faculty members were renowned scholars in various fields of mechanical engineering such as fluid mechanics, heat transfer, solid mechanics, manufacturing, materials, design, and internal combustion. It was indeed a unique privilege for me to learn from the masters of these fields and later to become one of their colleagues. Much of their contributions dealt with issues related to engineering problems that had been created in the late 19th and the first half of the 20th century, which were related to the development of automobiles, electric power plants, mass production, ship building, aerospace, etc. Many of these professors were the best in their respective fields. There were also great scholars at other universities working on similar problems. In fact, in the 1950s under the sponsorship of the Ford Foundation, MIT trained many young engineering professors to increase the supply of engineering professors with PhDs, because many professors did not have advanced degrees. To achieve this goal, brand new PhDs, mostly graduates from MIT, were appointed as "Ford assistant professors" at MIT and taught at MIT for about three or four years. Then they moved on to become faculty members at other universities. These professors and others made American engineering schools to be some of the best in the world, having authored many textbooks, etc. These engineering schools became pre-eminent in the world in the 1950s and 1960s. Given all these contributions, then the obvious question is: why should the MIT Department of Mechanical Engineering change?

The issue that had to be dealt with in the MIT Department of Mechanical Engineering in 1990s was the transition into new technologies and new problems that are important in the 21st century, and giving up some of the well-established fields in which the professors were well known. It was difficult to go through such a transformation for many reasons. It is always much more comfortable to enjoy the fruits of one's past labour, especially when money was coming in to work on refinements of one's past work. We had the best scholars who led the fields of internal combustion engines, solid mechanics, macro-heat transfer, textiles, machining, and so on. Since most important problems had been solved, many were engaged in the refinement and small advances. To initiate research in new fields, one had to have ideas and perseverance as well as work hard. While we were dwelling on these past issues, new fields were emerging in industry where mechanical engineers could help, if we had developed new tools, theories and methodologies that were applicable to these new problems. For example, in the 1980s, mechanical engineering professors at most universities did not work on problems related to semi-conductor manufacturing, optical devices, micro-device manufacturing, and information science and technology. Heat transfer problems encountered in semiconductor devices required entirely different physics in nano-scale heat generation and transport, which could not be handled based on macro-scale physics of heat generation and transport at nano-scale. Similarly, although the MIT Mechanical Engineering Department led the field of bioengineering, it was done using macroscale mechanical engineering disciplinary knowledge rather than combining that knowledge with knowledge in biology and other fields. We also did not cover optics, which is important in modern manufacturing and mechanical devices. "In-breeding" of the faculty members created some of these problems. Many of the professors in the Department of Mechanical Engineering had received one or more of their engineering degrees from MIT and therefore, the bandwidth of their collective expertise was relatively narrow and often limited to traditional subjects.

During the period 1991–2001, the Vector δ for the Department of Mechanical Engineering at MIT consisted of the following components:

1. Transformation of the discipline of mechanical engineering from a discipline that was largely based on physics to a discipline that incorporates physics, information, biology, and design.
2. Hiring of professors whose background was needed to deal with new issues of the 21st century. As a result, a large number of new professors of mechanical engineering hired did not have their doctorate degrees in mechanical engineering. In 2016, about 50% of the professors in the department had earned their doctorates in fields other than mechanical engineering. They learned about mechanical engineering from their colleagues while teaching mechanical engineering subjects.[5]
3. Stopping the in-breeding of the faculty by hiring most of the new professors from outside.
4. Renovation of physical space to create space to accommodate new research.
5. Emphasis on the two ends of the research spectrum to increase impact made by the research done in the department.

6. Changing the promotion review system to make them more rigorous.
7. Strengthening the interdisciplinary undergraduate mechanical engineering programme (called Course 2A), which increased undergraduate enrollment. In 2016, more than a half of mechanical engineering students were in Course 2A.
8. Strengthened multi-disciplinary research activities.

Challenges in Transforming the MIT ME Department

MIT has a system called the Visiting Committee for each department that gathers information and reports on the state of the department to the MIT Corporation (equivalent to what other universities would call the board of trustees of MIT). The chair of the Visiting Committee is a member of the Corporation. To gather information on the status of the Department, they hold meetings with three groups: tenured professors, un-tenured professors, and students once every one or two years. I think it is a good system.

Four months after I assumed the headship of the department, we had our first Visiting Committee meeting. After the meeting the tenured professors, the chairman of the Visiting Committee came to see me. He told me that 50% of the tenured faculty members voted to ask me to step down from the headship. He suggested that I should leave the headship in four months. I thought of stepping down, but my close colleagues and my wife thought that if I step down, my successors would not dare to make any changes in the future. Six months later when my colleagues saw the results of some of the transformation, they no longer raised this issue again. I stayed in the job for 10 years rather than three years I had originally intended. I give a lot of credit to then MIT President, Dr Charles M. Vest. Instead of asking me to resign, the MIT Corporation changed the chairman of the Visiting Committee. Mr Alex d'Arbeloff became the new chairman of the Visiting Committee, who later became the chairman of the MIT Corporation. Mr d'Arbeloff made many outstanding contributions to MIT and the Department.

After a couple of decades since the transformation, it is good to know that MIT's Mechanical Engineering Department is still ranked No. 1 and stronger than ever. Students are voting with their feet, making it one of the most popular departments to enrol for MIT undergraduates.

Conclusions

The value of having a great university in our midst is well documented. To become such a university, a university may have to transform itself to be on a different trajectory. The transformation should begin with a clear assessment of the factors that have prevented its progress. Based on the assessment, universities must transform to leap frog to be on a higher trajectory. Research universities that dwell only on their past accomplishments will eventually lag behind other universities that continue to leap frog. The trajectory of university development should include discontinuous jumps through timely adoption of innovative changes.

Three concepts are introduced in this chapter: the S-Factor, the S-Gap, and Vector delta. These ideas should solidify the concept of institutional development on a more quantitative basis.

The transformation of KAIST was used to illustrate the multi-faceted aspects of "systems" problems. Today, thanks to the difficult and sometimes painful changes made, KAIST ranks 6th in the world of most innovative universities.

Thanks to the major transformation it has gone through, the MIT Department of Mechanical Engineering continues to be the leading mechanical engineering department in the world.

Universities should strive to become the intellectual hubs where great ideas are created and implemented for public good. The great progress we made in many fields thanks to research at universities gives hope to the idea that we can create an ideal society. The conflicts we see in the world today and the disharmony in many nations that are bringing out the worst instincts of people are ultimately the reasons why our research universities must do a better job to show how a harmonious and just society can and should be created.

Notes

1. Most students at all universities are eager to get higher grades, but the pressure on KAIST students to achieve excellent grades was sometimes greater because of pressure from the students' parents and expectations from society.
2. There are many similarities between KAIST and MIT, but the MIT culture is somewhat different from that of KAIST because the students are responsible

for their tuition, etc. Many MIT graduate students pay their tuition by working as research assistants for professors with research grants.

3. See Dian Olson Belanger, *Enabling American Innovation: Engineering and the National Science Foundation* (West Lafayette, Indiana: Purdue University Press, 1998).

4. Some of these initiatives resulted in the creation of an opposition group called "Concerned Engineers of America", which sent a petition to the White House asking them to dismiss me. About 1,600 people signed it. The letter did not have any effect. I ended up staying in the Washington job for almost four years, although our family had to live on a limited income of a political appointee.

5. We hired new assistant professors based on their educational background, future promise, etc. However, I hired several mid-level professors (i.e. associate professors) from other universities (sometimes by visiting their laboratories to talk to their graduate students at their work) to recruit truly outstanding scholars. They are now leaders of the MIT Mechanical Engineering Department. About a half of them were not in mechanical engineering departments at their previous institutions.

Acknowledgement

The author is grateful to Professor M. Kathryn Thompson for reviewing this paper.

About the Author

Nam P. Suh is Cross Professor Emeritus, MIT, Cambridge, MA and Former President, KAIST (2006–2013), Daejeon, Korea.

CHAPTER ELEVEN

MULTI-CAMPUS INTERNATIONALISATION OF HIGHER EDUCATION INSTITUTIONS

GABRIEL HAWAWINI

Introduction

Leaders of higher education institutions (HEIs) around the world rank the internationalisation of their institutions among their highest priorities.[1] What does internationalization refer to in the context of higher education? How do HEIs internationalise their activities and why is it a priority for leaders of HEIs? We review the answers to these questions before turning to the examination of one particular channel through which HEIs internationalise: the establishment of campuses abroad.[2] We identify and describe three models of multicampus institutions: the branch model, the federal model and the global model. We follow this with a closer look at the global model adopted by INSEAD, the international business school with campuses in France, Singapore and Abu Dhabi. We then present four host-country models we refer to as the educational model, the academic model, the business model and the internationalisation model. These models are illustrated with the cases of Qatar for the educational model, Singapore for the academic model, Dubai for the business model and Abu Dhabi for the internationalisation model.

What Is Meant by the Internationalisation of Higher Education Institutions?

Internationalisation has been defined as "the process of integrating an international and intercultural dimension into the teaching, research and service functions of the institution".[3] This standard definition, however, emphasises the *inward* dimension of the phenomenon. It calls for bringing the world into the institution instead of taking the institution out into the world. A more outward-looking perspective defines internationalization as "*an ongoing process of change whose objective is to integrate the institution and its key stakeholders (its students and faculty) into the global knowledge economy*".[4]

Inward and outward internationalisation are usually complementary. An HEI would typically start its internationalisation process by introducing an international dimension into some of its teaching and research activities on its home campus. The process may stop at that stage or move to a second phase that calls for the adoption of outbound activities such as joint programmes delivered abroad and the opening of foreign campuses. Outbound activities rarely take place without some prior internationalisation at home.

How Do Higher Education Institutions Internationalise?

There is an array of initiatives an HEI can adopt to internationalise. They range from internationalising the curriculum and the student body to establishing academic joint-ventures with foreign institutions and opening campuses abroad.[5] The focus of this chapter is on outward internationalisation through the establishment of foreign campuses, a move that does not preclude the adoption of other international initiatives. As pointed out earlier, most institutions that have opened campuses abroad have also internationalised their home campuses by offering international courses and programmes and attracting foreign students and faculty on their home premises.

Why Do Higher Education Institutions Internationalise?

What motivates an HEI to establish a campus outside its home territory? This type of internationalisation initiative is clearly riskier to implement than, say, an international exchange programme or a dual-degree programme with a foreign institution. The former requires a larger investment and mobilises more institutional resources than the launch of the latter two programmes. It is also more complex to manage because of the geographical distance, the scale and size of the operation and the differences in cultures and business practices between the home and the host countries. It also carries significantly more reputational risk because the closing of a foreign campus would be a more visible indicator of a failed internationalisation strategy than the termination of an unsuccessful exchange programme or a dual-degree programme.

There are several reasons for an HEI to venture abroad. They can be classified by at least three distinct categories: academic, economic and, for some state-controlled HEIs, political.[6]

Academic motives. These are primarily driven by a desire to fulfill the institution's mission to educate potential students not only at home but around the world, especially those students who could not come to the home campus. In addition there is a need for the institution to remain academically relevant in an interconnected world, an objective that is easier to achieve if the institution has a physical presence abroad where its faculty and students can study and learn. Finally, there is the need to attract qualified students and faculty from around the world, a goal that is facilitated by a foreign presence and a broader international visibility.

Economic motives. These are mostly prompted by a desire to increase revenues by offering programmes to foreign students unable to travel to the home campus for financial or cultural reasons. One example of the latter is when some parents in the Middle East do not wish to send their daughters to study abroad. Another reason is to reduce the institution's operating risk via geographical diversification. This effect occurs when stronger demand for education in developing countries (where most foreign campuses are established) offsets weaker demand at home.[7] The stronger demand for education in developing countries stems from their faster economic growth rates and their large pool of younger students seeking a tertiary education. Another economic motive is the financial support from the host country that the guest institution could use to fund activities on its home campus. Finally, note that economic and academic motives are not mutually exclusive: an institution may open a foreign campus to satisfy both motives.

A political motive to go abroad is usually associated with state-controlled HEIs and dictated by national interests. This motive is well illustrated with the case of Russian HEIs which have established campuses in countries that are located in Russia's sphere of influence such as Armenia, Azerbaijan, Belarus, Kazakhstan, Kyrgyzstan and Tajikistan.

Alternative Models

The next two sections identify alternative models of multicampus HEIs with a closer look at the model adopted by INSEAD, the international business school with campuses in France, Singapore and Abu Dhabi. The following section explores the motives that drive host countries to attract foreign HEIs in their territory and describes alternative host-country models. The concluding section examines the potential for online education to reach out to students around the world as an alternative to opening campuses abroad.

Models of Multicampus Higher Education Institutions

In this section the terms "campus abroad" and "foreign campus" are first defined. This is followed by an examination of the number of such campuses operating worldwide as well as the home countries of the HEIs that have gone abroad. Finally, there is a review of alternative models of multicampus HEIs that explains why HEIs adopt different foreign campus models and how these campuses are structured and organized.

What Is a Foreign Campus?

A foreign campus is usually described as an 'entity that is operated in the exclusive name of a foreign HEI in which it engages in face-to-face teaching and delivers an entire academic program that leads to a degree awarded by the foreign education provider to students who have completed the program in the foreign entity.'[8] The defining feature of a foreign campus is the award by the foreign institution of its *own* degree to students who successfully completed a programme that has been delivered *entirely* in the *foreign* location. The facilities in which the campus is located can be provided by an agency of the host country or rented or owned (fully or partly) by the foreign HEI whose faculty can reside in the host country permanently or only during the duration of their teaching assignment. For example, Yale-National University of Singapore College located in Singapore is not considered a foreign campus of Yale University because Yale does not award a degree at the end of the programme, even though the programme has been developed by Yale and the teaching is delivered by resident Yale faculty (the degree is awarded by the National University of Singapore).[9]

A Look at the Data

As of June 2016, there were 258 foreign campuses around the world originating from 33 home countries and located in 76 host countries. The list of home countries and the number of campuses their HEIs operate abroad are summarized in Table 11.1.[10] There are five countries with more than 10 foreign campuses which, together, have 72% of all foreign campuses around the world. These are the United States, which tops the

Table 11.1. Home Countries with the Highest Numbers of Foreign Campuses (June 2016)

Home country (countries whose higher education institutions have campuses abroad)	Number (and percentage) of campuses abroad	
1. United States	89 foreign campuses	34.5%
2. United Kingdom	45 foreign campuses	17.4%
3. Russia	22 foreign campuses	8.5%
4. France	15 foreign campuses	5.8%
5. Australia	14 foreign campuses	5.4%
6. India	9 foreign campuses	3.5%
7. The Netherlands	9 foreign campuses	3.5%
8. China	8 foreign campuses	3.1%
9. Canada	6 foreign campuses	2.3%
10. Germany	5 foreign campuses	1.9%
11. Ireland	4 foreign campuses	1.6%
12. Malaysia	4 foreign campuses	1.6%
13. Egypt — Italy — Lebanon — Singapore South Korea — Switzerland — Turkey	2 foreign campuses	5.4%
20. Bangladesh — Belgium — Chile — Estonia — Iran Japan — Mexico — Pakistan — Philippines Portugal — Spain — Sweden — Taiwan — Venezuela	1 foreign campus	5.4%
Total number of home countries: 33	Total number of campuses: 258	

Source: Cross-Border Education Research Team (C-BERT).

list with 89 campuses, followed by the United Kingdom (45), Russia (22), France (15) and Australia (14).

What do these countries have in common? They all have a long history of well-established, reputable HEIs and, with the exception of Australia, either a past colonial presence abroad or strong political and economic ties with many countries around the world. These historical and commercial relationships can explain why these countries' HEIs have opened campuses in these host countries.

Despite the high risk associated with the opening and running of a foreign campus, there have only been 27 closures since the first reported closure in 1999.[11] This is about 10% of the 258 active and pending foreign campuses in June 2016, which is not a particularly high closure rate over a 17-year period considering that the HEIs that closed their campuses were generally lesser known institutions that were exclusively focused on teaching. There are a relatively small number of top institutions that have shuttered their foreign campuses. We can cite the cases of the University of New South Wales in Singapore (2007), George Mason University in the United Arab Emirates (2009), Carnegie Mellon University in Greece (2010), University of Waterloo in the United Arab Emirates (2013), Boston University in Belgium (2014), and New York University Tisch School of the Arts in Singapore (2015).[12]

Turning to the examination of alternative models of multicampus HEIs, three broad models have been identified which we refer to as the branch model, the federal model, and the global model. Their defining features are summarized in Table 11.2.[13] Each model's characteristics are shaped by the specific mission (implicit or explicit) that the HEI has adopted. And that mission is, in turn, the outcome of how leaders of HEIs look at economic and technological development across countries and think about the process of knowledge origination and dissemination around the world.

The Branch Model

Consider first the view according to which the level and speed of change in economic and technological development differ widely across countries, with developing countries constantly catching up with the

Table 11.2. Alternative Models of Multi-Campus Higher Education Institutions

		The branch model Teach the world	The federal model Experience the world	The global model Learn from the world
Underlying view of the world	Economic and technological development	The *speed* and *level* of economic and technological development differs widely across countries	Economic and technological development differs across countries because of societal and cultural differences	There are different *models* of economic and technological development across countries
	Knowledge location and dissemination	Knowledge, which originates mostly in the home institution, is universal and should be taught around the world	Different organisations and processes exist abroad. Faculty and students should be exposed to them	Knowledge is dispersed around the world. It should be "harvested" and blended together to create new, higher-value knowledge
Campuses around the world	Configuration	Foreign branches or satellites controlled by the home institution	A federation of semi-autonomous local campuses	An integrated and interconnected network of complementary campuses
	Governance	Foreign branches/satellites managed by the home institution	Campuses are local entities managed locally with central oversight	One institution with distributed managerial responsibilities across the network
Curriculum	Programme	Same in all campuses	Different in each campus	Seamless across the network
	Language	Same in all campuses (usually English)	Usually the language of the local campuses	Same across the network (English)
	Degree	Same or different across campuses	Multiples degrees	Same degree

(Continued)

Table 11.2.   *(Continued)*

International mission		The branch model Teach the world	The federal model Experience the world	The global model Learn from the world
Students	**Profile**	Mostly local	Majority are local/regional	International
	Admission	To the branch campus based on same or similar standards	To a local campus with the option to study on the other campuses	To the network based on common admission process and standards
	Mobility	Structured visits to the home institution if required by the programme	Movement between the campuses dictated by the programme structure	Seamless movement within the network
Faculty	**Recruitment**	Transferred from the home campus or recruited by the institution to serve on the branch campus	Recruited by the local campus to serve on that campus	Recruited internationally based on the same criteria
	Affiliation	With the institution but contract could be with the branch campus	With the local campus	With the institution (irrespective of posting in the network)
	Mobility	Limited	Limited	Seamless within the network
	Evaluation	According to standards set by the institution (that could be different for faculty serving on a branch campus)	Could vary according to standards established by the local campuses	Identical for all faculty members irrespective of their location in the network

developed nations as advances in technology and economic processes trickle down from developed to developing countries. Knowledge in this case originates in research centres and HEIs located in developed countries and should be transmitted to developing countries by HEIs whose international mission is to *teach* the world the knowledge that these institutions have generated and acquired at home. It should be pointed out that this teaching mission is not imposed by foreign institutions on the developing countries; as shown later, host countries are eager to attract these institutions and help them open these campuses.

An international mission that calls for the transmission of knowledge from the home campus to foreign campuses located in the lesser developed regions of the world is best accomplished through a branch model. In this case, the foreign campuses are satellites fully controlled and managed by the home institution. Curricula and degrees are developed in the home campus and delivered in the branches to local students who usually apply for admission to the branch campus and are accepted to that campus according to criteria that take into account the local market conditions. In general, admission to the local campus does not allow students to switch permanently to the home campus but they can go there to attend some classes over a limited period of time. Upon graduation, students are conferred a degree that is awarded by the home institution. Faculty members teaching in the branch campus are either transferred from the home campus for a period of time or recruited locally with a local contract that does not allow them to move permanently to the home institution. The locally recruited faculty is usually trained in a recognised university located in a developed country, often the HEI's home country, and evaluated according to standards set by that campus that may differ from those used to evaluate the faculty on the home campus.

An example of the branch model is the one adopted by universities that were invited by the Qatar Foundation to set up campuses in Doha's Education City to deliver bachelor degree programmes to local students who are awarded the same degree as the one conferred on students on the home campus. These universities include Carnegie Mellon University which offers degrees in business and computer science, Georgetown University in foreign service, Northwestern University in communication and journalism, and Texas A & M University in engineering.[14]

The major drawback of this form of internationalisation is that it may not help the HEI to benefit from its presence abroad to deepen its internationalisation at home because activities on the branch campus are focused on the delivery of programmes to local students with little mobility between the two locations.

The Federal Model

An alternative view considers how economic and technological development differs across countries because of societal and cultural differences, not because of differences in the speed at which countries develop. In this case, countries with similar levels of economic and technological development may have developed different organisational processes and adopted different ways to use and implement advances in technology. Students and faculty should be exposed to them in order to increase their awareness of these differences and enrich their knowledge. In this context, the international mission of an HEI is to offer its students and faculty the opportunity to *experience* the world.

This international mission is best served by a federal model of multi-campus higher education institutions that consists of semi-autonomous campuses that are well integrated in their local economy and managed locally with some central oversight from the main campus. Curricula and programmes are developed by locally recruited faculty and may differ across campuses. The language of instruction may be the local one and not that of the country in which the main campus is located. The student body is composed of two distinct groups: one group of local students who remain on the local campus for the entire duration of the programme and another group composed of foreign students who rotate between the campuses that make up the federation. The students who do not rotate receive a local degree while rotating students receive a degree awarded by the main campus (and possibly a dual degree). Faculty members are affiliated with the local campus and evaluated according to standards established in these campuses. They would be encouraged to spend time on some of the other campuses to experience teaching and research in different environments.

A school that illustrates the federal model is ESCP, a French business school whose main campus is in Paris with additional campuses located in six European countries: London (United Kingdom), Berlin (Germany), Madrid (Spain), Turin (Italy) and Warsaw (Poland).[15] As an example, students pursuing a 2-year master in management degree can obtain up to four national degrees by studying in four of the six ESCP campuses.

The Global Model

Consider now the view according to which there are different *models* of economic and technological development across regions of the world, not just differences in the speed and level of development across countries (the branch model) or societal and cultural differences between countries that have adopted similar approaches to development (the federal model). In this case, original knowledge is generated throughout the world, that is, knowledge "nuggets" can be found in multiple locations around the globe. And these locally generated "nuggets" should be "mined" in their different locations and "moulded" together to create new, breakthrough ideas and innovations.[16] In this context, the international mission of a HEI is to *learn* from the world, not *teach* the world (the branch model) or just *experience* it (the federal model).

This international mission is best served by the global model of multicampus higher education institutions that consists of an integrated and interconnected network of complementary campuses operating in a symbiotic fashion to the mutual benefit of the entire system. The global network is managed as a single institution with distributed managerial responsibilities across the campuses that constitute the network. Modular programmes are delivered across the network's campuses with a global curriculum that is designed to take advantage of the specificities of each campus location and the knowledge that is created in those locations.

The institution awards the same degree across the network to students who are centrally admitted to the institution, not to a particular campus. The student body is international with no dominant nationality or culture prevailing on any campus, with students allowed to move freely across the network's locations.

Faculty members are recruited internationally and contractually employed by the institution, not by a particular campus. They are thus affiliated with the institution irrespective of their actual posting in the network and can move across campuses to fulfil their teaching responsibilities and do their research. They are evaluated and promoted according to institutional standards, not campus-specific criteria. An example of the global model is INSEAD, which is examined in more detail in the next section.

A Closer Look at the INSEAD Global Model

INSEAD was founded in 1957 as a private, non-profit European business school.[17] The school's European mission prevailed until the early nineties with over 80% of its student intake — and the majority of its faculty members — coming from European countries.[18] By the mid-nineties the institution's leadership decided to internationalise the school beyond Europe in response to the rise in global business activities and the growing interest of non-European faculty and students for the school's programmes and its open learning environment.[19] But how should the school transform itself from being European to becoming global? There were two broad answers to this question: bring the world to Fontainebleau — where the school's campus is located — or take the school out of Fontainebleau and into the world beyond Europe where the school would establish new campuses.[20] Those who gave some thought to this process quickly realised that these two options were *not* mutually exclusive; they were actually mutually reinforcing because taking INSEAD beyond Europe would raise its international visibility which would in turn attract non-European students and faculty to its campus in France. In other words, setting up campuses beyond Europe would not only internationalise the institution, it would also internationalise its home campus.

The next question was, "where should the school go first?" The answer was straightforward: Asia would be the destination because the school had built knowledge and expertise on this part of the world thanks to its Euro-Asia Centre that had been established in the early eighties. This Centre acted as a bridge between Europe and Asia: it delivered executive education programmes to European companies active in Asia as well as Asian companies seeking to develop their managerial talent and expand abroad.

Four countries were identified as potential locations for an INSEAD campus: Hong Kong, Japan, Malaysia and Singapore. After a visit to each location and a comparative analysis of their respective merits, Singapore was chosen primarily because of its vision to develop an international educational hub open to students and faculty from around the world. This vision was perfectly aligned with INSEAD's internationalisation strategy to build a global knowledge and learning network as opposed to going abroad to educate the local student population. Other reasons that led the school to opt for Singapore were a favourable economic environment and affordable and attractive living conditions for expatriates and their families.[21]

Going to Singapore

Despite the strategically appealing logic of opening a campus in Singapore, the school leadership had to overcome a number of objections raised by some faculty members, students, alumni, board members and administrators. These objections are summarized in Table 11.3 with the counterarguments in favour of the move. The overriding concerns across all stakeholders were the potential damage to the school's reputation, a move away from its original European mission and a dilution of its historical roots in Fontainebleau. Would the school have to lower its standards to attract new students? Would the students be able to maintain a thriving learning and social environment if they have to commute between two distant campuses? Would the alumni network lose its cohesiveness as the number of graduates rises and spreads out around the world? Would a two-campus school located on two continents be too complex to manage? And could the school afford the investment and bear the associated risks? The counterarguments to these concerns, shown in the last column of Table 11.3, helped alleviate these legitimate concerns. But one of the most difficult to overcome was voiced by many faculty members, including some who favoured the project. They feared that the dual-campus structure would fragment the faculty between two distant locations and thus reduce the potential for exchanging ideas and cut the time that the faculty allocate to research (because of the need to shuttle between two campuses to teach), all of which would eventually lower the school's average research productivity. But this legitimate concern faded away over time as the number of faculty members on the Singapore

Table 11.3. Drawbacks and Advantages of INSEAD Campus in Singapore

	Potential drawback	Potential advantage
Reputation	A campus in Singapore will dilute the school's reputation (the implicit assumption is that the school may have to lower its standards to attract new students)	A campus in Singapore would enhance the school's visibility in Asia and thus strengthen its attractiveness and enhance its reputation
Faculty	The school may not be able to recruit faculty members who would want to settle permanently in Singapore; and even if it did, a second campus with permanent faculty will split the faculty and thus reduce the interaction among faculty members and decrease joint research activities and output	A campus in Singapore will enhance the school's ability to recruit Asian faculty (particularly Chinese and Southeast Asians whom the school has not been able to attract to its campus in Europe) and thus increase faculty diversity and enhance the potential for Asia-based research
Students	A campus in Singapore means more students and thus (1) lower admission standards and (2) the inability of students to get to know everyone on the programme, a phenomenon that will be aggravated by the constant movements of students between the two campuses	A campus in Singapore would allow the school to attract students who would have not considered applying to its programme in France thus increase the programme's size without lowering admission standards; these new students will increase diversity and enrich the programme
Alumni	The roots and soul of the school are in its original campus; opening a new one in another continent will destroy what makes the school unique and disengage its alumni	A campus in Singapore will increase the number and nationality of alumni and widen the geographical diversity of the school's network to the benefit of alumni
The Board	A campus in Singapore would make the school less European in contradiction to its founding mission to develop European managers and leaders	Since the school's founding in 1957 the world has become more global and more connected and thus the school should broaden its mission to encompass the world
Administration	A campus in Singapore will increase organisational complexity and intercultural misunderstanding and thus make the school less efficient and less manageable	The dual-campus structure will certainly be more complex to manage but it could also be an opportunity to improve efficiency on the campus in Europe and learn from intercultural exchange
Placement	The school does not have the relationships with Asia-based companies that are required to attract companies on its campus in Singapore to recruit its graduates	Many companies that recruit on the school's campus in Europe are also present in Asia and given the importance of Asia for business, their number should rise over time
Financials	The campus in Singapore will require a large investment that will significantly increase the school's financial and operating risks and thus threaten its long-term survival	A campus in Singapore would diversify the school geographically and thus reduce its risk exposure and protect its revenue stream from excessive volatility

campus rose and the interaction between faculty members across the two campuses turned out to be easier to maintain than expected. This was due to video-conferencing, the funding of visits to the other campus for the purpose of doing research, and the presence of doctoral students on the Singapore campus.

Why Has It Worked?

Despite the initial concerns and apprehensions, the new campus was inaugurated in October 2000 and quickly turned out to be an appealing destination to students and faculty alike. Their numbers, as well as revenues, climbed fast to reach half the figures for the campus in France after five years of operations.

In retrospect, to what factors could this successful outcome be attributed? We have identified at least ten factors that helped INSEAD achieve its objective. They should all be relevant to other HEIs wishing to open a campus abroad.

1. ***The institution's internationalisation strategy was aligned with its mission and built on the principle of "One School, Two Campuses".*** Even though the school was born with a mission to serve Europe, its underlying approach to management has always been that learning is best achieved when people of diverse backgrounds come together to study and exchange ideas in an open, non-dogmatic environment. As European companies expanded their business activities beyond Europe in the nineties, it was natural for INSEAD to broaden its mission from serving Europe to serving the world. The school began to offer executive education programmes in Asia in rented facilities. Opening a campus in Singapore where the school could also offer its MBA programme was a natural next step. The challenge was to adopt an internationalisation model that would preserve the unity of the institution and its programmes. The campus in Asia would operate seamlessly with the one in Europe, with faculty allowed unrestricted movements between the two locations and subject to the same evaluation and promotion standards irrespective of location, and students allowed to pursue their

programme seamlessly across the two campuses. This model of internationalisation was well captured by the motto "One School, Two Campuses" which the entire INSEAD community adhered to from the beginning.[22]

2. ***The institution's leadership team and the chairman of its governing board were fully committed to the school's internationalisation strategy.*** Academic institutions are known for their conservatism and their reluctance to adopt untested strategies that will take them into uncharted waters. They need a strong leadership with a clear vision to move them out of their comfort zone, particularly when the *status quo* is considered successful with no crises lurking in the horizon. INSEAD's leadership team in the mid-nineties believed that a physical presence in Asia would place the institution in a less assailable position than remaining focused on Europe with a single campus located in France. Fortunately, the chairman of the board at that time agreed with this vision and was ready to rally some of the board members who were hesitant.

3. ***There were a number of respected senior faculty members who acted as the project's champions.*** Strong leadership is a necessary but not sufficient condition to take an academic institution out of its comfort zone and into new territories. Without the full support of some members of the faculty who are opinion leaders, the process could stall and eventually die away. A key ingredient to a forward move is the presence of a group of respected senior faculty members who believe in the project and are ready to act as the project's champions. In the case of INSEAD, this condition was met when early on some key faculty members voiced their support and invested time to convince their colleagues who opposed the decision to open a campus in Singapore.

4. ***Some faculty members had developed an academic expertise on Asia.*** As pointed out earlier, a move to Asia was not an arbitrary jump into the unknown for INSEAD because, in the mid-eighties, the institution had established a centre to develop some expertise on Asia and deliver executive education programmes there. This meant that there were a group of dedicated faculty members and staff who were familiar with Asia in general and Singapore in particular and who could play a key role in the process of opening a campus in that city-state.

5. *There was among the senior faculty and staff a group of committed pioneers ready to move to Singapore.* Having project champions and Asia-experts on the faculty and staff was essential but there should also be among them a number of individuals who were ready to physically move to Singapore to get the project off the ground at least until the campus was up and running. Most of the faculty and staff associated with the Euro-Asia Centre moved to Singapore to get things going as soon as the decision was taken to go there. They were accompanied by faculty and staff who were not associated with the Centre, an important signal to the broad community that the campus in Singapore was an INSEAD project, not a Euro-Asia Centre one.

6. *Once the decision to go ahead was made, activities were rapidly ramped up.* It was also important to move as fast as possible to achieve scale on the new campus in terms of faculty and student numbers in order to avoid the temptation to delay the project. It would have been easier to postpone additional investments, and even abandon the project, if the resources already committed there were minimal. Another reason to reach scale quickly was to make sure that the contribution of the campus in Singapore to the institution's overall activities represented a significant percentage of the school's total budget to avoid positioning the new campus as a junior partner dominated by the campus in Europe. Also, more students in Singapore meant that the new campus would break even faster and quickly become economically self-sufficient.

7. *Financial support from the host country was not the primary reason to establish a campus abroad.* A somewhat less obvious factor that contributed to the success of the project was that the institution had to commit a significant amount of its own funds to launch the project and sustain it during its early phase of development. Funding a project with the institution's own resources was a powerful incentive to remain focused on achieving the plan to quickly reach financial self-sustainability.

8. *The institution's objective was fully aligned with the host country's objective.* One key factor for success was the alignment of the institution's objective with that of the host country. As pointed out earlier, the host wanted to attract foreign HEIs to Singapore to turn the

city-state into an international educational hub and develop a rich academic community. This objective was perfectly aligned with INSEAD's vision of setting up an international campus populated with students and research faculty from around the world as opposed to delivering a programme to local students using a large number of commuting faculty members.

9. ***Some of the school's best teachers were assigned to teach on the new campus***. It was important to send a strong signal to students that some of the institution's best teachers would be directly involved in the courses delivered on the campus in Singapore in order to immediately dispel any thoughts that the faculty on the new campus would not be as strong as the one in Fontainebleau.

10. ***A strong signal was sent to the faculty that research on the new campus was as important to the institution as research on the campus in Europe***. It was made clear to the faculty that the criteria for performance evaluation and promotion were the same irrespective of where faculty members were located. A presence on the campus in Singapore would not provide the faculty with bonus points for promotion based on the pretext that they took the risk to move there when the new campus was being developed. Again, the "One School, Two Campuses" motto had to prevail.

Host-Country Models

In this section we discuss the countries that have successfully attracted foreign HEIs into their territories. Which are these host countries and why did they want to attract foreign HEIs?

A Look at the Host Countries

The data on the number of host countries around the world and the number of foreign HEIs in each of these countries is summarized in Table 11.4.[23] As of June 2016, there were 76 countries hosting a total of 258 foreign campuses. The host country with the highest number of foreign campuses is China with 36 campuses representing close to 14% of the total, followed closely by the United Arab Emirates (34 campuses).

Table 11.4. Host Countries with the Highest Numbers of Foreign Campuses (June 2016)

Host country (countries in which foreign campuses are located)	Number and percent of foreign campuses in the host country		Country with most foreign campuses
1. China[1]	36 foreign campuses	14.0%	U.S. (14)
2. United Arab Emirates (UAE)[2]	34 foreign campuses	13.2%	U.K. (8)
3. Malaysia	12 foreign campuses	4.7%	U.K. (9)
4. Singapore	12 foreign campuses	4.7%	U.S. (5)
5. Qatar	11 foreign campuses	4.3%	U.S. (7)
6. South Korea	8 foreign campuses	3.1%	U.S. (5)
United States	8 foreign campuses	3.1%	U.K. (3)
8. France	6 foreign campuses	2.3%	U.S. (4)
United Kingdom	6 foreign campuses	2.3%	U.S. (3)
Uzbekistan	6 foreign campuses	2.3%	Russia (3)
11. Armenia	5 foreign campuses	1.9%	Russia (5)
Germany	5 foreign campuses	1.9%	U.S. (2)
Italy	5 foreign campuses	1.9%	U.S. (3)
South Africa	5 foreign campuses	1.9%	Netherlands (2)
15. Greece	4 foreign campuses	1.6%	U.S. (4)
Kazakhstan	4 foreign campuses	1.6%	Russia (4)
Spain	4 foreign campuses	1.6%	U.S. (3)
18. Australia — Canada — Japan Mauritius — Pakistan — Panama — Thailand	3 foreign campuses in each of 7 countries	8.1%	U.S. (8) in 5 countries
25. Bahrain — Belarus — Ecuador — Ghana Indonesia — Israel — Kuwait Kyrgyzstan — Mexico — Russia St Lucia — Switzerland — Tunisia — Turkey	2 foreign campuses in each of 14 countries	10.9%	U.S. (12) in 8 countries
39. 38 host countries	1 foreign campus in each of 38 countries	14.7%	U.S. (12) in 12 countries
Total number of host countries: 76	Total number of foreign campuses: 258[3]		

Notes:

[1]Includes 4 campuses in Hong Kong.

[2]Includes 25 campuses in Dubai, 6 campuses in Abu Dhabi, and 3 campuses in Ras Khaimah.

[3]Includes 25 campuses in the process of being established in 2016.

Source: Cross-Border Education Research Team (C-BERT).

Three additional countries host more than 10 foreign campuses: Singapore (12 campuses), Malaysia (12 campuses) and Qatar (11 campuses). In general, the world's regions with the highest numbers of foreign campuses are East Asia and the Gulf countries in the Middle East.

We have seen in Table 11.1 that the countries that have established the highest number of campuses abroad are the United States (89 campuses), the United Kingdom (45 campuses) and Russia (22 campuses). As indicated in the last column of Table 11.4, the United States is not only the country with the highest number of foreign campuses; it is also the country with the *widest* and *deepest* foreign presence: its HEIs have the highest number of foreign campuses in 35 out of 76 host countries (46% of the total). The next two home countries with the highest number of foreign campuses in a given host country are the United Kingdom (11 cases) and Russia (7 cases). As pointed out earlier, these two countries have a historical and political relationship with the host countries in which their HEIs have established their campuses (United Arab Emirates, Malaysia, the United States, Mauritius and Pakistan in the case of the United Kingdom, and Uzbekistan, Armenia, Kazakhstan, Belarus, Kyrgyzstan, Tajikistan and Azerbaijan in the case of Russia).

Alternative Host-Country Models

We have identified four alternative host-country models based on the primary motive that is driving the host country to invite foreign HEIs to set up campuses in its territory. They are the educational model (to educate the local high-school graduates), the academic model (to develop a richer local academic community), the business model (to serve the local international business community) and the international model (to position the country as an attractive educational and cultural destination). Their defining features are summarised in Table 11.5 and examined below.[24]

There is, however, an overriding motive for all host countries to attract top universities: the presence of these institutions is a major contributor to the economic development and growth of the area in which they are located. There are no great and prosperous cities without great universities. A recent study that looked at the locations of nearly 15,000 universities in about 1,500 regions across 78 countries concluded that

Table 11.5. Alternative Host-Country Models

	Educational model	Academic model	Business model	Internationalisation model
Primary host-country motive	Educate local high-school graduates	Develop a rich local academic community	Serve the expatriate business community located in the country	Position the country as an attractive educational and cultural destination
Typical host-country	Qatar	Singapore	Dubai	Abu Dhabi
Majority of students	Local nationals	International students	Local expatriates	International students and local nationals
Number of foreign campuses	11	12	25	6
Country of origin of foreign institutions	Canada — France, The Netherlands, United Kingdom, United States	Australia — China — France, India — United Kingdom, United States	Australia — France — India, Iran — Ireland — Lebanon, Pakistan — Russia	Egypt, France, United States
Name of some foreign institutions	Carnegie Mellon University, Cornell University, Georgetown University, Northwestern University, Texas A&M University	Culinary Institute of America, Curtin University, ESSEC Business School, INSEAD, Manchester Business School	CASS Business School, Heriot-Watt University, London Business School, Michigan State University, University of Exeter	INSEAD, La Sorbonne (France), New York University, Al Azhar University (Egypt)
Degree of host-country support	High	Moderate	Moderate	High
Major challenge for the host country	Attracting qualified local nationals and providing them with attractive employment opportunities upon graduation	Integrating the foreign institutions into the local academic community	Attracting qualified guest institutions and monitoring the quality of their educational offerings	Ascertaining that foreign institutions will enhance the country's position as an attractive educational and cultural destination

"doubling the number of universities per capita is associated with 4 percent higher *future* gross domestic product per capita". And the source of that growth "is not simply driven by the direct expenditures of the university, its staff and students" but also by "an increased supply of human capital and greater innovation".[25]

The Educational Model

In this case, the host country has a clear objective: it wants to provide high-quality tertiary education to its local high-school graduates. Raising the quality and reputation of local universities takes time and would be more difficult to achieve than attracting top universities into the country. Sending local students to study abroad has its own challenges: some students may not want to go abroad to study. As pointed out earlier, this might be the case of female students from some Middle East countries. Furthermore, those who do go abroad may decide to remain in the host country if more attractive employment opportunities are available there.

The educational model is best exemplified by the case of Qatar discussed earlier. The country has been successful in attracting some of the world's top universities to establish a campus in Doha's Educational City by providing financial support, outstanding facilities and full control over the admission process and the programmes offered, with the condition that the guest university awards the same degree as its home campus. A major challenge for the guest universities and their hosts is to enroll enough qualified local students and help them find attractive local employment opportunities upon graduation.

The Academic Model

According to this model, the host country's objective is to create a richer and more diverse local academic community, attract foreign HEIs that deliver degrees in fields where the local HEIs are absent, and position the country as an attractive international educational hub.

Singapore is a good example of this model.[26] Its two oldest universities, the National University of Singapore and Nanyang Technological University, are among the best in the world. In 2000, the city-state established in cooperation with US universities (the Wharton School of the University of Pennsylvania and Northwestern University) the Singapore Management University (SMU), an HEI that specializes in management, law and political studies. But the establishment of SMU did not stop Singapore from inviting five management schools to set up campuses in its territory (INSEAD, ESSEC, Manchester Business School, Baruch College of the City University of New York and the SP Jain School of Global Management). Other foreign institutions have been invited to open a campus in Singapore to deliver degrees in fields where local institutions are absent such as video-game development and digital-interactive media (New York University Tisch School of the Arts.[27] and the DigiPen Institute of Technology) and hospitality and tourism (University of Nevada Las Vegas College of Hotel Administration and The Culinary Institute of America).

A major challenge for the host country is to integrate these guest institutions into the local academic community and create bridges between them and local institutions.

The Business Model

The primary motive, in this case, is a desire on the part of the host country to serve the international business community that has settled in its territory. This situation would occur in a country with a large international business community whose employees and children need access to quality higher education delivered in English by reputable HEIs.

Dubai, a member of the United Arab Emirates, is a good example of this host-country model. It has the second largest number of foreign campuses in the world, representing 10% of all foreign campuses worldwide.[28] The challenges for the host country is to regulate this multitude of HEIs, maintain quality standards across institutions, avoid unhealthy competition between them, and coordinate their activities in order to create a coherent educational environment.[29]

The Internationalisation Model

The final host-country model is referred to as the internationalisation model because the primary motive for the host is to position the country as an attractive educational and cultural destination. Abu Dhabi, another member of the United Arab Emirates, exemplifies this model. It has attracted three top HEIs to its territory (New York University, Paris-Sorbonne University and INSEAD) in which a significant number of students are international rather than local. And in addition to HEIs, it has attracted top cultural institutions such as Le Louvre and the Guggenheim museums.[30]

Concluding Remarks

This exploration of the internationalization of HEIs through foreign campuses concludes by raising the question of whether the growing phenomenon of online education may eventually render the foreign-campus model obsolete. After all, an HEI can offer its programmes online to any qualified student located anywhere in the world at a presumably lower cost per student than that associated with the opening of physical campuses.[31]

It is often pointed out that one advantage of a physical campus is that students from around the world could gather at the same location to study together and work in groups to exchange ideas and learn from each other's cultural background. But one could argue that an online group assignment, during which a small number of students could interact with one another to solve a problem while remaining in their respective countries, can provide more learning and cultural insights than if they were working together in the same physical classroom. This is the case because, in a virtual classroom, the students are in their respective countries and are thus unaffected by the norms and cautiousness of a face-to-face group and not influenced by the cultural environment of the country in which the physical classroom is located.[32]

In any case, it is doubtful that the virtual international classroom will completely replace the physical one because some students will always want to study on a physical campus with students from other countries. The most likely scenario, which most experts predict, is that the two forms will coexist either in combination in the same programme (the so-called hybrid model in which some classes or courses are delivered online and others are delivered in the classroom) or in their exclusive forms in which they will each serve different segments of the higher education sector.

Notes

1. See AACSB (2011), De Meyer et al. (2004), Hawawini (2016), Spring (2009), Stearns (2008) and Wildavsky (2010).
2. See ACE (2009).
3. See Knight (2003).
4. See Hawawini (2016) for a critical review of alternative definitions of the process of internationalization by HEIs.
5. Academic joint ventures include student and faculty exchange programmes as well as joint-degree or dual-degree programmes. See Hawawini (2016) for a more extensive list of internationalisation initiatives.
6. See Hawawini (2016) and Stier (2004).
7. We show later that most foreign campuses are established in developing countries by HEIs located in developed countries (see Table 11.1 and Table 11.4).
8. This is a rephrased statement of a definition given by the Cross-Border Education Research Team (C-BERT) to an entity it refers to as "an international branch campus". See C-BERT (2016). Note that in this chapter we do not use the label "branch campus" to refer generically to a foreign campus. We use it instead to refer to a specific model of a multicampus HEI as shown later in this section.
9. Another example of an institution with facilities abroad that is not reported in the C-BERT (2016) list of HEIs that operate foreign campuses is the French business school Skema <http://www.skema.edu/skema/campuses>. It has facilities in Brazil, China and the United States but is not listed because the foreign students who study in these locations do not complete an entire programme on these premises and Skema does not offer its own degrees to local students.
10. The data is compiled by the Cross-Border Education Research Team (C-BERT) and updated regularly through the year. See C-BERT (2016) and <http://globalhighered.org/branchcampuses.php> where the latest data can be found (downloaded by the author in June 2016). Note that the 258 campuses include 25 campuses that are in the process of being established.
11. The earliest closure reported in the data set (see previous footnote) is the Royal Melbourne Institute of Technology that closed its campus in Malaysia in 1999.
12. Note that 5 out of the 6 cases occurred after the financial crisis of 2008 and the ensuing recession.

13. Table 11.2 is adapted from Hawawini (2016).
14. See <https://en.wikipedia.org/wiki/Education_City>.
15. See <www.escpeurope.eu>.
16. See Doz, Santos and Williamson (2001).
17. INSEAD is an acronym based on the school's French full name known as Institut Européen d'Administration des Affaires, which means European Institute for Business Administration.
18. Initially, the percentage of French students was high but this ratio dropped over the following 40-year period as the relative intake of European students from countries other than France went up making the school less "French" and more "European" over the years.
19. A key element in this growing interest was the school's increasing visibility and reputation bolstered by high rankings and favourable reviews in the international press. See Barsoux (2000).
20. Fontainebleau is a small city of about 15,000 inhabitants located in a forest 40 miles south of Paris.
21. Other considerations include the following: Singapore set-up costs were the lowest and its administrative processes the least restrictive; the school was provided with a desirable location in a science and educational park in which to build its campus; and there was a relatively large and growing international community, good international schools for children and the possibility of employment for the spouses of faculty and staff. See INSEAD case studies (2003) and (2008).
22. To emphasize the fact that the student population on the campus located in Singapore would have a similar international make-up as the one on the campus in France (as opposed to being a campus for Asian students), the campus was called INSEAD Asia campus (as oppose to "Asian campus"). And the original campus was renamed the INSEAD Europe campus (as opposed to the "European campus").
23. The source of the data is from the Cross-Border Education Research Team (C-BERT). It is available online at <http://globalhighered.org/branchcampuses.php>.
24. We could have added a fifth model, which we identified in the previous section, where the host-country is historically and politically tied to the home country but one could argue that in this case the host country is constrained in its choice of foreign HEIs it can attract on its territory.

25. See Valero and Van Reenen (2016).
26. See Olds (2007).
27. New York University Tisch School of the Arts opened in 2007 but closed in 2015.
28. See note 2 in Table 11.4.
29. Note that more than a quarter of all campuses that closed (7 out of 26) during the period 1999 to 2016 were located in Dubai, a statistic that reflects both the ease of entry into the UAE educational market and its highly competitive environment with respect to attracting students.
30. See <https://en.wikipedia.org/wiki/Cultural_policy_in_Abu_Dhabi>.
31. See for example the case of the University of the People, an online, non-profit, tuition-free, degree-granting higher education institution that had, at the time of this writing, over 5,000 students in 200 countries and growing fast. See <www.uopeople.edu>.
32. See Hawawini (2016) who argues that international students in a physical classroom tend to assimilate with the dominant culture of the host country.

References

AACSB (2011). *The Globalization of Management Education*. Bingley, UK: Emerald Group Publishing Limited.

ACE (2009). *U.S. Branch Campuses Abroad*. American Council on Education.

Barsoux, Jean-Louis (2000). *INSEAD: From Intuition to Institution*. Macmillan Press.

Cross-Border Education Research Team (13 June 2016) C-BERT Branch Campus Listing. <http://globalhighered.org/branchcampuses.php> Albany, NY: Kevin Kinser and Jason E. Lane.

De Meyer, Arnoud, Patrick Harker, and Gabriel Hawawini (2004). "The globalization of business education in Gatignon H". In J. Kimberly, ed., *The INSEAD-Wharton Alliance on Globalizing*. Cambridge University Press.

Doz, Yves, Joe Santos, and Peter Williamson (2001). *From Global to Metanational*. Harvard University Press.

Hawawini, Gabriel (2016). *The Internationalization of Higher Education and Business Schools: A Critical Review*. SpringerBriefs in Business.

"INSEAD: One School, Two Campuses: Going to Asia" (2003). Case study.

INSEAD (2008). Harvard Business School Case Study 9-308-009.

Knight, Jane (2003). "Updated internationalization definition". *International Higher Education*, 33, pp. 2–3.

Kwok, Chuck and Jeffrey Arpan (2002). "Internationalizing the business school: A global survey in 2000". *Journal of International Business Studies* 33, no. 3, pp. 571–581.

Olds, Kris (2007). "Global assemblage: Singapore, foreign universities, and the construction of a global education hub". *World Development* 35, no. 6, pp. 959–975.

Spring, Joel (2009). *Globalization of Education*. New York, NY: Routledge.

Stearns, Peter (2008). *Educating Global Citizens in Colleges and Universities: Challenges and Opportunities*. New York, NY: Routledge.

Stier, Jonas (2004). "Taking a critical stance toward internationalization ideologies in higher education: idealism, instrumentalism and educationalism". *Globalisation, Society and Education* 2, no. 1, pp. 83–97.

Valero, Anna and John Van Reenen (2016). "The Economic Impact of Universities: Evidence from Across the Globe". National Bureau of Economic Research, Working Paper 22501 (August).

Wildavsky, Ben (2010). *The Great Brain Race: How Global University are Reshaping the World*. Princeton University Press.

About the Author

Gabriel Hawawini is Emeritus Professor and former Dean, INSEAD.

CHAPTER TWELVE

A SINGAPORE UNIVERSITY CATERING TO THE NEEDS OF A POPULATION AMIDST A VOLATILE AND CHANGING ECONOMY

CHEONG HEE KIAT

Introduction

On 14 April 2005, a new university was established in the island republic of Singapore. It was not the usual university that the Government of Singapore sets up to provide for the university education needs of the population. The new university, called SIM University (or UniSIM in short), was different from all the other publicly-funded ones (called Autonomous Universities or AUs) at that time in several key aspects. It was a private not-for-profit university, not receiving any state funding, and it catered to the learning and qualification needs of the adult population. It had a policy of admission that was much more inclusive than the other AUs, allowing in many more who did not manage to go to university before starting work, but graduating only those who could meet its standards that closely mirrored those of the existing AUs. It was, in essence, Singapore's first university dedicated to continuing education.

It was the first time ever that post-independent Singapore allowed the establishment of a private university that focused on education for working adults and adult learners. And, it proved to be popular with learners as it expanded its repertoire of applied programmes and its collaboration with industry and the public sector. Fortuitously, it functioned in a period when a growing emphasis was placed in the country on applied learning and on continuing education to meet the rapidly changing needs of employment. In 2017, UniSIM was re-structured as a publicly-funded university (i.e., an AU) and re-named as the Singapore University of Social Sciences (SUSS), bringing it into the national university system that, up to then, was made up of five AUs.

This is the story of a university which is geared to meet continuing learning needs in a rapidly-changing socio-economic and demographic landscape of Singapore, and its transition from a private to a publicly-funded university. While effort is made to trace the evolution of the university, there is inevitably a referencing to what was there before and what is there today, sometimes mixing of the two; also, while UniSIM was the name used in the first twelve years, the new and long-term name of the university is SUSS — thus, SUSS will be used, where appropriate, in this paper to represent both UniSIM, the old, and SUSS, the new.

Genesis

UniSIM had its roots in the OUUK (Open University of the United Kingdom) programme that was run for about 12 years from 1992 by the Singapore Institute of Management (SIM). Back then, SIM was already running degree programmes of its overseas partner universities mainly for those who wanted to continue studying after high school or polytechnic but could not get a place in the state universities. One of its partner universities was the OUUK, which was invited to offer its programmes under the Open University Development Programme (OUDP). The OUDP was different from other partner university programmes as it was set up under the auspices of Singapore's Ministry of Education (MOE). There was a desire for a degree pathway for MOE's many teachers who did not have a degree and SIM was picked to provide this pathway through the OUDP. The OUDP offered programmes in only a limited number of areas suitable to equip teachers in their areas of teaching in the schools, such as English Language & Literature, Mathematics and Information and Communications Technology (ICT).

Eventually, OUUK granted SIM the status of an Open University Centre (OUC) which came with a good degree of academic autonomy. With this in hand and a successful run of 12 years, SIM asked the MOE for a licence to start its own university. This privilege is held very tightly by MOE, so it was quite to the surprise of many when MOE agreed that a university be started by SIM, though only the OUC was to be recognised and used as the foundational block for the new university. Also, the new university was to continue running on a privately-funded mode and offer only part-time programmes for working adults and adult learners. On hindsight, this was a bold move by MOE, but more importantly, it signalled a shift from long-held policies and underscored the importance of providing degree programmes through part-time studies. It also heralded a diversification and enrichment of the local university system, and a recognition that there is merit in having people go back to school only after gaining work experience and a maturity that would enhance their learning. Non-degree holders in the teaching profession were no longer the main target; many more could find opportunities to upgrade their skills and knowledge at tertiary level.

Vision, Mission and Core Values

So, UniSIM came into being, a not-for-profit, private university and registered as a charity. In the same year, MOE granted to UniSIM the status of an Institution of a Public Character for one of its funds, which afforded donors to that fund additional and generous tax exemptions. From its inception, UniSIM saw itself as a provider of education and training to adults who have missed out on the opportunity for a university education. All applicants who satisfied a minimum set of criteria were admitted — these were less onerous than those required by the other AUs but deemed sufficient academic preparation for the rigour of university studies imposed by UniSIM.

In pursuit of this objective, UniSIM adopted the following Vision and Mission statements and core values:

Vision: Serving society through excellence in flexible learning for adults.
Mission: To provide opportunities for professionals and adult learners to upgrade their qualifications, knowledge and skills through a wide range of relevant programmes.
Core Values (SPIRIT): **S**pirit of learning, **P**assion for excellence, **I**ntegrity, **R**espect and trust for the individual, **I**nnovation, **T**eamwork

These were crafted and adopted when UniSIM was first formed, and have remained largely unchanged even after its new AU status.

Growth

At its inauguration, UniSIM inherited the 4800 or so students who were still in the OUDP programmes. The university had a grand total of ten incumbent faculty members supported by several hundreds Associate Faculty members who taught classes in the evenings while functioning in their regular jobs. Counting the President, who came over from the Nanyang Technological University and the Provost, who joined from the Singapore Management University, the faculty strength was twelve!

One of the first actions taken was when the incumbent OUUK students enquired if they could be awarded a UniSIM degree also. A choice was then given: choose between graduating with an OUUK or a UniSIM degree after completing their OUUK programme which UniSIM would continue running, even though it would not admit any more students for an OUUK degree. A surprising 89% chose eventually to receive the UniSIM degree! Yet, it should not have been that surprising — Singaporeans are pragmatic. Our students took the long view and saw their future in a qualification and an institution that has a Singapore brand and an MOE endorsement. It was an early success for the university.

In the years following, UniSIM experienced dramatic growth in its enrolment (Figure 12.1). There were several reasons for this: (a) though

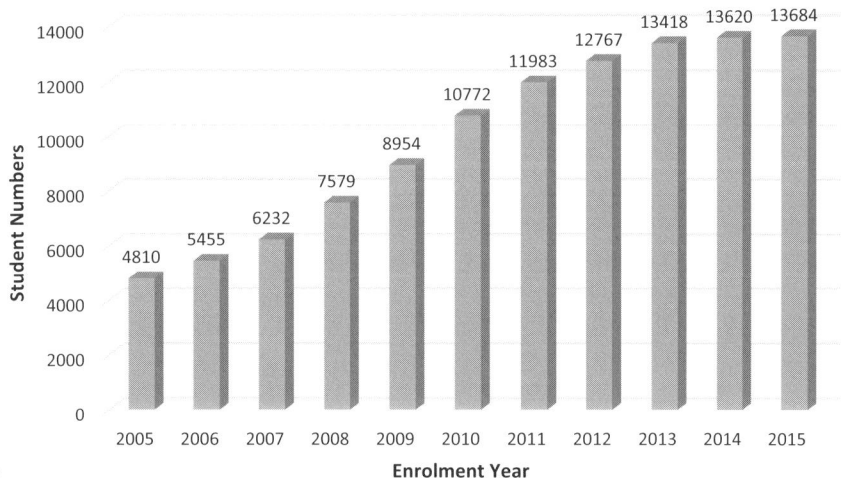

Fig. 12.1   UniSIM student enrolment 2005–2015.

private, UniSIM was government-endorsed, (b) a local degree was offered, (c) UniSIM introduced many more programmes in other fields which catered to a wider section of the working adults, (d) other measures were taken to widen access, such as introducing two admissions per year instead of one and offering programmes in courses (or modules) to enhance flexibility for students, (e) it was less expensive than pursuing studies overseas and less disruptive in terms of continuity of employment and personal life, and (f) the Singapore Government decided to subsidise tuition fees of students coming to UniSIM, which made (e) even more so.

The latter was a very significant development in Singapore's university education. Hitherto, state funding was given only for full-time studies at the AUs, targeted at fresh school-leavers and diploma graduates from the local polytechnics. In 2008, the government announced a tuition fee subsidy of 40% for students taking part-time programmes at UniSIM and other AUs. Then, in 2011, this was increased to 55%. With this move, UniSIM still did not receive any funding from MOE, but the greater affordability for university studies encouraged and enabled many more to study at UniSIM. Importantly, the move signalled (or at least was perceived as) a shift in government thinking about the place part-time studies have in continuing education and the skills upgrading needed by the future workforce. And, indeed, UniSIM found that as it explored and collaborated with industry, there was a great need to improve employee skills and give those who can the chance to obtain a degree.

Philosophy

The OUDP was set up primarily to uplift the qualifications of school teachers who had entered the profession without a basic degree, and who had gained experience as career teachers. As more teachers were brought into the system who were university graduates, there was a felt need for, as well as a recognition that, these non-graduate teachers should be given the chance to upgrade to enhance their standing, knowledge, and progression in the teaching profession. However, there were many others in the workforce with the same desire, and UniSIM threw open the doors to these who wanted the upgrading. Up till then, a local university education was available mostly to those who went straight to university after finishing high school or polytechnic. Even then, the number of seats available in the public universities was limited, and aspiring students had to compete for a seat, with academic ability being the main criterion for selection. And, even then, a student might not be admitted into a desired programme discipline, such was the disparity in demand for certain disciplines and the supply of places.

With UniSIM, it was altogether different. There was choice as the university ventured to open places in the many disciplines where upgrading was needed in the market, and as many places as there were qualified applicants. So, each applicant applied only for one programme and most got admitted into the programme chosen — "most" because for some disciplines, like early childhood education, social work, and counselling, there were other considerations for selection related to the sensitivity of these professions. Giving our students the choice of programme is an important and enabling feature of the UniSIM philosophy — the students come with a work experience, know what they are suited for or passionate about, have determined a trajectory for their careers, and getting their choice of studies is a strong motivating force in pursuing and completing their studies. What is worse than being assigned to a programme of last resort or that has little connection with personal affinity for the discipline?

But, choice is just one facet of the university's philosophy. The educational and operating philosophies of the university were developed over a period of time. The undergirding principles were choice for the students, an applied education, an open system of admission that gives pathways and opportunities not locally available at the time, good quality and rigour in standards, standards expected of a Singapore university, flexibility in the way our students can do their learning, promotion of continuing learning. What enables then is high modularity of our programmes, a unified IT-enabled administrative and student support system, strong learning support, faculty aligned to our type of provisions, speed to market, strong links with industry. These basic tenets are encapsulated in Table 12.1. All of these enable the university to have inclusivity as its essence (Figure 12.2).

Two distinct groups of people were served by UniSIM: the aspiring learners (the working adults) who see their educational goals as a means to fulfil their career goals; and the other adult learners who are seeking quality-of-life enhancement in knowledge and skills. The first group has been predominant, but the goal is, in line with the vision to serve society

Table 12.1.   Basic Tenets (SIM University, 2011)

The basic tenets in the pursuit of this philosophy are:
a. Multiple pathways to learning and qualification catering to learners with a diversity of educational qualifications and work experience. Multiple points of entry and exit, without sacrificing academic rigour and degree award standards;
b. Modular structure of programmes, with individual component courses carrying credit units (cu) of various sizes that can be accumulated or stacked towards a degree qualification over a maximum period of eight years;
c. Flexible, multi-modal learning environment — learn at one's own pace, place and time, using three main modes: comprehensive study materials, enhanced online provisions and scheduled face-to-face (F2F) sessions;
d. Good teaching and learning (T&L) support systems that cater to the diverse learning needs of our students;
e. Strong application of technology in all academic and administrative processes to facilitate interactions with stakeholders and enhance student experience;
f. Promotion and actual provision of lifelong learning — provision of education in as many modes and styles as are appropriate to the needs faced in the working lives, and beyond, of the adult learner;
g. Applied learning, supported by partnerships with external organisations — working closely with employers, community groups, government bodies, NGOs, private organisations and other educational institutions, to develop and offer academic programmes and courses relevant to industry or society, and to pursue applied research.

at large, to expand the latter group, to acculturate Singaporeans to embrace lifelong learning as a recreational activity that is worthwhile paying for. In the Singapore context, this will take years, perhaps a generation or two, but beating the path towards that is key to opening up the continuing education market for others such as retirees and stay-at-home spouses. As UniSIM students were adults of at least 21 years of age and resident in Singapore, they were either Singapore citizens or permanent residents, with a very small percentage of foreigners on professional or employment or dependant passes.

System

What system was implemented to enable UniSIM to deliver its education model? There are several features that UniSIM homed in on, viz., a flat and lean structure, applied and innovative programme curricula, a

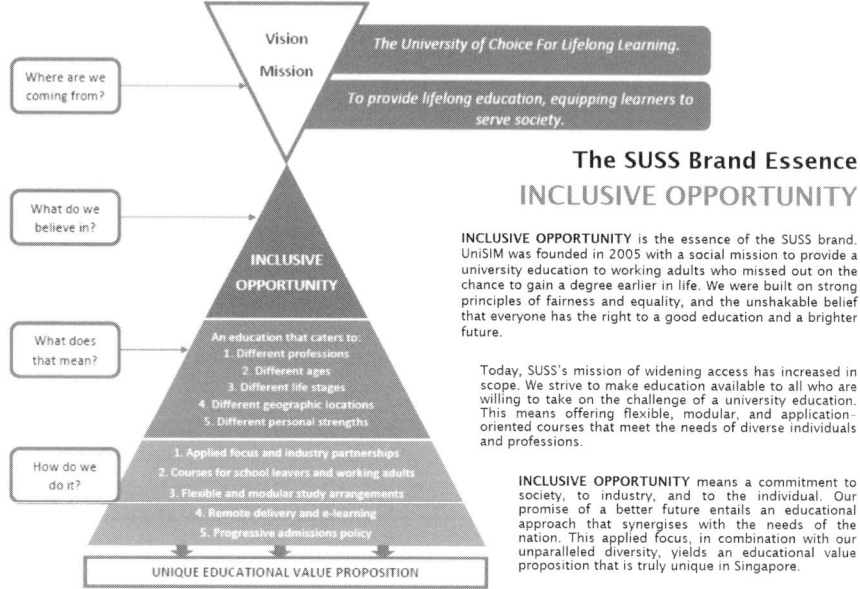

Fig. 12.2   SUSS's inclusive essence.

standardised production framework, rigorous quality assurance, applied pedagogy, heavy reliance on industry involvement, a "distributed" approach in resourcing and delivery, extensive use of technology for online delivery and to operate the value chain of processes, a focus on teaching & student support, flexibility — mobile, anytime & anywhere, programme modularity, mix & match programme offerings, and speed to market, as well as a culture of teamwork and shared goals among employees. Some of these are described elsewhere (SIM University, 2011; Cheong, 2013 and 2015).

Flat & Lean Structure

Being self-funding, UniSIM had to be a lean and efficient organisation while keeping quality and giving as much back to the students as financially feasible. It was critical that the university maintained a fairly flat structure, partly due to its lean manpower but also to facilitate quick decision-making and speed of implementation. Today, as then, there are four clusters, viz., academic, administrative, learning support and corporate helmed by the Provost, Registrar, Vice-President (Learning Services) and the President, respectively. The Academic cluster initially had four schools, viz., SASS, SBIZ, HDSS and SST, and OGS in graduate studies and CFAR, the centre for applied research.[1] In 2015, a fifth school, the School of Law (SLAW), was added, as was the Centre for Continuing & Professional Education (CCPE). The OGS and CCPE tap on the schools to offer graduate-level and continuing education programmes, respectively. The CFAR administers the research activities of the university and works with the schools to promote applied research among the faculty and with external partners.

The President, together with key officers, form the small executive committee which makes decisions regularly and expeditiously. The formation of a tightly-knit community is facilitated by an open-door policy where there is open communication and access between the lowest and highest levels of staff.

Applied and Innovative Programme Curricula

Because it serves the working population, UniSIM (and SUSS) develops an array of programmes to meet various needs. These include the usual programmes found in other AUs for career advancement, programmes that are not offered by the AUs due to small demand or unsuitability for fresh school-leavers but which industry needs, niche disciplines which UniSIM develops as part of its social mission and not available in the other universities. Such disciplines include Tamil Language and Literature, Malay Language and Literature, Counselling, Human Factors in Safety and Early Childhood Education; programmes sought by industry partners for employee development, such as the Management and Security Studies programme for the Singapore Police Force and the Building & Project Management programme for the building and construction sector. A significant portion of these programmes is profession-centred, e.g., business analytics, electronics, biomedical engineering, aerospace systems, translation and interpretation, counselling and social work. UniSIM's modular flexible model and its ability to mix and match courses to form new programmes enables it to provide programmes in an innovative and responsive way.

A rigorous programme development process takes into account not just academic requirements but industry/market demand, possible strategic collaborator(s) and accreditation. Market relevance is achieved through various means, including: (a) market orientation of courses and assignments, (b) input from practitioners, (c) regular curriculum updating, (d) engagement of many associates who have relevant industry experience, (e) partnering with industry to provide exposure to students, and (f) aligning curricula to the requirements of professional bodies. Each programme is managed by a Head of Programme (HoP) who is a full-time faculty member. All programmes are outcome-based and assessments are mapped to learning outcomes of the courses. They are externally assessed and reviewed every five years; course reviews are undertaken every two to three years, ensuring timely refreshing to industry needs.

Where applicable, the university seeks accreditation of its professional programmes at the earliest opportunity. Over the years, this has been achieved for several programmes,[2] while others offer, within their curricula, opportunities for students to gain a professional certification that gives them an additional advantage in the workplace.

All undergraduates take a university core which is a broadening component that enables students to acquire communication skills and other general abilities. Many programmes now have the combination of a major and a minor — our graduates need to be broadened not just at the liberal education level but also at a disciplinary level; and the minor, which is at the own choosing of the student, can afford that broadening. Apart from the career-oriented programmes, a General Studies programme is offered that encourages learning for its own sake. It is a unique programme that allows anyone above 18 years old, with a minimum educational background, to select courses of study leading to the award of certificates, or to progress to a Diploma or a Degree in General Studies. The student may choose from a whole range of courses, but must attain advanced-level proficiency in some courses to qualify for a degree.

The slogan that SUSS uses for its programmes is "learn today, apply tomorrow". Programmes are geared towards building up expertise in the students, who already hold jobs, which they can bring to their workplace. They leverage on the collective student experience for peer-learning and contextualising lessons, the linking of projects and assignments to work practices and problems, and enable students to apply their new-found knowledge quite immediately at their workplace, enhancing their learning. This is unlike in the traditional universities where students apply their learning at the workplace only on graduation, three to four years since starting their learning. In that respect, the university's offering and pedagogy is hitherto not available in the Singapore university system.

Standardised Production Framework

At the outset, the university adopted a standardised way in which programmes are to be developed and run, and students are to be supported academically and administratively. This is akin to the "MacDonald's" approach, after the global fast-food chain, in which processes are pervasively followed, formats and templates are the norm, selection of students and teachers are mainly standardised. Faculty unaccustomed to this mode will scoff at the loss of "academic autonomy" but it assures minimum standards in a setting of large vagaries in the quality and ability of students and associates. So, applicants are admitted if they have the minimum qualification (except for some sensitive disciplines), associates are required to go through a standard selection and training process, study guides are used for every course and associates have to follow the same curriculum and teaching regime, and common marking rubrics are used. New faculty members can ease into their work with minimal guidance. Such standardisation also gives speed of implementation, common standards to work towards and objectivity in audits. But, it is not all fixed. So, for instance, variety in teaching occurs in how associates interact with, and support, their students, and the different experiences that they bring into the classroom.

Quality Assurance

As a private university, UniSIM had to be registered with the Council for Private Education, satisfying the mandatory registration requirements prescribed under the Private Education Act (2009), and subjected to a regulatory regime of minimal operating requirements, reporting and audit. At the same time, because of the MOE tuition fee subsidy and the fact that UniSIM was operating under licence from MOE, it was also subjected to an academic quality audit regime called Quality Assurance Framework for Universities. Viewed positively, these regimes serve to nudge UniSIM along a high quality orientation, and indirectly enhance our reputation as an institution that is transparent and accountable to its stakeholders.

UniSIM's quality assurance framework (Cheong, 2015) applies to the whole academic value chain from admission through the delivery of programme to graduation. While programme origination and curricular development are done by the Schools, the Academic Board exercises the highest authority on academic matters, and is accountable to the Board of Trustees. Various channels of sensing and feedback, apart from the usual feedback from students, are utilised to gauge how the university is performing with a view to introduce improvements.

Supporting Learning

Adult learners require support that differs from those on traditional full-time studies. To provide the appropriate support for them, it is critical to understand their learning needs; these are shaped by several factors, as encapsulated in Table 12.2.

The pedagogical and support systems adopted are designed to enable students with different academic background and learning styles to cope with university studies and to do so within their normal employment duties and other life schedules. They also have to be helped to embrace new technology-based modes of Teaching and Learning (T&L), and increase the ownership of their learning. The part-time students are likely

Table 12.2.   Learning Needs of SUSS Students (SIM University, 2011)

a. The relatively more inclusive admission requirements, which bring in students with a wide spectrum of academic abilities and background experience;

b. The independent learning required of the students, with reduced direct teaching and supervision by faculty;

c. The time constraints they face, being mostly employed full-time while studying, limiting how much and how efficiently they learn;

d. Their connection with industry which requires SUSS's programmes to follow suit;

e. Their need to have flexibility in following classes and in pacing the progression of their studies to fit their other commitments.

to face greater learning difficulty than the usual cohorts of school-leavers accepted by the AUs: many are generally not as academically-inclined, and some may have left off formal education for a substantial period of time. To a large extent, the stress level of students is a function of the number of courses they have chosen to take each semester.

SUSS's part-time Associates, being key providers of academic instruction, are given professional, administrative and technical support to improve the quality of their contributions. Through flexible contract arrangements, the university has flexibility on enlarging or reducing class sizes and releasing or retaining Associates. While managed by the HoPs, the performance of Associates is also tracked by the Teaching & Learning Centre (TLC) with the objective of providing support for their instructional ability. The TLC also provides support to help students adapt to university studies and to at-risk students specifically, working with the schools to identify learning difficulties, at-risk students and adopting new approaches which are informed and enriched by research.

For adult learners, support services other than academic are important to facilitate their studies and give a positive learning experience. At SUSS, these include helpdesk services, a detailed class and assessment schedule and an individual curriculum plan for each student, academic counselling at the schools and professional services that can be tapped from SUSS's Counselling Centre.

Multi-modal 'Distributed' Model of Resourcing and Delivery

A central theme of SUSS's programme offering is "Quality Education, Anytime, Anywhere". Towards this end, SUSS delivers learning in several modes:

(a) self-study print-based study guide and accompanying textbook for every course. These study guides have now been made into iStudy-Guides (iSG), an EPUB3 digital version of the Study Guide with on-board videos, weblinks, formative quizzes, e-illustrations and elements for annotations by students. Textbooks are increasingly offered as e-versions, so that all study materials can be fully and conveniently carried on a mobile device.

(b) Face-to-face (F2F) classes, though attendance is not compulsory. Classes for the part-time programmes are conducted in the evenings and on weekends.

(c) Online discussions and peer learning activities conducted on SUSS's Learning Management System (LMS) — this was BlackBoard from the beginning, but has since been migrated to the Canvas LMS in 2016.

(d) Tutor-marked assignments that enable students to keep up with their courses and learn from tutor comments on their work.

The bulk of the teaching is done by the associates. Besides associates, SUSS leverages on external institutional providers to deliver some courses, chiefly those of the partner education institutions in collaborative programmes, and also professionally-oriented ones where a professional or industry certification also becomes obtainable by the students. This approach recognises organisations outside the university which have the pockets of expertise that SUSS does not have, nor would readily develop. In fact, SUSS joins hands selectively with such organisations to offer co-branded degree programmes that leverage on courses and expertise at these organisations.

In terms of facilities, SUSS's campus is presently co-located with SIM's, using a lease-based arrangement (Figure 12.3). It also leverages on its partners. For example, SUSS uses laboratories at the polytechnics and

Fig. 12.3   SUSS campus.

specialised companies for its technology programmes — an approach that is not only cost-effective but gives its students access to up-to-date equipment, operated in a real-world work environment.

Heavy Reliance on Technology

SUSS being new in an age of technological innovation in learning, the opportunity was taken to develop an online learning capability which would eventually be the main vehicle for teaching and learning rather than as a supplementary mode as is usually found in traditional universities. To achieve this, SUSS invested heavily in the BlackBoard LMS (now Canvas LMS). The goal for this thrust is to make learning accessible, empowering and effective. Over the years, content, delivery and interactions have been moved online to increase accessibility, encourage self-learning, reflection and peer-to-peer and student-tutor interactions; gradually, synchronous didactic F2F sessions will be reduced, provided instead as recorded sessions for download to desktop and mobile devices, allowing students to sit in, and even participate, in sessions regardless of geographical location. F2F sessions are organised using what is commonly called 'flipped' classroom mode, with students expected to have read their materials beforehand, and actively participating in interactions and sharing their experiences. The majority of SUSS's courses now adopts a "blended" delivery mode {comprehensive materials that are available online + online learning components or downloadable interactive materials + some interactive F2F sessions that are not didactic in nature}.

The quality of e-Learning is much emphasized. The university has developed measurements/benchmarks of quality and effectiveness of its blended or online courses, stepped up training of faculty and Associates to equip them with the desired skills to design, develop and deliver T&L online, and enhanced training of students for online learning.

Technology is also extensively used for the end-to-end administrative value chain. Students have a one-stop access to university services through the Student Portal while an Associate Portal with the relevant functions serves both the Associates and the full-time faculty members who teach.

Increasing Flexibility in Learning

In the long-term, flexibility for SUSS's students is best served by a high-quality system that includes end-to-end e-enabled services to students and an interactive e-Learning environment. Towards this end, all courses are now presented in full-e or blended mode, without F2F didactic teaching, and all courses have iSGs. E-services and e-learning are mobile-enabled, and in time, students should expect to access all they need just from their mobile devices.

This is not without difficulty. In the early days, faculty buy-in was hesitant, they needed skilling in interacting with students in online mode, there was a very large number of courses to convert, and a shortage of technical manpower to achieve this. Moreover, feedback from students had indicated that many students, particularly the older ones, were still not ready for online learning, and mindsets needed to be changed.

Besides the technological element, flexibility is a distinctive feature in SUSS's academic programmes — they are modular, stackable to qualifications at various levels, students choose the number of courses in any semester and their pace of learning, and even unhindered transfer to another programme if the original proves to be a mistaken choice.

Besides the flexibility already provided to the part-time students, flexibility for its full-time students has also been built in, giving them the option to finish their studies on a part-time basis.[3] The modular structure allows learners to take courses piecemeal, on a need basis, progressively according to ability, or programmatically to attain a qualification. Participants are allowed to read courses individually or as a group for certification or towards a degree, if they so choose. Flexibility is accorded by having day and evening classes to allow participants to study full-time or part-time, as well as alternate or blend between the two. In addition, SUSS's online mode allows participants to engage in independent learning at their own time, pace and space.

Heavy Reliance on Industry Input

As mentioned previously, SUSS actively seeks good collaborative partnerships in the development and delivery of applied education in a wide range of industry-relevant areas. This takes the form of programme advisory, course development, programme audit, teaching services, use of industry facilities, providing internships, employer feedback, etc.

Associates are a critical component of our teaching and learning framework. They comprise a healthy mix of professionals from industry and institutions of higher learning. In a classroom where both associates and part-time students come with their own experiences, the sharing is rich indeed. SUSS now has about 1,000 Associates on its active list. As these come from a variety of backgrounds, a high degree of quality control is needed to assure consistency of delivery of teaching. This is achieved through careful selection, adequate preparation and required training, close monitoring, active retention or discontinuation of service.

Speed to Market

In its first ten years, the university developed more than 50 new programmes, this being made possible because of its modular programme structure and the "speed-to-market" modus operandi that a private university afforded. This speed is aided by the well-defined processes in place as described earlier. The modularity of programmes allows for a mix-and-match approach to programme development and quick deployment using existing courses that suit a new programme.

Integration

As mentioned earlier, SUSS takes the approach of recognising that much content and expertise exist in organisations and individuals outside of its cloisters and in the marketplace. It thus judiciously harnesses this expertise, through collaborative partnerships, in programme development and delivery. By so doing, several objectives are aimed for, viz., providing greater study choice and enrichment for students, augmenting SUSS's capability and achieving responsiveness to the market, enhancing its image and standing, bringing in good practices and innovative teaching processes, and creating platforms for interactions between staff of partnering institutions.

But, there is more than that. SUSS actively works with organisations to bring their employees into our programmes as part of their career progression framework. So, it recognises training done in those organisations for credit, even a set of in-company training as a minor that will offset almost one quarter of its degree requirements. In addition, SUSS has tailor-made programmes for employees of large organisations. An example is a BSc in Management & Security Studies created for members of the Singapore Police Force (SPF) — in this partnership, the SPF (and later the Home Team NS) needed to equip its non-degree officers in security know-how as well as in management for career advancement, so SUSS organised a security studies minor, added its business management major, and the new programme was born. To date, about 200 SPF officers have completed the programme. Another is a collaboration with the Nanyang Academy of Fine Arts (NAFA) in which NAFA's visual communication diploma holders may finish a Bachelor of Visual Communication with Management programme at SUSS. The diploma is recognised for credits and the students get business management training while deepening their professional ability through advanced modules done at NAFA and recognised by SUSS. Yet another is a fast-tracked aerospace systems programme specifically tailored for personnel in the Republic of Singapore Air Force. Finally, SUSS runs a successful fast-tracked professional conversion programme to turn mid-career professionals into accredited social work graduates. Such alliances integrate the university with industry and vice-versa, combining the expertise and training from both for a degree programme.

Holistic Learning

Taking all the above, SUSS now offers a broad and holistic range of learning to a wide range of interested parties, viz., learning that is flexible, outcome-based, goal-oriented, applied, multiple-pathed, supported, online, inclusive and distributed when and where they are, and parties that include fresh school-leavers looking for full-time education, working adults looking for part-time studies and/or continuing education, employers looking to raise their employees' capability, and the general public looking for the pleasure of casual learning. SUSS is becoming an institution which is serving the community, yet with the community also being part of its raison d'être and involved in its mission and operation.

Making a Mark

Given its admission philosophy, UniSIM had an image of a "second chance" university. Together with its "newness" on the university landscape, it faced issues of branding and academic recognition. The negative perceptions come from several quarters — un-informed/mis-informed, sometimes fussy, parents and aspiring students, the general public's mixed views about private universities, and particularly employers who view degrees not obtained through full-time study as being of "suspect quality". This was compounded by UniSIM's strategy of increasing e-Learning as a primary means of delivery and to allow greater flexibility in learning, again something not well-understood generally. With its co-location on the SIM property and the closeness in name and degree offerings to SIM Global Education (SIM's private education provider of partner overseas university programmes), there was identity and brand confusion.

Despite that, SUSS's reputation today is strong as a lifelong learning university and a provider of good upgrading opportunities for working adults. SUSS is not in the league of the large research-intensive universities, but is firmly recognised for its applied and continual learning focus. It was not a surprise then that the MOE had chosen first to subsidise our students' tuition fees and then turned SUSS into an AU as the country finds an increasing need for continuing education and lifelong learning.

In 2014, while still a private university, UniSIM was tasked by the MOE to run programmes for full-time studies; this followed a study by the government on expanding cohort participation in local university education (MOE, 2012). It was an endorsement of the relevance and standards attained by the university. The steady-state enrolment of such students will be substantially smaller than that of the part-time enrolment, and programmes will be confined to those which are in demand or of critical need in the future.

In terms of finances, the university is regarded as lean and mean — using only income largely from student tuition fees and an annual supplementation from SIM in the first 10 years to fund operations. Through prudent spending which management keeps a close eye on and a deliberate reliance on a substantial out-sourced mode to supply its operations, the university has been able to turn in a modest operating surplus in all the years except one. At a cost per student very significantly less than those in the other AUs, SUSS has shown to be value-for-money in higher education provision and a model for future affordable university education. But, it is more in the educational value-add that SUSS should be judged — it takes in many who did not get the chance of pre-employment university studies, and indeed some who did not get a place in an AU but later on found success in the workplace, gives them a chance and turns them into graduate-level contributors to the workforce.

Second Beginning

In 2017, legislation (Parliament, 2017) was passed in the Singapore Parliament to re-structure UniSIM and accord it the status of an Autonomous University (AU) under the ambit of the MOE. While this meant that the university will leave SIM, what was significant was that UniSIM would not remain as a private university and would receive some government funding directly for its operations. Given public perception that places greater value on education at an AU, the change was a status elevation and a fillip for the university. A new name (and a new logo — Figure 12.4) was also adopted for UniSIM: the Singapore University of Social Sciences (or SUSS). SUSS is to be an applied university, with a focus on the social sciences and a leader in lifelong learning. These will be its niches in the higher education eco-system here and SUSS will complement the other AUs. The name ties in well with the university's social mission and is in harmony with what it has been doing. There are very few universities named specifically in social sciences, and in that respect, SUSS will again be untraditional and a possible model for the future.

Fig. 12.4   From UniSIM to SUSS.

Future

Whither the future for SUSS?

The opportunity to offer full-time programmes gave SUSS a new buzz and a chance to bring something different to a traditional avenue to an undergraduate degree. Presently, full-time programmes are offered in Accountancy, Finance, Marketing, Supply Chain Management, Human Resource Management, Social Work, Early Childhood Education and Business Analytics, all already in our stable of part-time programmes. While these may be viewed as regular programmes like in the other AUs, some features set them apart, viz., all students must have (a) an overseas experience, (b) a minimum 6-month work attachment, (c) a service learning stint, (d) a minor which must be taken with the part-time students (except for Accountancy). The latter makes it possible for full-time students with little or no work experience to learn from their more experienced and mature part-time counterparts, and vice versa. Students who find a job, possibly after the work attachment, are allowed to finish their programme part-time while they work.

In designing the full-time programmes, a 3H's education philosophy was formulated: Head — strong disciplinary fundamentals with an applied focus, Heart — socially aware and conscious, and going beyond intellectual ability to make positive changes to society, and Habit — independent self-motivated learning as a lifelong habit. It is the goal of SUSS to produce graduates with the 3Hs so they can be better prepared to serve in the workplace and in society.

As an AU, SUSS functions within Singapore's university eco-system to complement the other AUs, contributing to providing, by 2020, 40% of every cohort of local students with a shot at university education fresh out from school. It will remain an applied university with a strong focus on adult education and lifelong learning. In 2014, following an extensive study (MOE, 2014), the Singapore Government launched the SkillsFuture movement, to prepare the Singapore workforce to face the future world of employment. The financial commitment was huge and aimed at preparing the workforce for the future (Budget, 2015; ST, 2015). Essentially, continuing education and training (CET), with an applied focus, will be the order of the day, a necessary and on-going activity of every individual. In this context, the universities have a signal role to play, bringing out skills training speedily and responsively, to help the workforce adapt quickly and move into the new jobs. In this endeavour, SUSS is well-positioned to take a lead. Indeed, it has embarked on work-study programmes, earn & learn programmes for polytechnic graduates to stay in their jobs while learning part-time for their degrees, professional conversion programmes and credit-bearing training provisions, many stackable towards a degree later on. SUSS offerings will include professional certifications, in-company continuing education programmes, customised learning for special interest groups and bite-size courses. Many of these will count for credits in SUSS's programmes. Crucially, SUSS will develop a framework for progression of learning and training accreditation that will enable a learner to earn credits for skills recognition as well as towards a degree. A focus will be an integration of learning at the workplace with academic learning at SUSS, fostering a two-way flow between theory and practice. The university's pervasive blended learning pedagogy and strong online capability provide further support to its SkillsFuture participation. Its applied orientation and industry focus are aligned with skills upgrading and mastery and the ability to meet both industry needs and personal aspirations. In the long run, SUSS aims to be a sought-after training arm of industry, and a regular source of skills and knowledge refreshing for individuals. It hopes to grow a trend that is already happening elsewhere (Merisotis, 2016; EIU, 2014).

SUSS also will work towards pedagogical innovations and research to better understand and provide for adult learning. In SUSS's view, formal learning should not be dichotomised from work (*ST*, 2014) — there isn't a stark shift from formal studies to work, rather a looping in and out of learning and work all through adult life. In support of better learning, SUSS has embarked on learning analytics to understand how it may enable effective learning among its students. With this and the use of artificial intelligence, and its proprietary iStudyGuides and learning system, the goal is to put in place an adaptive, evidence-based and supportive self-learning system that our students can have with them wherever they go.

The focus areas that SUSS was entrusted with on its becoming an AU, viz., applied, social sciences bias, and lifelong learning, align nicely with its 3Hs philosophy. The social sciences dimension is of particular interest as it gives SUSS a niche and competitive focus. In SUSS, "social sciences" is interpreted in a broad way — the concern with the community and society, and the individuals who make up that community, and the development and well-being of the community. Many disciplines impact society and its development, the ones that are closely related to traditional social sciences and others from management, languages, to IT and even technology. So, rather than merely deepen its pure social sciences disciplines, the university has the opportunity to give a strong social sciences understanding and inclination as a horizontal skill in all its graduates whatever the discipline. The importance placed on the social dimension is timely and apt given that in the end, with all the technological changes, demographic shifts, geo-political changes and job dislocations, it is the people who matter.

Finally, SUSS will remain asset-light. In the future, its "distributed" model of operation will be strengthened as it draws on, and embraces, expertise and resources outside traditional university domains.

Conclusion

The re-structuring of UniSIM into SUSS came against a backdrop of disruptions in several domains, viz., a rapidly ageing demographics, jobs threatened by technological and other changes, the uncertainty of the nature of future jobs, social dislocations and disruptions arising from the changes mentioned, increasing social/religious tensions, and on top of that, the increasing cost of higher education and poor preparation of graduates with the right skills for the workplace (Barber *et al*, 2013). As SUSS gears up for the future, it is optimistic that it is in a good position to contribute to Singapore's growth and well-being as the country grapples with these issues. SUSS can become a model for relevant, inclusive, value-for-money and affordable university education of the future. Whether through online learning, flexible modes, multiple pathways, a hub-and-spokes provision with satellite learning centres in employment and business hubs, or learning provisions for all ages and through all stages of life, SUSS will bring the university to the people and make its mark as the lifelong learning university for the people.

And so, the story continues ……..

Visit SUSS at <www://suss.edu.sg>

Notes

1. Schools of Arts & Social Sciences (SASS), Business (SBIZ), Human Development & Social Services (HDSS) and Science & Technology (SST), Office of Graduate Studies (OGS), and Centre for Applied Research (CFAR).

2. Programmes that are accredited include those in Electronics and Aerospace Systems (with the Engineering Accreditation Board of the Institution of Engineers Singapore under the auspices of the Washington Accord), Facilities and Events Management (with International Facility Management Association & Royal Institution of Chartered Surveyors), Building & Project Management (with Singapore Institute of Surveyors & Valuers and Royal Institution of Chartered Surveyors), Human Factors in Safety (recognised by the Ministry of Manpower for Workplace Safety & Health officer registration), Accountancy (with Accounting & Corporate Regulatory Authority and the Singapore Accountancy Commission), Finance (with the Financial Planning Association of Singapore), Social Work (with Singapore Association of Social Workers), Counselling (with Singapore Association of Counselling). Within their curricula, opportunities are given for students to gain a professional certification, such as those for SAP, Oracle and Red Hat in ICT.

3. UniSIM was invited by MOE to run programmes for full-time students in selected programmes that it was already offering on a part-time basis. See also section on 'Making a mark'.

References

Barber M., K. Donnelly & S. Rizvi (Mar 2013). *"An avalanche is coming — higher education & the revolution ahead"*. Institute for Public Policy Research, UK.

Budget statement (March 2015). *"Developing our people"*. Budget Statement by Minister of Finance, Singapore Budget 2015. <http://www.singaporebudget. gov.sg/budget_2015/pc.aspx1>

Cheong, H.K. (2013). "Quality assurance at SIM University (UniSIM), Singapore". In I. Jung, T.M. Wong, & T. Belawati, eds., *Quality Assurance in Distance Education and Elearning: Challenges and Solutions from Asia*. Asian Association of Open Universities and Sage Publications, pp. 3–24.

Cheong, H.K. (2015). "Raising the bar, extending the reach in Singapore higher education", in J. Sim, ed., *Beyond 50: Re-imagining Singapore*. Really Good Books Publishing House, pp.179–190.

Economist Intelligence Unit (EIU) (Mar 2014). "Higher education in the 21st century: Meeting real world demands", 28pp.

Merisotis, J. (2016). "Credentials reform: How technology and the changing needs of the workforce will create the higher education system of the future". *Educause Review*, May/Jun, pp. 26–34.

Ministry of Education, Singapore (July 2012). "Report of the Committee on University Education Pathways Beyond 2015 (CUEP)", 80pp.

Ministry of Education, Singapore (August 2014). "Report of the Committee on Applied Study in Polytechnics and ITE Review (ASPIRE)", 37pp.

Parliament of Singapore (2017). Singapore University of Social Sciences Act 2017, No. 24/17, 10pp.

SIM University (December 2011). "Self-Assessment Report, Quality Assurance Framework for UniSIM".

Straits Times Singapore (27 Feb 2015). "SkillsFuture: How you can benefit from it".

Straits Times Singapore (28 Feb 2014). "Earn and learn for life", The Long Interview.

About the Author

Cheong Hee Kiat is President of the Singapore University of Social Sciences.

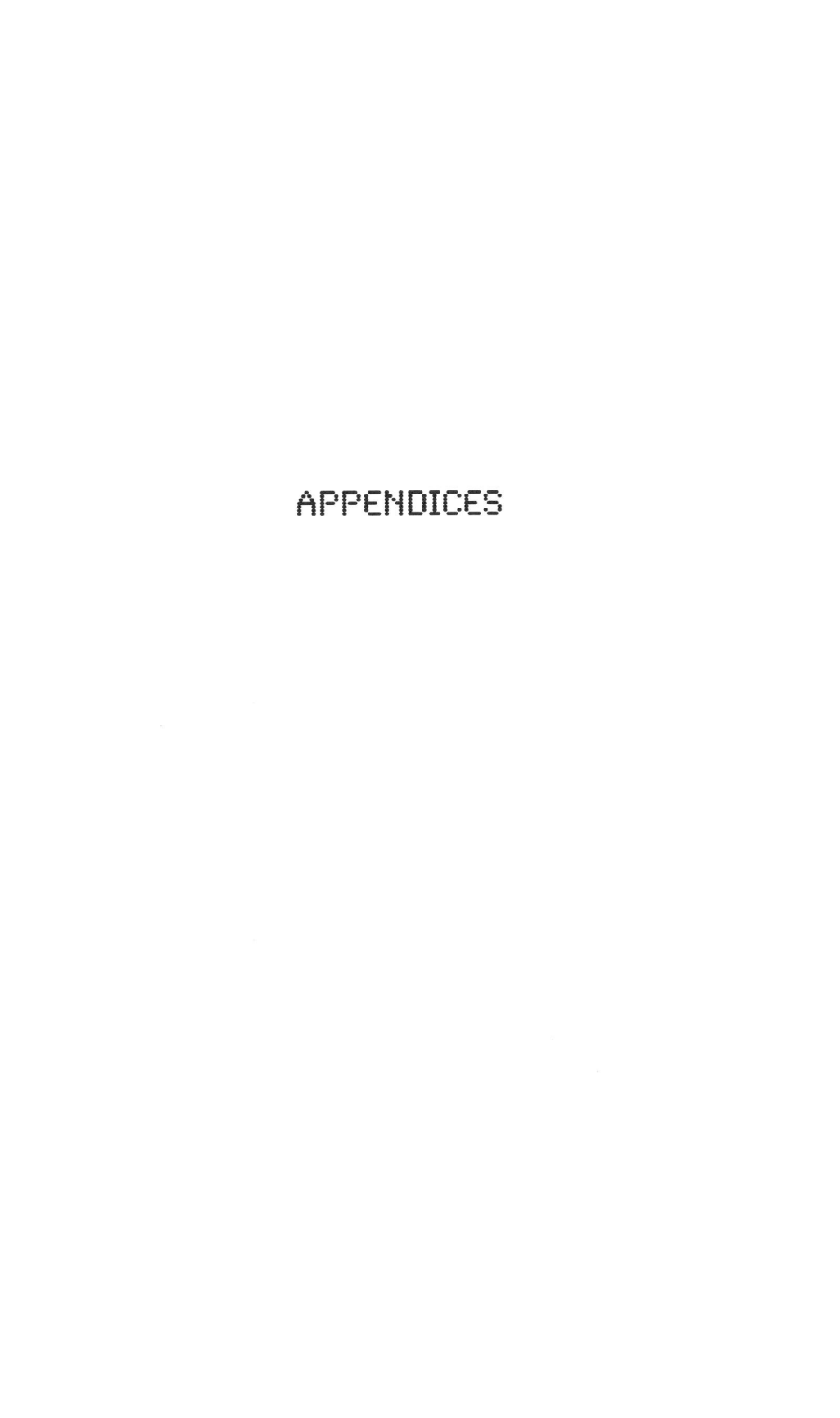

APPENDICES

ADVISORY COUNCIL OF THE UNIVER-CITIES CONFERENCE 2016

"Univer-Cities: Strategic Dilemmas of Medical Origins and Selected Modalities"

Professor Bertil Andersson, Nanyang Technological University President and Trustee, Nobel Foundation.

Professor Dr Cham Tao Soon, Chancellor, SIM University, Founder President of NTU and The Singapore Academy of Engineers. Recipient of the 2006 United Kingdom's Distinguished Engineering International Medal.

Dr Gordon Johnson, Fellow of The Royal Asiatic Society and President (2009–2012); and former Deputy Vice Chancellor, University of Cambridge.

Professor Dr Lilia Labidi, Visiting Research Professor at the Middle East Institute (National University of Singapore), and former Minister for Women's Affairs in the Tunisian cabinet post-Arab Spring.

Professor John H McArthur, Dean Emeritus and George F. Baker Professor of Business Administration, Harvard Business School; Duke University Health System Board of Directors; Koç University Board of Overseers; Chairman of Asia Pacific Foundation of Canada; and Officer of the Order of Canada.

Professor Dr Rudolph A Marcus, Arthur amos Noyes Professor of Chemistry, California Institute of Technology, Nobel Prize in Chemistry 1992.

Tan Sri Dato' Seri Professor Dr Sharifah Hapsah Syed Hasan Shahabudin, Vice Chancellor, Universiti Kebangsaan Malaysia and Chairperson, National Council of Women's Organisation, Malaysia.

Professor Lap-Chee Tsui, OC, FRS, Vice Chancellor and President of The University of Hong Kong, discoverer of the gene causing cystic fibrosis and past President of Human Genome Organisation.

Cross Professor Emeritus Dr Nam Pyo Suh, Massachuses Institute of Technology and president (2006–2013) of the Korea Advanced Institute of Science and Technology (KAIST).

Professor Richard Bender is the former Dean of the College of Environmental Design and Chair and Professor of Architecture at UC Berkeley.

Anthony SC Teo
Univer-Cities Conference Chairperson
Chevalier of the Ordre des Palmes
Académiques
ascteo23@Univer-Cities.com

PROGRAMME OF THE UNIVER-CITIES CONFERENCE 2016

2016
Univer-Cities

Core-dynamics of Univer-Cities
with medical origins - are they different,
complex and integrative?

13 - 14 November 2016

CONFERENCE ON
UNIVER-CITIES

Program

Hunter Medical Research Institute

		Location
8.15am	Registration and coffee	Atrium
9am	Welcome to Country **Mr Joe Griffin** Community Engagement Officer, The Wollotuka Institute, The University of Newcastle Welcome address **Professor Caroline McMillen** Vice-Chancellor and President, The University of Newcastle	The Caves
9.15am	**Keynote address** *Univer-Cities in the 21st Century Revisited.* **Sir Leszek Borysiewicz** Vice-Chancellor, University of Cambridge (video in absentia)	The Caves

Conference session one

		Location
Complex and deeper community intertwining and the trans-disciplinary impact on the academic evolution in comprehensive or niche institutions whose origins emanate from medicine and physiology to rarer the ones in contemporary times.		
9.30am	Chair: **Adjunct Professor Anthony SC Teo** Lee Kuan Yew School of Public Policy, National University of Singapore Panelists: **Laureate Professor John Aitken** Pro Vice-Chancellor, Health and Medicine, The University of Newcastle *Dilemma and Strategy - Shaping the University of Newcastle, Australia.* **Professor Dr (Med) Frank Rühli** Head of Evolutionary Medicine, University of Zurich *Univer-City of Zurich from an evolutionary medical perspective, 1850-2015.* **Dr Gordon Johnson** Former Deputy Vice-Chancellor, University of Cambridge, 2001-2010 *Cambridge – from medieval university to bio-medical campus: science, medicine, city and university – a long view.* **Professor Bertil Andersson** President, Nanyang Technological University *Rising Top Young University NTU, Singapore - From Engineering and Business to Contemporary Start-Up Medical School Complementing the Regional Medical Hub and the Silvering Population.*	The Caves
10.45am	Morning tea	Atrium
11.15am	Chair: **Tan Sri Dato' Seri Emerita Professor Dr (Med) Sharifah Hapsah Syed Hasan Shahabudin** President, National Council of Women's Organisations of Malaysia **Keynote address** *Nuevo Experience of UON: From Medicine, Public Health and Beyond – Regionality and Inter-Continentality.* **Professor Caroline McMillen** Vice-Chancellor and President, The University of Newcastle	The Caves
12.15pm	Lunch	Haggarty Space

Conference session two

		Location
Univer-Cities Conference 2013 Updates on USA and Canada with new emerging Univer-Cities from Hong Kong and Paris-Singapore.		
1.30pm	Chair: **Dr Gordon Johnson** Former Deputy Vice-Chancellor, University of Cambridge 2001-2010 Panelists: **Ms Emily Marthinsen** Assistant Vice-Chancellor and Campus Architect University of California Berkeley **Mr John Parman** Senior Associate, Gensler *University of California in the Bay Area: Present and Future of a Public University.* **Dr Roseann Runte** President and Vice-Chancellor, Carleton University *Universities of Carleton and Ottawa's impact on Canada's National Capital Region – City of 'Bright' versus Paris' 'Light' (video in absentia).* **Emeritus Professor John Malpas** Former Vice President, The University of Hong Kong *Reinventing the University of Hong Kong in mortar and spirit with deepening engagement of the entrepreneurial fragrant city.*	The Caves
2.45pm	Afternoon tea	Haggarty Space

Conference session three

		Location
Strategic and evolving implications of the single key node Eco-system of globalizing Univer-Cities		
3.15pm	Chair: **Laureate Professor Graeme Jameson AO** Director, Centre for Multiphase Process, The University of Newcastle Panelists: **Professor Asit Biswas** Distinguished Visiting Professor, Lee Kuan Yew School of Public Policy, National University of Singapore, and Stockholm Water Prize Winner and Practitioner *Could a Single Factor Water Policy Impact a City and Redefine a Whole New Univer-City Relationship: Case of Singapore.* **Cross Professor Emeritus Dr Nam Pyo Suh** Massachusetts Institute of Technology *Strategy for Developing an Innovative University: S-Factor, S-Gap, and Vector Delta.*	The Caves
4.30–5pm	Closing remarks and handover to 2019 Univer-Cities Conference host **Adjunct Professor Anthony SC Teo** Lee Kuan Yew School of Public Policy, National University of Singapore	The Caves
5pm	Conference close	
5.10pm	Transport departs for conference dinner	

ABOUT THE UNIQUE UNIVER-CITIES DESIGN

About the unique Univer-Cities design

Yeo Chee Kiong translated the theme of Univer-Cities: Strategic Implications for Asia into a design where institutions of higher learning are depicted in twin-skyline cityscapes.

The book cover design focuses on a stylized sky-line of a city with a built-in core of institutions of higher learning - idiomatically referred to as seats of learning. His hypothesis is that through human history, the idea put to record from early Sumerians and Egyptians has been the discipline of thinking and writing. He represented them through the form of chairs and tables.

The book title 'Univer-Cities: Strategic Implications for Asia' is portrayed in SYNCHRO LET font. It visually places the accent on the contrast of light, darkness and dots reminiscent of the lights of a city - an interpretation of a night skyline of a 'univer-city' scape. A more intriguing imagination is a twist of double-helix - every univer-city has its distinctive DNA.

Publications

Univer-Cities: Strategic Implications for Asia – Readings from Cambridge and Berkeley to Singapore

Univer-cities: Strategic Implications for Asia aims to redefine the multi-faceted symbiotic relationship between universities and host cities. The four readings in this book will invite readers to challenge the traditional view of what a university is as a place, and re-define the university as a space; drawing discoverers, creators, and seekers who are keen to preserve and enhance the value of higher education in Asia. This reader will also show how universities can make a huge and innovative impact on the immediate, surrounding, and global communities that are drawn into the ambit of its campus and sought out by the university in inter-univer-city and trans-displinary linkages.

Written by worldly academic leaders and professionals from Berkeley, Cambridge, Canberra and Singapore — who are prominent in fields of higher education strategy, campus cum urban planning, design, and architecture — the readings will shed some light on the future and power of univer-cities.

Imperial College Press, 2014

Univer-Cities: Strategic View of the Future – Readings from Berkeley and Cambridge to Singapore and Rising Asia

This follows on from the very well-received Volume I Univer-cities: Strategic Implications for Asia - Readings from Cambridge and Berkeley to Singapore edited by Anthony SC Teo and published in 2013. The early discussions on the topic "univer-cities" sparked considerable interest, leading to the Inaugural Univer-Cities Conference 2013.

Volume II is the result of papers presented at the inaugural Univer-Cities Conference 2013. Founded by Anthony SC Teo, the Conference was held under the auspices of Nanyang Technological University and the Lee Foundation in Singapore. The inaugural address was delivered by His Royal Highness Raja Dr Nazrin Shah and was followed by presentations by eminent scholars and thought leaders from universities all over the world.

World Scientific Publishing, 2013

INDEX

Aboriginal doctors, 29
Abraham Lincoln, 97
Abraham Zalesnik, 17
Abu Dhabi, 177
academic freedom, 55, 82
academic hub, 83
academic model, 177, 196
Academic motives, 179
Adam Sedgwick, 48
Addenbrooke's Hospital, 7
adult learners, 205, 207, 210, 216, 217
advanced technology platforms, 42
ageing, 36
Alex d'Arbeloff, 174
Alison Richard, 9
Antoine Van Agtmael and Fred
    Bakker, 34
applied learning, 205
ARC, 37
armature, 14–16, 21, 95, 96
AstraZeneca-MRC Centre for
    Lead(ing) Discovery, 7
Autonomous Universities, 205, 224
Avenue of Ideas, 108

Babraham Institute, 56
Baruch College of the City University
    of New York, 199
BBSRC, 37
Berkeley Global Campus, 91
bioengineering, 39
bioinformatics, 39

biology, 42
biomaterial science, 39
bio-medical field, 46
Biomedical Translation Fund, 34
Bologna 2020, 81
Boston University in Belgium, 182
BRAIN initiatives, 37
Branch Model, 182
budget, 79
business model, 177, 196
Business philosophy, 145

Cable, 18, 39
Cambridge, 31
Cambridge Bio-medical Campus, 6
Cambridge Silicon Fen, 6, 7
Cambridge University Hospitals-NHS
    Foundation Trust, 7
campus abroad, 180
cancer, 36
Cancer Research UK, 7
Carleton University, 105
Carnegie Mellon University, 185
Carnegie Mellon University in
    Greece, 182
chemistry, 42
Christopher Marlowe, 18
citation indices, 33
City of Bright, 109
civil rights, 134
collaborative ecosystem, 34
College Structure, 61

collegiality, 5, 20, 21
collegiate academic leaders, 2
Committee on Economic, Social and
   Cultural Rights, 132
Commitment to equity, 40
communication, 114, 115, 120
community-based medicine, 70
community-based medicine initiatives,
   63
complex neurological conditions, 36
Confucius Institute in Australia, 18
Constitutional Court, 134
Contamination, 130, 146
continuing education, 205, 209, 211,
   213, 222, 223, 225, 226
Convergence, 36–38
convergence culture, 42
Convergence ecosystem, 37
core values, 83
Cornell Tech, 91
corridor, 107
Co-working, 94
creative class, 103
creativity, 82
Culinary Institute of America, 199
cultural enrichment, 45
Cultural rights, 132, 134, 135
Curriculum Reform Centennial
   Campus, 113

David Maddison, 29
Dean Maddison, 5
Delta Vector, 15
dementia, 36
Department of Engineering at the
   University of Cambridge, 37
Dermot Kelleher, 70
design, 109
de-siloing of university structures, 42

Developing countries, 136, 138, 141,
   145
DigiPen Institute of Technology, 199
digitalization, 82
dilemma of leadership, 19
dilemma of strategy, 19
Discovery Centre, 105
disruptive innovations, 6
diversified research funding model,
   41
Doha's Education City, 185
Don Cartledge, 12
Double Helix, 56
Dr Charles M. Vest, 174
Drinking water, 134–139, 141, 147,
   148
Dr John Caius, 54
Dr Lee Seng Tee, 68
Dubai, 199
Duke-NUS Graduate Medical School,
   59
duo-univer-city, 16
dynamic duo, 12, 13
dynamic equilibrium, 6

E. Brynjolfsson, 6, 22
Economic
   rights, 132, 134, 135
economic development, 108
economic growth, 45
Economic motives, 179
eco-system, 12, 15, 91
educational model, 177, 196
educational paradigms, 161
e-learning technologies, 70
emerging technologies, 82
Energy, 132, 141
engineering, 36
engineering focus, 3

Engineering Genius Bar at MIT, 36
Engineering Research Centers (ERC), 170
entrepreneurial, 94
entrepreneurial culture, 42
entrepreneurialism, 41
entrepreneurs, 107, 157
Environment, 129–131, 135, 140, 141, 143, 146, 147
equity and equal opportunity, 28
ESCP, 186
ESSEC, 199
Euro-Asia Centre, 17, 188
Eutrophication, 130, 147
evolutionary biology, 78
evolutionary medicine, 21, 77, 78
evolving ecology, 2
expertise, 42

Faculty of Health and Medicine, 28
Fairtrade, 146
Federal Model, 186
Five Peaks of Excellence, 7, 8
five pillars, 3
flexibility, 209, 210, 212, 217, 219, 220, 223
Floods, 129
F.M. Balfour, 48
Fontainebleau, 188
Ford assistant professors, 172
Ford Foundation, 172
foreign campus, 180
France, 177
Francis Crick, 56
fundamental research, 161
funders, 45
funding, 46, 79, 82
fund-raising endowments, 8
Future of Health convergence, 36

Gan Kim Yong, 68
geology, 42
George Mason University in the United Arab Emirates, 182
Georgetown University, 185
Georgia Tech's Parker H. Petit Institute for Bioengineering and Bioscience, 37
Global Impact Clusters, 39
Global Innovation Hub, 28
global knowledge and learning network, 189
Global Model, 187
Global spaces, 105
global university, 31
global warming, 153
GNFC, 146
governance, 64, 83
Governing Board, 64
government, 38
Graduate Destination Survey, 30
Grand Hall, 123, 124
Great Lakes, 130
Greenpeace, 146
Groundwater, 130, 139, 140
Gu Pei Hua, 14

Habit, 225
health economics, 39
Heart, 225
Heng Swee Keat, 68
Henri-Claude de Bettignies, 17
Henry Henslow, 47
heritage, 111, 115, 117, 120
h-index, 33
Hitchison-MRC Research Centre, 7
home countries, 181
host countries, 181
Host-Country Models, 194

Human, 137, 143
    need, 131–136
    right, 131–137, 143, 146, 147
human rights, 11
Hunter Medical Research Institute, 5

Ian Chubb, 35
ICT, 73
Ideological debate, 143
impact, 161
impact factors, 33
impact on society, 34
Imperial College London, 60, 63
Improved sanitation, 140, 141
Improved sources of water, 137, 138, 148
Inclusive Opportunity, 212
incubators, 151, 157
Industrialised countries, 130, 131
industrialisation, 163
Industrial Revolution, 129
industry, 38
information technology, 70
innovation, 4, 6, 34, 94, 147, 153
    disruptive, xii, 2, 6, 21, 34, 82
innovation of technologies, 157
innovative changes, 175
innovative universities, 156
innovators, 108
INSEAD, 17, 177
institutional development, 175
intellectual firepower, 32
Intellectual property, 41
interconnected, 45, 104
interconnection of research and
    everyday life, 81
inter-continental visions, 3
interdisciplinary, 79, 104
interdisciplinary convergence, 38

interdisciplinary hubs, 105
interdisciplinary innovation
    ecosystem, 41
interdisciplinary mode of working, 31
interdisciplinary research, 79, 80, 83
interdisciplinary research agenda, 40
international connectivity, 105
International drinking water supply
    and sanitation decade, 136
internationalisation model, 177
international model, 196
Investments, 145, 147
Inward and outward
    internationalisation, 178
Isaac Newton, 47
iStudyGuides, 217, 226

Jack Ma, 18
James and Catherine Patten seminar, 36
James Clerk Maxell, 48
James Watson, 56
Jan Carlstedt-Duke, 62
Jennifer Martin, 5
Jenny Higham, 70
J. J. Thomson, 48
John Addenbrooke's, 55
John Blyth, 4
John Neville Keynes, 51
Justin, 16

knowledge capital, 108
Korean Government, 163
KPIs, 32, 41

Lake Biwa, 130
Land Grant College system, 97
land-grant universities, 89
Lap Chee Tsui, 12

Learning Commons, 122, 123
learning community, 115, 116, 122
Lee Foundation, 61
Lee Kong Chian School of Medicine, 60
liberal education, 13
lifelong learning, 211, 223, 227
life sciences, 83
Light Rail Transit, 104
Li Kashing, 12
Li Kashing Cancer Centre, 7
Lim Chuan Poh, 64
local health services, 38
Lord Rayleigh, 48
Louis XIV, 101

Main Campus, 111, 112, 115–117, 120, 121
Manchester Business School, 199
Mar del Plata Action Plans, 137
Mark Zuckerberg, xiii, 14, 87, 88
Mary Ritter, 64
mathematics, 47
Maurice Wilkins, 56
Mayor Michael Bloomberg, 91
Mayor Willie Brown, 93
MD degree, 29
medical origins, xiii, 3
Medical Research Future Fund, 34
Memorial University, 12
metabolic disease, 36
metropolises, 96
Michael Crow, 19
Michael Foster, 48
MIT, 169
MIT Department of Mechanical Engineering, 172
Mobile Harbor (MH), 169
mobility, 94

models
    28 combination, 15
modularity, 210, 212, 221
Monash University's Institute of Medical Engineering, 37
MRC, 7, 37
MRFF, 34
MSTEAMδ, 18
MSTEM, 18
multidisciplinary projects, 34
multidisciplinary research, 5
Multinational companies, 145, 146
multi-professional teams, 63
multi-univer-cities, 16

Nanyang Technological University, 198
Nanyang Water and Environmental Research Institute (NEWRI), 11
National Earthquake Research Center, 170
National Health Service, 54
National Innovation and Science, 34
National Robotics, 37
National University of Singapore, 181
natural environment, 115, 117
natural sciences, 36, 42
network, 108
New Centennial College, 12
New Futures Strategic Plan, 31
New Silk Road, 3, 18
Newton's Principia, 47
new venture firms, 157
New York University Tisch School of the Arts in Singapore, 182
NGOs, 132, 148
Ng Wun Jern, 11
NHMRC, 37
NHMRC project grant, 35
Nicholas Dirks, 91

Niels Bohr, 4
NIH, 37
NIH-Biomedical Research Centre, 7
NIMBELS, 72
NITHM, 73
Nobel Prize, 56
Non-English speaking nations, 33
Northrop Frye, 108
Northwestern University, 185
NSF, 37
NTU, 63
NTU-ICL Lee Kong Chian School of
    Medicine, 7
nucleation, 5, 20, 36

Old Dominion University, 105
One School, Two Campuses, 192
online, 212, 218–220, 222, 226, 227
On-Line Electric Vehicles (OLEVs), 169
Oxford, 31

Paradoxes, 2, 4
Paris-Sorbonne University, 200
partnership, 46
part-time studies, 207, 209, 222
pathways, 210, 227
Patricia Chan, 87
Pericles Lewis, 14
PhD scholarships, 41
Philip Matthias, 14
physics, 42
Planning Principles, 114
Political motive, 179
political sensitivities, 53
political will, 135, 148
Pontifical Academy of Sciences, 3, 11
postgraduate coursework, 29
Premier Chretien, 17
President Su Guaning, 60
private donations and bequests, 49

Private sector, 132, 139, 143–148
problem-based, 29
Problem Based Learning, 8
problems, 175
professional incentives, 40
Public colleges, 89
public funding, 49, 50
public policy, 45
Public sector, 143–148

Qatar, 177
Qatar Foundation, 185
QS (Quacquarelli Symond, Ltd.), 155
qualitative assessment, 161
qualitative measures, 153
quality assurance, 212, 215, 216
quality of life, 11
quantifiable metrics, 153
quantitative measure, 161

Rainforest Alliance, 146
regional council, 108
research funds, 152
restructuring economies, 21
return on investment, 152
Reuters, 154
Rhode Island School of
    Oceanography, 12
Richard Bender, 90
Richard Florida, 108
Richard Walker, 46
Rights
    civil, 134
    cultural, 132, 134, 135
    economic, 132, 134, 135
    social, 132, 134, 135
"Right time, right place", 5, 12
River
    Cuyahoga, 130
    Han, 163

Nile, 129
Rhine, 130
Tigris-Euphrates, 129
Trent, 130
Yellow, 129
robotics, 168
Rockefeller Foundation, 54
role of the university, 45

Salesforce, 94
sanitation, 11, 133–137, 140, 141, 146, 147
Saxon White, 5
seed funding, 41
sewer systems, 145
S-Factor, 157
S-Gap, 159
Silicon Valley, 95
SIM University, 205
SIM University (UniSIM), 212
Singapore, 177
Singapore Management University, 199
Singapore University of Social Sciences (SUSS), 21, 205
Sir Clifford Allbutt, 53
Sir George Paget, 53
Sir Hugh Anderson, 53
Sir Keith O'Nions, 64, 67
Sir Leszek Borysiewicz, xiii, 4–6, 10, 19–21, 32
Sir Wilfrid Laurier, 103, 107
SkillsFuture, 225, 226
Social rights, 132, 134, 135
social and economic impact, 35
social compact, 21
Social Sciences, 79
society, xi, xxxvii, xxxviii, 5, 45
at-large, 6, 151
changes to, 225

democratic, 151
engaging, 36
equal, 16
future of, 89
ideal, 175
impact on, 32, 34, 35, 227
relevance to, 37
responsibility to, 10
service to, 3, 207
shifts in, 52
stakeholders, 4, 33, 42
trends, 82
value for, 145
specialized areas of research, 33
speed of development, 45
SP Jain School of Global Management, 199
Starman Dilemma Proposition, 6
state funding, 50, 89
STEAM, 3
Steel City, 28
STEM, 2
STEMM, 18, 38
STEMM budget, 41
Stephen Hawking, 4
Stephen Smith, 70
Stockholm Water Prize, 3
strategic freedom, 82
strategic goals, 82
strategic vector deltas, 8
strategy dilemma, 4, 5
subsidies, 143, 144, 147
sustainability, 109, 116, 119, 120, 146
sustainable funding, 81
systems, 175

Tan Sri Dato Dr Lee Kong Chian, 61, 67
teaching and learning (T&L), 211, 216, 217, 219, 220

team-based learning, 8, 70
teamwork, 94
technical infrastructure platforms, 41
technologies, 5, 7, 206, 211, 212, 216,
    219, 227, 228
    "brilliant", 6
technology entrepreneurs, 97
technology innovation, 152, 161
Texas A & M University, 185
Third World Centre for Water
    Management, 138, 142
Thought Leader of Focus, 10
Tigris-Euphrates
    river, 129
Times Higher Education, 155
Toh Kian Chui, 66
Top Innovative Universities, 154
top-ranked universities, 153
T. Piketty, 157
tradition, 52
trans-disciplinarity, 32
trans-disciplinary, 2, 8
trans-disciplinary educational
    programmes, 41
trans-disciplinary research, 5
transformations, 152
transformative learning, 71
trans-institutional partnering agree-
    ments, 40
transit-linked development, 97
translational medicine, 80
tri-univer-cities, xlii, 14–16
Trudeau
    Pierre Elliot, 16
    Justin, 16

UC 2019, xv, 10, 21
UC Merced Campus, 90
UCSF Mission Bay, 93
UCSF Research Campus, 93

undergraduate, 29
unified campus, 115, 116
UniSIM, 205
United Arab Emirates,, 199
United Nations (UN)
    Conference on Human
        Settlement, 136
    Children's Fund (UNICEF), 137,
        138, 141
    General Assembly, 133, 134, 137
    Serity Council, 133
    Water Conference, Mar del
        Plata, 136, 137
Univer-cities Project, 45
University District, 114
University Grants Committee, 50
University of Hong Kong (HKU),
    111–115, 119, 125
University of Nevada Las Vegas
    College of Hotel Administration,
    199
University of New England, 29
University of New South Wales, 27
University of New South Wales in
    Singapore, 182
University of Newcastle, 27
University of the People, 203
University of Waterloo in the United
    Arab Emirates, 182
university rankings, 153
University Street, 116, 117, 119
urbanisation, 140
urban planning, 83
USAID, 163
US National Science Foundation, 169
UTZ, 146

Vancouver Declaration, 136
Vector Delta, 16, 19
Vector δ, 160

venture capital, 152
Versailles, 102
vertical campus, 94
Victor Fung, 12
Virginia Commonwealth University,
    105
Vision 2026, 80

Wastewater
    collection, 134, 140
    contamination, 129, 130
    infrastructure, 147
    management, 141, 145, 147
    reuse, 136, 141, 143
    treatment, 130, 134, 139–141,
        143, 148
water, 11
    conservation, 145
    footprints, 145
    pricing, 132, 139, 143
    quality, 129–131, 136–139, 141
    utilities, 135, 138, 139, 144, 145

Weizmann Institute of Science, 36
Wellcome Trust-MRC Cambridge
    Stem Cell Institute, 7
Western countries, 130
Wilfred Laurier, 16
William Cavendish, 49
William Whewell, 48
World Bank, 132, 137
World Health Organization (WHO),
    137, 138, 141
World University Rankings 2016, 60
Wyss Institute for Biologically
    Inspired Engineering, 37

Xi Jinping, 2

Yale-National University of Singapore
    College, 180
Yale University, 36, 180
Yong Loo Lin School of Medicine, 59

Zuckerberg-Chan, 14